537246

KU-511-179

ONE WEEK LOAN

Einstein's Wake

Einstein's Wake

Relativity, Metaphor, and
Modernist Literature

MICHAEL H. WHITWORTH

OXFORD
UNIVERSITY PRESS

This book has been printed digitally and produced in a standard specification
in order to ensure its continuing availability

OXFORD
UNIVERSITY PRESS

Great Clarendon Street, Oxford OX2 6DP

Oxford University Press is a department of the University of Oxford.
It furthers the University's objective of excellence in research, scholarship,
and education by publishing worldwide in

Oxford New York

Auckland Bangkok Buenos Aires Cape Town Chennai
Dar es Salaam Delhi Hong Kong Istanbul Karachi Kolkata
Kuala Lumpur Madrid Melbourne Mexico City Mumbai Nairobi
São Paulo Shanghai Taipei Tokyo Toronto

Oxford is a registered trade mark of Oxford University Press
in the UK and in certain other countries

Published in the United States
by Oxford University Press Inc., New York

© Michael Whitworth 2001

The moral rights of the author have been asserted

Database right Oxford University Press (maker)

Reprinted 2004

All rights reserved. No part of this publication may be reproduced,
stored in a retrieval system, or transmitted, in any form or by any means,
without the prior permission in writing of Oxford University Press,
or as expressly permitted by law, or under terms agreed with the appropriate
reprographics rights organization. Enquiries concerning reproduction
outside the scope of the above should be sent to the Rights Department,
Oxford University Press, at the address above

You must not circulate this book in any other binding or cover
And you must impose this same condition on any acquirer

ISBN 0-19-818640-1

SOUTHAMPTON SOLENT
UNIVERSITY LIBRARY

SUPPLIER Blackw

ORDER No

DATE 14\3\08

To

BRIAN *and* BARBARA WHITWORTH

Preface

EINSTEIN developed his Special and General Theories of Relativity at the same time as modernist writers began their literary careers, 1894 to 1916; his theories received the greatest publicity in Britain as modernist literature came to maturity, in the years 1919 to 1931. The coincidence is often alluded to, and the dates 1905 (the Special Theory) and 1916 (the General Theory) are often included in chronologies of the period. Einstein is often named, along with Nietzsche, Bergson, Freud, and others, as part of a familiar litany of intellectual forefathers. Yet, unlike philosophy and psychoanalysis, the physical science of the period has very rarely been considered in any detail in its relation to literature.

The word 'relativity' has been a trap for many, in that it encourages a premature conceptualization of the field as one concerned with relative and absolute truth. Rather than focus on 'relativity', this study examines the metaphors which shaped Einstein's theory and the scientific ideas associated with it. The popular conception that Einstein 'made everything relative' cannot be ignored, as it was current during the period, but the metaphors are more important. This study places 'relativity' in its scientific rather than its philosophical lineage, and so includes treatments of theories which were not Einstein's, in particular, the second law of thermodynamics, the school of epistemology known as descriptionism, and the new theories of matter from 1895 to 1913. The term 'relativity' is often taken to provide a point of contact between Einstein and the ideas of complementarity and uncertainty developed in the quantum mechanics of the mid 1920s; Bohr, Heisenberg, and Schrödinger are often mentioned alongside Einstein as part of the intellectual atmosphere. However, the 1920s quantum theories appeared after the canonical works of high modernism. This study assumes (and argues in passing) that statistical thermodynamics and descriptionism are the more important sources for concepts of uncertainty and complementarity.

Individual responses to science are important, but the meanings of those responses are shaped by the literary culture and by literary form more generally, and for this reason, rather than organize my chapters author-by-author, I have arranged them on a thematic basis. I return repeatedly to certain authors, particularly Joseph Conrad, Virginia Woolf, T. S. Eliot and D. H. Lawrence. Though my title glances at James Joyce, he is less prominent than might be expected, because he was less closely connected with the literary periodicals I have examined, and because, compared to Eliot and Woolf, he was unproductive as a critic and theorist.

The Introduction explains the methodological assumptions of the study, particularly as regards its treatment of metaphor and the importance placed on the literary periodical. Chapter 1 examines the popularization and dissemination of science in the period, and asks why scientific knowledge was important to the literary reader. The following two chapters, on entropy and descriptionism, examine particular sciences in more detail, emphasizing the earlier part of the period. Chapter 4 emphasizes a particular historical period, 1914 to 1919, for the thematic purpose of examining the relations of literature and science. The following three chapters return to particular physical theories, arranged in a broadly chronological pattern. Chapter 5 considers theories of matter from 1895 to 1913, and their relation to ideas of the self; Chapter 6 approaches Einstein's special theory of relativity through the concept of simultaneity; Chapter 7 opens up the general theory of relativity to critical enquiry, focusing on the reception of non-Euclidean geometry and exploring the relation of geometrical metaphors to ideas of literary form.

This book continues research begun as my D. Phil. thesis under the supervision of David Bradshaw, to whom I am grateful both for his supervision and for his continued interest in my work; I wish also to thank the external and internal examiners of that thesis, Gillian Beer and Christopher Butler, for their advice, Oxford University Press's anonymous readers for their helpful suggestions, my editor Sophie Goldsworthy for her patience, and Matthew Hollis for seeing the manuscript through to publication.

During the course of writing this work, I have enjoyed conversations about it with Liz Barry, Tom Corns, Gowan Dawson, Elle Leane, Nicola Luckhurst, and Jessica Maynard, and with the participants in the Ninth and Tenth Annual Conferences on Virginia Woolf, the Twentieth-Century Graduate Seminar organized by the English Faculty, University of Oxford, the 1999 Leiden October Conference, and the First European Conference of the Society for

Literature and Science; I hope the work does justice to their suggestions.

I would like to thank the English Department, University of Wales
Bangor, for granting me the study leave in the second semester of
1999–2000 which allowed me to complete the text. For assistance
with books and archives, I am indebted to the staff of the Upper
Reading Room, Bodleian Library; the staff of the library, University
of Wales, Bangor; Michael Bott and staff, Special Collections,
University of Reading; Eamon Dyas and staff at the *TLS* archive; Sue
Holland, Simon Powell, and Kirsty Carr at City University; David
McKitterick and staff at Trinity College Library, Cambridge; and
Julia G. A. Sheppard at the Wellcome Library, London.

For accommodation and entertainment in Oxford, I would like to
thank Mark Stanton and Lindsey Gillson, and Jenny and Derek
Ferguson. For literally constructing the solid table on which I wrote
the first three chapters, and for metaphorically providing the table
on which the other chapters rest, I dedicate this book to my parents.

M.H.W.

Acknowledgements

PARTS of Chapters 2 and 3 have previously appeared as 'Inspector Heat Inspected: *The Secret Agent* and the Meanings of Entropy', *Review of English Studies* 49 (1998), 40–59, and I am grateful to Oxford University Press for permission to reproduce this material. I am also grateful to Navin Sullivan for permission to quote from a previously unpublished letter by his father, J. W. N. Sullivan; to Cambridge University Press and the Wellcome Institute for quotations from unpublished letters by A. S. Eddington; and to the Needham Research Institute for quotations from a letter by Joseph Needham. I have been unable to trace the copyright holders for the letters by Jacob Isaacs quoted in Chapter 1, and would welcome information enabling me to contact them.

Contents

Introduction

God us keep
From Single Vision and Newton's Sleep.[1]

THE study of literature and science raises an ontological problem: faced with two terms which are commonly understood as antithetical, we must explain in what sense we are comparing like with like; the problem appears particularly acute when we are examining the relation of literature to a mathematical science such as physics. As regards the present study, the short answer is that we are not so much examining relativity and modernism as examining certain metaphors in their textual and historical context; that these metaphors may be found both in scientific theories and in descriptions of modernist literary form is particularly convenient. However, this response merely invites further questions. What is the relation between the metaphorical and the literal? How do the metaphors in question come to be found in both literature and science? Were they deployed consciously or unconsciously? How can a history centred on language take into account forces which are irreducibly material?

The practice of studying literature and science has produced a substantial body of theoretical reflections, but although certain themes recur, there are many explicit and implicit differences of methodology and terminology. Theoretical reflection is perhaps inevitable in a discipline which takes scientific theories as its object of study; equally inevitable is the recognition that literary theories serve very different purposes from scientific ones. During the period when literary theory was winning widespread institutional acceptance in Britain and North America, from the mid 1980s to the early 1990s, the discipline gave particular prominence to questions of theory.[2]

---

[1] William Blake, from a letter to Thomas Butts, 22 Nov. 1802, *Poems of Blake*, ed. W. H. Stevenson (London: Longman, 1971), 475.

[2] Especially Stuart Peterfreund (ed.), *Literature and Science: Theory and Practice* (Boston: Northeastern University Press, 1990); but also the introductions to Ludmilla Jordanova (ed.), *Languages of Nature* (London: Free Association Books, 1986); George Levine (ed.), *One Culture: Essays in Science and Literature* (Madison: University of Wisconsin Press, 1986), N. Katherine Hayles (ed.), *Chaos and Order: Complex Dynamics in Literature and Science* (Chicago: University of Chicago Press, 1991).

Theory mattered, in that it seemed to offer the discipline a means of breaking with its origins in the philological annotation of scientific references for the purposes of scholarly editions.[3] Though such annotations may be profitably expanded into articles and chapters, they do not provide sufficient foundations for more sustained histories or analyses. As several critics have noted, often with a note of regret, the characteristic form of literature and science studies has been the collection of essays.[4] It is possible to defend such a format, on the basis that literature has always interacted with science through a process described by Gillian Beer as 'fugitive appropriation'.[5] However, even if a full-length study were to restrict itself to fugitive appropriations, it would need to account for the divergency of the modes of appropriation: literary fugitives flee the bank vaults of science in all directions, and a single searchlight cannot track them down. Though structuralist and post-structuralist theory provided a common discourse for the discussion of these problems, its largely ahistorical character was unsympathetic to the fundamentally historical nature of the raw materials. Such problems as it solved were not the most significant.

Writing in 1989, Shuttleworth and Christie recognized this problem: they held out some hope for the future theorization of the discipline, but argued that such theorization would have to be based on essentially historical groundwork, and was not possible at that time.[6] While at the time such cautionary remarks were a necessary corrective to the more exorbitant claims of literary theory, they too require qualification, in that they might seem to encourage the absolute separation of empirical groundwork and stratospheric theory. I would argue that empirical research and abstract theorization need to develop in parallel, with theorization taking the form of preliminary hypotheses and working methodologies. This does not mean, in relation to a book, that theory and practice can be seamlessly interwoven. It is necessary to begin by articulating key

    [3] George S. Rousseau, 'Literature and Science: The State of the Field', *Isis*, 69 (1978), 582–91.

    [4] Marina Benjamin (ed.), *Science and Sensibility: Gender and Scientific Enquiry 1780–1945* (Oxford: Blackwell, 1991), 9; Peterfreund (ed.), *Literature and Science*, 5.

    [5] Gillian Beer, 'Science and Literature', in R. C. Olby, G. N. Cantor, J. R. R. Christie, and M. J. S. Hodge (eds.), *Companion to the History of Modern Science* (London: Routledge, 1990), 783–98 (p. 797).

    [6] John Christie and Sally Shuttleworth (eds.), *Nature Transfigured: Science and Literature 1700–1900* (Manchester: Manchester University Press, 1989), 11–12.

assumptions, by attempting to resolve contradictions between incompatible assumptions, and by outlining practical methodologies which are consistent with those assumptions.

The metaphors under consideration become interesting when they shape ideas about literary form. The essential aim of this study is not to catalogue literary content, such as representations of science in modernist works, nor to reconsider Einstein as an icon of the modern age.[7] Nor is it to examine citations of scientific 'facts' in literary works, except when those facts stand in some significant relations to the literary form of the work. The catechism in the 'Ithaca' chapter of Joyce's *Ulysses* contains many scientific facts, but as a form the catechism is ecclesiastical in origin, and stands in no significant relation to contemporary scientific research, nor to the facts examined in 'Ithaca', nor to the structure of Joyce's novel as a whole. I am not concerned with the 'poetry of knowledge'.[8] It follows that I am not essentially concerned with 'correcting' modernist misapprehensions of scientific facts. Though it must be recognized that the distinction between a fact and a theory is often difficult to determine, and that misunderstandings of theory can be fruitfully pursued, correcting basic factual errors is usually a sterile exercise.[9] Scientific facts in literary texts need to be understood primarily as a rhetorical ploy, one form of what Barthes termed the 'reality function'; the literary context evacuates them of their content.[10] Of course, the way that a literary writer treats scientific facts, scientists, and discussions of science in his or her works is not to be ignored: it can indicate the level of receptivity to more significant scientific ideas, though as I show in Chapter 4, attitudes to science and attitudes to its ideas are very often entirely contradictory.

There are three positive reasons for focusing on literary form. Firstly, it facilitates generalization. While content is a matter of individual conscious choice, literary forms are shared, and are often unconsciously adopted. Though my discussion returns repeatedly

[7] For such studies, see Roslynn Haynes, *From Faust to Strangelove* (Baltimore: Johns Hopkins University Press, 1994); Alan J. Friedman and Carol C. Donley, *Einstein as Myth and Muse* (Cambridge: Cambridge University Press, 1985), 180–7.

[8] Robert Crawford, ' "The glow-worm's 96 per cent efficiency": Hugh MacDiarmid's Poetry of Knowledge', *Proceedings of the British Academy*, 87 (1995), 169–87.

[9] e.g. June Deery, 'Cultural Trespass?: Aldous Huxley's Forays into Modern Physics,' *University of Dayton Review*, 21/3 (Spring 1992), 73–84.

[10] Roland Barthes, 'The Reality Effect', in Tzvetan Todorov (ed.), *French Literary Theory Today*, trans. R. Carter (New York: Cambridge University Press, 1982), 11–17.

to four authors—Joseph Conrad, Virginia Woolf, T. S. Eliot, and D. H. Lawrence—the emphasis on form makes the discussion resonant, applicable to works treated more cursorily and to works excluded or overlooked. Secondly, formal innovation was particularly prized by modernist writers, as well as by contemporaneous theorists of painting. This second factor might seem to work against the first: it might be argued that, precisely because of their formal self-consciousness, modernist writers did not absorb concepts of form unconsciously, and so remarks pertaining to any given writer may be severely restricted in their applicability. In practice, though, this seems not to have been the case, because, whatever the formal innovations of a given work, the underlying family resemblances remained relatively stable. Thirdly, the physics of the period preferred to 'explain' natural phenomena in formal and statistical rather than materialistic and deterministic terms.[11] Indeed, insofar as we expect an 'explanation' to have some sort of content at its centre—the mysterious mechanism or efficient cause—the very term 'explain' is inadequate. As we shall see, many scientists preferred to think in terms of 'description' rather than 'explanation'. The second law of thermodynamics, though pre-Einsteinian, represents the beginnings of this tendency: we can produce a formal statistical description of the behaviour of a group of atoms without understanding the mechanical 'law' they are individually obeying. Later, Einstein was to describe gravitation as a formal distortion of space rather than explain it as a mechanical force transmitted by an all-pervading ether.

Although the parallel between the literary and the scientific preference for form is intriguing, I am inclined to grant these factors less significance than the first, ahistorical consideration. But literary form presents a problem: in itself, it is always inaccessible to literary criticism; one can only quote and discuss metaphors of form. Similar considerations apply to the mathematical sciences: although mathematical formalizations are reproducible on the page in a way that literary form is not, reproducing them does not make them suitable objects for critical discourse. We are forced, then, to discuss the metaphors embedded in scientific theory. The 'curvature' of Einstein's space is a metaphor, one that asks us to imagine space curving by

<hr />

[11] Gerald Holton, *Thematic Origins of Scientific Thought* (Cambridge, Mass.: Harvard University Press, 1973), 113; *The Advancement of Science, and its Burdens* (1986; Cambridge, Mass.: Harvard University Press, 1998), 53.

analogy with our experience of material objects curving. The discussion of such metaphors will seem illegitimate to the scientist who insists that a theory is equivalent to nothing more nor less than its mathematical formalization. Literary purists may likewise feel that to discuss metaphors of form is to lose touch with the form itself. Certainly, metaphors of form can be misleading, deliberately or otherwise, but they are the only tangible material available for discussion. Because, as we will see, all scientific theorization is dependent on metaphor, regardless of whether it values 'formal' explanation, the thematic preferences of modern physics are of secondary importance.

It is important to emphasize that this is a study of certain metaphors, rather than of scientific theories *per se*. Although it examines the theory of relativity and related themes, the mode of analysis means that the concept of 'relativity' plays only a small part. It is necessary to consider the conception that Einstein had 'made everything relative', but it is less important than the component metaphors of relativity theory. Even though the main motivation for studying those metaphors is their importance to science, this study cannot address the theories as the scientists would have understood them. The analysis of theories into their component metaphors cuts them along lines which would have been largely unfamiliar to scientists. Of course, here as elsewhere, 'understanding' is a complex term. Each of us has many understandings of the ideas which are central to our professional activities, each understanding being relevant to different contexts: the context of sitting an examination, the context of pedagogic exposition, or the context of practical problem solving, for example. Called upon to provide a popular account of a theory, a scientist may employ explanations which in another context he or she would not regard as valid. In analysing theories into their component metaphors, one may be usefully guided by scientific texts, but one may produce results that would have seemed quite alien to a scientist. Psychoanalysis provides a general and unsystematic analogy, in that the process of analysis resembles the process of dream interpretation. As we cannot call upon the patient to free associate, we must create the associations ourselves, drawing upon adjacent cultural materials, working from the manifest content (scientific expositions) to the latent content (metaphors).

It is questionable whether any adjudicatory authority should be granted to the scientist (as a generalized figure), or to individual scientists, in a study which is closer in its assumptions to the history of science. It is not necessary to have any understanding of the history of science to be a fully qualified, or indeed a highly successful, scientist. If the 'science' presented by the history of science in its modern forms is unrecognizable to the practising scientist, this need not imply that one or the other discipline is superior in authority, merely that their accounts of the discipline fulfil different purposes.

Many recent historians of science would argue that these metaphors are not 'science' because they have been abstracted from their institutional context: as Gooday notes, since the late 1970s there has been a change of 'methodological sympathies', away from 'theory-centred philology' towards 'laboratory-centred anthropology'.[12] The possibility of understanding a scientific theory in a truly 'scientific' way is not a function of the individual scientist's consciousness, but a function of the theory's existence in an institutional context. The institution secures the assumptions which frame the theory, reinforcing tacit agreements as to the theory's field of valid application, and the definitions which underlie it. There is no response that can absolutely negate this objection, and it must be noted that, to the extent that this study examines science detached from its institutional context, it falls short as sociology of science. However, two points must be noted. Firstly, the institutional basis for Einstein's theories of relativity was relatively slight; indeed, rather than attributing the genesis of the theory to Einstein's genius, one could also point to his relative institutional freedom in the crucial years of his career. Moreover, in its early years the theory was understood essentially in astronomical terms, and so was free from the practical, industrial concerns which were placed on a theory such as thermodynamics; this was to change for ever with the invention of atomic power and atomic weaponry. Secondly, while the validity of scientific theories is secured largely by forces which are peculiar to the scientific institution, it is secured additionally by forces which have a larger scope, operating beyond the doors of the institution: for example, in the seventeenth century, the notion of 'truth' itself was sustained by the idea of gentlemanliness.[13] No

[12] Graeme Gooday, 'The Premisses of Premises: Spatial Issues in the Historical Construction of Laboratory Credibility', in Crosbie Smith and Jon Agar (eds.), *Making Space for Science: Territorial Themes in the Shaping of Knowledge* (Basingstoke: Macmillan, 1998), 216–45.

[13] Steven Shapin, *A Social History of Truth: Civility and Science in Seventeenth-Century England* (Chicago: University of Chicago Press, 1994).

matter how peculiar the institution of science, there will be a degree of continuity with the outside world. Metaphors abstracted from science are no longer wholly identical to science, nor are they wholly divorced from it.

The focus on metaphor leads to a distinctive theorization of the relation of science and technology, and although the present work does not pursue these connections in every chapter, it is important to clarify this issue. The discipline of literature and science has tended to focus on 'pure' science, and relatively few studies have included technology within the field.[14] The wariness about technology, in Britain at least, is due partly to the literary legacy of the Victorian 'sages'. As we shall see in Chapter 4, their warnings about the irreconcilability of civilization and the 'mechanical' seemed for many to be confirmed by the 1914–18 war; in this respect, the discourse under examination and the metadiscourse used to examine it share a common history. In North America, 'science' has been used far more commonly to refer to 'technology', and the discipline has been more open to considerations of applied science. These, however, are contingent factors; there are also sound theoretical reasons why technology needs to be treated differently. While the discourse of pure science can be treated as a textual object, technology is irreducibly non-textual. The texts surrounding new technologies have been very successfully studied, but such texts are not the thing in itself.[15] Such studies are justifiable, however, on the grounds that a corpus of such penumbral texts allows us to reconstruct the metaphors by which the technologies were understood. For example in considering the discourse of 'dissipation' surrounding steam engines, we understand the metaphors of investment and loss which inform later discussion of the sun as a dissipative body.

The connections between the thermodynamics of steam engines and later thermodynamic theory are a commonplace in the history of science, but with the new physics it is less clear which are the appropriate technologies to relate to a given theory, and a more

---

[14] Notable exceptions include Lisa Steinman, *Made in America* (New Haven: Yale University Press, 1987), Cecelia Tichi, *Shifting Gears: Technology, Literature and Culture in Modernist America* (Chapel Hill: University of North Carolina Press, 1987), and Joseph W. Slade and Judith Yaross Lee (eds.), *Beyond the Two Cultures: Essays on Science, Technology and Literature* (Ames, Iowa: Iowa University Press, 1990).

[15] Carolyn Marvin, *When Old Technologies Were New: Thinking About Electric Communication in the Late Nineteenth Century* (New York, Oxford: Oxford University Press, 1988).

speculative method is required in order to make the connections. The technology which is physically or institutionally closest to a scientific theory is not necessarily the most relevant in terms of its metaphors. ('Physically closest' refers to equipment used in the scientist's own laboratories; 'institutionally closest' refers to equipment used in the scientist's discipline, which the particular scientist has access to indirectly, through published results, for example.) Institutionally speaking, Michelson and Morley's interferometer appears to have been close to Einstein's special theory of relativity, but thematically speaking telecommunications were much closer.[16]

It is important to recognize that in treating technologies as nodes in an economy of metaphorical exchange, we are treating them as no different from any other material social practice. The only reason for privileging technology over other practices is that scientists have tended to be more aware of it than have other citizens. If, however, the new experience of shopping seems as close to theories of perception as the obvious technologies (the camera, for instance), then there is no reason why it should not be introduced into the argument.

The notion that metaphor could have a role to play in science will strike many as paradoxical, though it is an accepted part of the theorization of literature and science. That the idea seems paradoxical is due to a set of deeply embedded dualisms in post-Renaissance culture. The dualism of the literal and the metaphorical supports, and is supported by, the dualistic oppositions of the objective and the subjective, the sciences and the arts, nature and culture, fact and value, and so on. These dualisms lead us to believe that the literal truth about nature can be told only by science, and that the role of metaphor in science is merely expository. Metaphor, according to this view, is decorative; scientific language is unadorned.

The difficulty with such accounts is that they provide no means of actually distinguishing literal from metaphorical statements. The often-expressed idea that our conceptual system contains 'dead' metaphors goes some way to acknowledging the complexity of the relation between literal and metaphorical, though at the same time it merely displaces the problem of distinguishing: we still need to know how to distinguish a 'dead' from a 'living' metaphor. As Max

---

[16] Stephen Kern, *The Culture of Time and Space 1880–1918* (London: Weidenfeld and Nicolson, 1983), 6. Moreover, the interferometer's appearance of proximity derives from the 'experimenticist' account of Einstein's work: Holton, *Thematic Origins*, 275–80.

Black has argued, it is better to regard all language as 'dormant' metaphor.[17] Such metaphors may be woken by a suitable critical process. Lakoff and Johnson explain why metaphor is so all-pervasive in thought: 'Because so many of the concepts that are important to us are either abstract or not clearly delineated in our experience (the emotions, ideas, time, etc.), we need to get a grasp on them by means of other concepts that we understand in clearer terms (spatial orientation, objects, etc.).'[18] The abstract concepts under discussion here are not the complex abstractions of modern science, but far simpler abstractions which preceded and have largely been incorporated into it.

The literalist might be tempted to see scientific 'progress' as a continuing process of stripping away science's inherited metaphors in order to reach the truth. On this view, if the ideas of modern physics seem paradoxical, it is because they contradict our inherited base of metaphors. However, even if one wishes to retain the idea of 'progress' in science, one need not view it as a process of removing metaphorical wrappers from 'literal' nature. One may equally well see it as a process of replacing one metaphor with another. There is still 'progress', as the new metaphor allows the scientist to understand the range of known phenomena more economically than did the old.

New concepts are by definition less clearly delineated than existing ones, so metaphor has a crucial role in allowing the scientist to 'grasp' new concepts as he or she attempts to theorize a new area of knowledge, or retheorize an old one. The best known illustration is Darwin's theorization of evolution by natural selection. The very phrase 'selection' implies a selective agency, and Darwin understood the natural process by analogy with 'artificial selection'. Just as farmers selected for breeding the livestock which produced the best wool, or highest milk-yields, so nature 'selected' those organisms which best suited their environments. This metaphor implicitly personifies Nature; in a crucial passage in Darwin's 'Sketch of 1844',

---

[17] Max Black, 'More About Metaphors', in Andrew Ortony (ed.), *Metaphor and Thought* (Cambridge: Cambridge University Press, 1979), 19–43 (p. 26); see also N. Katherine Hayles, 'Self-Reflexive Metaphors in Maxwell's Demon and Shannon's Choice', in Peterfreund (ed.), *Literature and Science*, 209.

[18] George Lakoff and Mark Johnson, *Metaphors We Live By* (Chicago: University of Chicago Press, 1980), 115. These underlying metaphors may sometimes manifest themselves as similes; for the purposes of the present study, the distinction of simile from metaphor is relatively insignificant.

the process of personification is even clearer, as Nature is explicitly a 'Being' with God-like powers of perception and foresight.[19]

Though Lakoff and Johnson's account of metaphor is undoubtedly the most accessible, it does not fit every situation that one encounters in dealing with modern science. Lakoff and Johnson describe metaphor as the definition of the abstract in terms of the concrete. This is unsuitable as an account of metaphor in science, where the new objects to be described are undeniably material: for example, atoms, or fields of force. They seem 'abstract' only in so far as they are not graspable by unaided human senses; they are not abstract in the sense that time or love are abstract. It might be better to define metaphor as the definition of the intangible in terms of the tangible. However, while this definition is probably sufficient for most of the instances contained in the following chapters, it is still imperfect: the metaphor 'the atom is a miniature solar system' models one intangible thing on the basis of another. It is better still to define metaphor as the definition of the unfamiliar in terms of the familiar. At the time that the 'solar' atom was theorized, the solar system was the more familiar concept.

My proposed definition has the disadvantage that 'familiarity' is a much vaguer concept than Lakoff and Johnson's 'concreteness' or my own 'tangibility', because it seems to beg the question 'familiar to whom?' This seeming disadvantage may be turned to good account, however, in that it allows us to understand how the felicity of a metaphor is relative to the cultural group in which it functions. The description of an abstract entity in terms of a 'concrete' one will be meaningless to a cultural group which is unfamiliar with the concrete term. As Lakoff and Johnson concede, in relation to their own innovative metaphor 'love is like a collaborative work of art', the concepts involved vary widely from culture to culture.[20]

Similar considerations apply to Lakoff and Johnson's idea that, among the various domains of experience which metaphors may be used to describe, certain domains are 'natural kinds of experience'.[21] This concept needs to be subjected to sceptical questioning, because two of the underlying assumptions of this study are that our

---

[19] Darwin, 'Essay of 1844', in Darwin and Alfred Russel Wallace, *Evolution by Natural Selection* (Cambridge: Cambridge University Press, 1958), 91–254; Gillian Beer, *Darwin's Plots: Evolutionary Narrative in Darwin, George Eliot and Nineteenth-Century Fiction* (London: Routledge and Kegan Paul, 1983), 68–71.

[20] Lakoff and Johnson, *Metaphors We Live By*, 142.   [21] Ibid., 117.

concepts of the 'natural' since the Renaissance have very often derived from science, and that science in turn has derived its concepts from 'culture'. While Lakoff and Johnson assume that there is a concept called 'human nature' which produces the 'natural kinds of experience', this study assumes that human nature is continually, albeit slowly, changing. There are no unchanging Platonic ideas, only concepts mediated through linguistic signs. Lakoff and Johnson themselves seem confused on the relative importance of the cultural and the natural. They list examples of natural kinds of experience 'which require metaphorical definition', but add that these are 'natural kinds of experience *in our culture*'.[22] To many working in cultural and literary studies, their list will seem heterogeneous: love, time, ideas, understanding, arguments, labour, happiness, health, control, status, and morality. Some, such as concepts of love and labour, have changed within living memory. They have not, it is true, altogether vanished, but a concept does not become a 'kind' merely because it has a continuous history. Lakoff and Johnson also list examples of the more 'concrete' natural kinds which provide structures for the more abstract ones: physical orientations, objects, substances, seeing, journeys, war, madness, food, and buildings. Again, while the set of possible physical orientations has presumably changed little in evolutionary history, the domains known as 'war' and 'madness' have changed immensely in the last few centuries. Familiarity and concreteness vary not only from culture to culture, but also from historical moment to moment.

Recognizing the relativity of the concept of 'familiarity' (and of 'concreteness') allows us to qualify Lakoff and Johnson's claim that metaphor is directional, that 'we tend to structure the less concrete and inherently vaguer concepts (like those for the emotions) in terms of more concrete concepts, which are more clearly delineated in our experience'.[23] It is unclear from this statement whether the abstractness (or concreteness) of a 'concept' is a function of its position in the linguistic system, or a function of its use in a particular speech-act; unclear whether its abstractness is universal or local. It is necessary, of course, for the participants in any successful speech-act to have tacit agreements about what they consider familiar and unfamiliar. However, the directionality of the metaphors in such an act is relative to those local agreements, not to any global system. To

---

[22] Ibid., 118.   [23] Ibid., 112.

return to Lakoff and Johnson's example 'love is like a collaborative work of art': one can imagine circumstances where the speakers have little conception either of art generally, or of collaborative art in particular, and where they are relatively familiar with love. In those circumstances, 'a collaborative work of art is like love' would be a more felicitous metaphor than Lakoff and Johnson's example; it might not be the most felicitous metaphor for a collaborative work of art, but that is another matter.

Lakoff and Johnson overlook such instances of reversal because their account of metaphor is concerned with everyday acts of understanding. Its unstated governing principle is economy of effort: metaphor works to assimilate the unfamiliar to existing conceptual schemes, 'grounding' it in familiar patterns. Lakoff and Johnson break with this principle at one point, suggesting that metaphor can work to defamiliarize, and can defamiliarize something as familiar as love. However, in doing so they produce an example ('love is a collaborative work of art') in which the principle of economy runs most risk of being compromised by the cultural relativity of the metaphors.

It is clear that reversibility does not apply to every metaphor. In particular, those metaphors which Lakoff and Johnson term 'ontological' and 'orientational' metaphors seem more strongly directional than others. For example, we habitually speak of the emotions using orientational metaphors: happiness is described as 'up', depression as 'down';[24] it is not possible, however, to describe orientation using metaphors of emotion. Nevertheless, the reversibility of the less deeply rooted metaphors allows us to understand how metaphors can circulate between science, literature, and other areas of culture. Not only can scientists understand new phenomena in terms of familiar material objects and social institutions, but non-scientists can defamiliarize the familiar, reconceiving it in metaphors provided by new scientific theories. Some of these defamiliarizations are common thoughts: many people must have reversed the 'solar atom' metaphor and wondered, fancifully, if the solar system itself is an atom; at least one person wrote a pamphlet on the subject.[25] From a scientific and a practical point of view, such speculations are meaningless and eccentric, but they represent an

---

[24] Lakoff and Johnson, *Metaphors We Live By*, 15.
[25] Florence Langworthy, *Reflections on the Structure of the Atom* (London: Watts and Co., 1926).

important imaginative process for writers exploring new literary forms.

Lakoff and Johnson's account of metaphor may be developed in order to resolve some methodological problems in the discipline of literature and science. The most prominent problem concerns intention: did a given writer intend to adopt a given metaphor, or did he absorb it 'unconsciously'? This problem is one particular instance of the larger conflict between 'atomistic' and 'zeitgeist' approaches to the intellectual background to literature, and is one I shall return to shortly.[26] The most influential accounts of Victorian literature and science have focused on authors whose reading of science is well documented, notably George Eliot and Thomas Hardy; these studies have represented their literary appropriations of science as deliberate processes.[27] However, such an approach cannot be applied to the relation of Charles Dickens and evolutionary theory: the evidence for Dickens having shown an interest in Darwin is scant and ambiguous. Nevertheless, there are striking formal similarities between his narratives and contemporary science, and so critics have had recourse to the idea of the unconscious absorption of the intellectual atmosphere.[28] Similar problems affect our theorization of scientific creativity. For most schools of science, metaphor has no formal role to play in theorization, so scientific papers do not reflect deliberately on metaphor choice. Nevertheless, one can discern metaphorical structures in the theories. Similarly, in Holton's account of scientific theorization and themata, the themata appear to be an unconscious inheritance; scientists make a conscious decision only to the extent that they allow themselves to be led by their themata.[29]

A second problem, not unrelated, arises when the author or scientist is influenced by something in his social environment which cannot be readily summarized as a metaphor. The experiences of

[26] Sanford Schwartz, *The Matrix of Modernism: Pound, Eliot, and Early Twentieth-Century Thought* (Princeton: Princeton University Press, 1985), 3.

[27] Beer, *Darwin's Plots*; Sally Shuttleworth, *George Eliot and Nineteenth-Century Science* (Cambridge: Cambridge University Press, 1984).

[28] George Levine, *Darwin and the Novelists: Patterns of Science in Victorian Fiction* (Cambridge, Mass.: Harvard University Press, 1988); Kate Flint, 'Origins, Species, and *Great Expectations*', in David Amigoni and Jeff Wallace (eds.), *Charles Darwin's The Origin of Species: New Interdisciplinary Essays* (Manchester: Manchester University Press, 1995), 152–73.

[29] Holton, *The Advancement of Science*, 53.

telecommunication and of smooth high-speed travel are the most striking examples: both have profoundly changed our understanding of time and space, yet both seem more readily categorizable as 'experiences'. We should perhaps avoid the vagueness that comes with a term such as 'experiences', and attempt to uncover the metaphors which structure our experiences. In doing so, we can bring greater specificity to the discussion, and greater precision. However, although as critics we may be able to become more conscious of the metaphors involved, our doing so does not make the original participants any more conscious of them. We find ourselves in another version of the dichotomy of conscious intention and unconscious absorption.

Though the dichotomy presents two divergent images of the creative mind, they share a common factor. In the intentionalist model, the conscious mind stands outside and manipulates the metaphors. In the unconscious absorption model, the metaphors rise up into a conscious mind and influence it. Both models imply a division between metaphor and rational control: the metaphor appears to be a contaminating influence, unless it can be properly manipulated. The 'contamination' may of course be creative and productive, but it is always less than rational.

Lakoff and Johnson's account of 'metaphors we live by' presents a model in which rational discourse occurs *because of* metaphors, and not in spite of them. Their account stops short of a linguistic theory of 'subjectivity', but it may straightforwardly be assimilated to one; it goes without saying that 'subjectivity' in such a theory can no longer be understood in opposition to 'objectivity', as both are linguistic modes of representation. The respect in which Lakoff and Johnson's account falls short of a linguistic theory of the subject may be summarized by reference to their title: in saying that we live 'by' metaphors, they employ a metaphor of adjacency, as if the house of being and the convenience store of metaphor were next-door neighbours. Their own analysis of the English usage of 'with' supports this, in that it uncovers a metaphorical bond between accompaniment and instrumentality.[30] A properly linguistic theory of the subject demands a subject who is not merely living adjacent to metaphors, but who is living 'within' them; even this way of putting it does not fully convey the imbrication of the subject within the structure of language. In

---

[30] Lakoff and Johnson, *Metaphors We Live By*, 134–5.

fairness to Lakoff and Johnson, living 'by' metaphors could also be understood by analogy with living 'by' rules: in so far as we internalize the law, 'by' becomes more appropriate.

Though Lakoff and Johnson largely concern themselves with our understanding of the world around us, in their final chapter they turn to the question of self-understanding: 'Just as we seek out metaphors to highlight and make coherent what we have in common with someone else, so we seek out personal metaphors to highlight and make coherent our own pasts, our present activities, and our dreams, hopes, and goals as well.'[31] Once again, they present a model in which a subject external to language goes in search of metaphors. Elsewhere though, they refer to our 'implicit and typically unconscious conceptions of ourselves'.[32] This lends support to an account in which, so to speak, the personal metaphors go in search of us. The subject's self-understanding is structured by language prior to any higher level quest for self-knowledge. One need not accept every aspect of Lacanian theory to adopt a linguistic theory of the subject, one in which the subject is 'spoken' by language rather than (or as well as) speaking it.[33] I take my cue from Christie and Shuttleworth's suggestion that the future theorization of science and literature may lie in the idea of subject formation, and associate this remark with Althusser's account of subjects interpellated into ideology.[34] It is notable that Lakoff and Johnson's brief examination of the role of 'personal ritual' in sustaining a coherent sense of self has much in common with the Althusserian terminology of 'practices'. Practices, in Althusser's account of ideology, are the material form which ideology takes. Lakoff and Johnson's account differs from Althusser's in that it does not explain how practices are embodied in institutions. It differs more fundamentally, in that it does not seek to explain how 'rituals' sustain the power of a hegemonic class; nor does it consider how rituals diminish the lives of the people who fall into them.

---

[31] Ibid., 232–3.   [32] Ibid., 235.

[33] For an introduction, see Elizabeth Wright, *Psychoanalytic Criticism: Theory in Practice* (London: Methuen, 1984), 107–13. The key primary texts are J. Lacan, 'The Function and Field of Speech and Language in Psychoanalysis', *Écrits: A Selection*, trans. Alan Sheridan (London: Tavistock, 1977), 30–113, and Louis Althusser. 'Ideology and Ideological State Apparatuses', *Lenin and Philosophy* (London: New Left Books, 1971), 121–73.

[34] Christie and Shuttleworth (eds.), *Nature Transfigured*, 11–12.

By developing a theory of the relation of the subject to metaphor, we can sketch a modified account of scientific theory formation. The 'strong' form of such an account would argue that all scientific theory is anthropomorphic. On encountering new phenomena, and on forming new theories, the scientist understands the unfamiliar by comparing it to that which is nearest to hand and most familiar: the human subject. Lakoff and Johnson's theory comes close to this, but takes the human *body* as its primary reference point; I argue that while our models of the self must take the body into account, they are not circumscribed by it. In saying that 'the human subject' is the nearest and most familiar thing, I do not wish to imply an ahistorical model of 'human nature'. There are many subject positions, through history and across cultures, and I use the definite article merely to indicate a general type of tool. In the period examined in the following chapters, there were many possible modernist subject positions. It is precisely the plurality of subject positions which makes change in scientific theory possible. As Ian Small has said, 'when there is more than one intellectual model of "man" at any one historical moment—as in the last decades of the nineteenth century—then there will invariably be competition between epistemologies'.[35] And, one might add, competition between scientific theories, and competition between ideas of literary form.

The 'weak' form of the account would differ in that it would still allow a role to metaphor. On encountering new phenomena, or forming a new theory, the scientist has recourse to comparisons drawn from a wide range of sources: these include the human self, and its metaphors; but they also include metaphors which are of limited importance in subject formation, but of great importance in culture, society, or in other, established sciences. As the present account is intended as an exploratory sketch of a theory, it is not necessary to choose between the 'strong' and 'weak' forms. The chapters that follow will refer to this account when relevant, but are not intended to be a systematic implementation of it. I shall consider in the Conclusion the factors which limit the usefulness of a systematic theory.

Theories of subject-formation cannot in themselves solve every problem in the theorization of science and literature. For most of its life, the discipline has lived in the shadow of C. P. Snow's phrase 'the

[35] Ian Small, *Conditions for Criticism* (Oxford: Clarendon, 1991), 29.

two cultures': Snow's contention that the 'arts men' could not understand something as simple as the second law of thermodynamics has set an agenda in which all scientific theory is presumed to be occult knowledge unless proven otherwise.[36] Even if Snow's reductive binary division were true in the 1950s, it does not hold true for other historical periods. Gillian Beer has argued that in the nineteenth century, scientists shared 'a common language with other educated readers and writers of their time', 'a literary, non-mathematical discourse which was readily available to readers without a scientific training'.[37] However, the question becomes more difficult when we deal with mathematical physics, both in the nineteenth and twentieth centuries. If we must accept Snow's agenda, how are we to account for communication between the two cultures?

It is not enough to say that scientists and artists share a common linguistic system. Although they may live by a common stock of metaphors, the intellectually innovative ones are those least likely to be shared. Here, we must depart from post-Saussurean continental theory: one of its weaknesses has been its tendency to focus on the abstract linguistic system, and to overlook particular material speech acts. Another weakness has been its tendency to understand *langue* as a single ideal form shared by all speakers of a given language, and to ignore the existence of dialects within it. If we understand Lacanian 'entry into the symbolic order' in traditional psychoanalytical terms, then we are unable to distinguish between the different symbolic orders which different individuals might enter, according to the social networks in which they live. If our knowledge of linguistic structure is derived from our experience of particular material speech acts, and if these acts occur in a society which is stratified on the lines of class, gender, and profession (to name but three), then our knowledge of the language will differ according to the strata we occupy. If we are to employ the model of the speaking subject, we need to recognize that each subject is shaped by his or her community, or rather, by a set of intersecting communities.[38] We cannot interpret utterances without referring to

---

[36] C. P. Snow, 'The Two Cultures', *New Statesman and Nation*, 52 (6 Oct. 1956), 413–14; 'The Two Cultures and the Scientific Revolution', *Encounter*, 12/6 (June 1959), 17–24, and 13/1 (July 1959), 22–7.

[37] Beer, *Darwin's Plots*, 6–7.

[38] Lesley Milroy's *Language and Social Networks* (Oxford: Basil Blackwell, 1980) is the classic sociolinguistic examination of social networks.

linguistic systems, but we must attempt to choose the system(s) appropriate to the utterance in question.

With this modified Saussurean model in mind, we may return to the question of atomistic and *zeitgeist* approaches to intellectual history, and attempt to recover something useful from both. The disadvantage of the atomistic approach, taken to an extreme, is that it reports utterances, but does not determine their significance in relation to any larger system. The disadvantage of *zeitgeist* (or 'intellectual atmosphere') is that, like the classical Saussurean idea of *langue*, it is monolithic, and provides no means of discriminating between different social networks. We might tentatively replace *zeitgeist* with the model of the 'field of force'. Although, as Luckhurst has argued, this model could simply allow *zeitgeist* to return 'in scientific guise', the 'field of force' has the advantage that it allows us to model both dissemination and impermeability.[39] For the model to be useful, we must understand the field of force as being propagated through a heterogeneous, discontinuous medium: in certain places, there are material obstructions which attenuate its full force. Like the *zeitgeist* model, it allows us to ascribe scientific knowledge to an author in the absence of particular reports of reading or of conversations. Moreover, in those cases where we have fragmentary evidence of scientific knowledge, it allows us to understand its larger significance. However, the model forces us to map the medium of propagation, noting the material paths through which the ideas could have been transmitted: we cannot assume that an entire society would have been saturated uniformly in the new knowledge.

Snow's binary division of society into scientific and literary cultures is reductive and simplistic. There were subdivisions within the two cultures: in the 1920s, there were divisions between those who accepted relativity and those who clung to the ether hypothesis; between modernists and traditionalists; and between Bloomsbury modernism and Vorticism. Moreover, certain communities traversed the disciplinary boundaries. Some of these communities corresponded to actual social networks of friends, such as the Bloomsbury group, but others had only a virtual existence, existing by affiliation to a particular literary or generalist periodical. For example, Herbert Read's self-discovery and self-definition as a modernist were sustained by the actual social network of the Leeds Art

---

[39] Nicola Luckhurst, *Science and Structure in Proust's* A la recherche du temps perdu (Oxford: Clarendon, 2000), 69.

Club, and also by the virtual community of A. R. Orage's *The New Age*: he understood himself, in part, as a *New Age* reader.[40] A central assumption of this study is that the periodical is as important as the book, and that the generalist periodical is as important as the more often mentioned 'little magazine'.[41] It is gradually being recognized within the discipline that the study of periodicals allows us to reconstruct actual and virtual social networks more numerous and complex than Snow's phrase allows. It allows us to reconstruct the local *zeitgeist* of a particular social network, rather than a generalized *zeitgeist* which never informed the work of any individual. It allows us to pursue intertextual relations within that network without losing sight of the materiality of *parole*. However, though it returns us to *parole*, it allows us to do so without isolating individual authors or works from their context. The physical structure of the periodical, unlike that of the book, allows us to conceptualize texts as interacting with their neighbouring texts.

The centrality of the periodical has several practical methodological consequences, while the focus on particular periodicals in this study produces emphases and omissions which may be unexpected. Studies of modernism's intellectual context, if they give science any significant coverage at all, have tended to rely on books written after 1945.[42] These, it is true, often present a clearer and cleaner narrative of the development of the new physics than those books written at the time. However, the very process of clarification involves a refraction of the period's history through the concerns of the post-war period. After 1945, relativity theory was closely associated with the

---

[40] James King, *The Last Modern: A Life of Herbert Read* (London: Weidenfeld and Nicolson, 1990), 29–31, 39.

[41] Peter Faulkner, *Modernism* (London: Methuen, 1977), 19–20; Malcolm Bradbury and James McFarlane, 'Movements, Magazines and Manifestoes', in Bradbury and McFarlane (eds.), *Modernism 1890–1930* (London: Penguin, 1990), 192–205; Lawrence Rainey, *Institutions of Modernism* (New Haven: Yale University Press, 1998), 39, 91–9.

[42] Such overviews most commonly cite Werner Heisenberg's *Physics and Philosophy* (New York: Harper and Row, 1958), *The Physicist's Conception of Nature* (London: Hutchinson, 1958), and *Physics and Beyond* (New York: Harper and Row, 1971), along with Fritjof Capra's *The Tao of Physics* (New York: Bantam, 1975), and *The Turning Point* (New York: Simon and Schuster, 1982), and Gary Zukav's *The Dancing Wu Li Masters* (New York: William Morrow, 1979). One of the few exceptions is Randall Stevenson's *Modernist Fiction: An Introduction* (Hemel Hempstead: Harvester Wheatsheaf, 1992), which gives a broad overview of intellectual context without losing sight of specific contemporary texts; Stevenson's primary sources for science are Russell's *ABC of Relativity* (1925) and Eddington's *The Nature of the Physical World* (1928).

creation of the atomic bomb.[43] Quantum theory was seen to embody the spirit of the new physics far more fully than Einstein's theory. The concept of complementarity was believed to have changed man's understanding of his relation to nature, a theme taken up uncritically in later 'new age' science writing.[44] These concerns do not reflect what was available to writers in the 1930s, still less in the 1920s: not only do the post-1945 writers expound physical theories which were not developed until the mid and late 1920s—far too late to influence the canonical works of high modernism—but they attach values to them which were not those of the period itself. By giving contemporary periodicals a central place, we avoid such anachronisms.

It would be perverse to exclude books altogether. There was an immense upsurge in popular science writing in the period following the proof of Einstein's theory of relativity; the best-sellers by Jeans and Eddington were to become the 'tribal books' of physics for decades to follow.[45] However, the sheer number of titles presents the problem of knowing which texts might have informed a given social network, and therefore which metaphors might have informed their literary work. Some metaphors, such as the 'curvature' of space, are deeply rooted in the theory itself, but these 'deep' metaphors take many local forms, which have variable distribution. The use of 'flatlanders' to introduce the idea of curved spacetime was relatively common; the image of a distorting fairground mirror was not. We might be tempted to consult the best-sellers, particularly Eddington's *The Nature of the Physical World* and Jeans's *The Mysterious Universe*, but their being best-sellers tells us only about the total national population, not the particular social networks responsible for modernism. The elitist attitudes common in those networks meant that the very popularity of those books, particularly Jeans's, counted against them.[46] By studying reviews in literary periodicals, we may map the distribution of each title. It turns out that Eddington and even Jeans were received quite favourably in the literary periodicals at first; but it is the fact of their being widely reviewed in the right places which makes them important, not their

[43] Friedman and Donley, *Einstein as Myth and Muse*, 154–6, 171–6.

[44] e.g. Danah Zohar, *The Quantum Self* (London: Bloomsbury, 1990).

[45] Holton, *The Advancement of Science*, 165; Whitworth, 'The Clothbound Universe: Popular Physics Books, 1919–39', *Publishing History*, 40 (1996), 53–82.

[46] Whitworth, 'The Clothbound Universe', 70–5.

gross sales. The focus on periodicals can give some texts unexpected prominence: though E. A. Burtt's *The Metaphysical Foundations of Modern Physical Science* was, according to one historian of science, neglected by the scientific journals of the time, it was reviewed in six literary journals in the year of its publication, and mentioned in a novel by Aldous Huxley three years later.[47] Similarly, the present study gives more prominence to the popular science writer J. W. N. Sullivan than might seem justified by the sales of his books, primarily because his writings were so prominent in the literary community of the time.[48] If we accept that metaphors are disseminated only through material utterances, then we need an accurate bibliographical history; but the histories that are true for the community of scientists or for the population as a whole are not necessarily true for the literary community.

By emphasizing the importance of the periodical I do not intend to deny the important of conversation in the dissemination of metaphors; however, periodicals are the best means of supplementing the fragmentary records we have of actual meetings and conversations. In certain cases, the virtual communities of contributors correspond very closely to actual social networks. During the period in which Leonard Woolf was the literary editor of the *Nation*, it was virtually the house magazine of the Bloomsbury group. Vanessa Bell, feeling somewhat excluded, reported that it seemed 'like a drug': 'Everyone reads it and discusses it in and out and theres [sic] always a lot of gossip about each article or review.'[49] Murry's *Athenaeum* combined contributors from several circles, who, in spite of feelings of suspicion and superiority, met and talked at

[47] Lorraine Daston, 'History of Science in an Elegiac Mode', *Isis*, 82 (1991), 522–31; the reviews appeared in *The Calendar of Modern Letters*, *The Dial*, *The Nation and Athenaeum*, *The Spectator*, *TLS* and *The Weekly Westminster*, the allusion in Huxley's *Point Counter Point* (1928; London: Chatto and Windus, 1935), 269. Another review, by William Empson, appeared in *The Criterion* in 1930.

[48] For biographical information on Sullivan, see Whitworth, '*Pièces d'identité*: T. S. Eliot, J. W. N. Sullivan and Poetic Impersonality', *English Literature in Transition*, 39 (1996), 149–70; David Bradshaw, 'The Best of Companions: J. W. N. Sullivan, Aldous Huxley, and the New Physics', *Review of English Studies*, 47 (1996), 188–206, 352–68; for details of his sales, Whitworth, 'The Clothbound Universe', 59–60. His writings were more prominent than his name, in that his pieces for the *TLS* appeared anonymously, as did some of those for the *Athenaeum*; I have identified these contributions using the *TLS* archives at Wapping, and the marked copies of the *Athenaeum* at City University, London.

[49] Bell, letter to Roger Fry dated 29 Dec. [1923], quoted in Hermione Lee, *Virginia Woolf* (London: Chatto and Windus, 1996), 447.

various venues during its life; Sullivan, its science writer, had a great reputation as a conversationalist, and is recorded by Mansfield as discussing relativity with Murry in April 1919.[50] An interesting talker will do much more than repeat the substance of his or her latest article or review, and so we must accept that the periodicals provide an imperfect image of conversations in these social networks; but in the absence of any more thorough transcription, they at least indicate that scientific topics were available for discussion.

Periodicals can also help us to speculate more accurately on conversations between individuals who were not part of the same print communities. For example, when Sullivan met Ezra Pound in Paris in August 1922, he reportedly gave a 'lucid explanation' of Einstein's theory, or at least, in Pound's sceptical phrase, 'something he says is Einstein'.[51] To understand how Sullivan managed to interest Pound, we might turn to his *Aspects of Science*, published in March 1923; but there is nothing in the book to indicate that it collects articles dating from April 1919 to September 1922. Only with a detailed bibliography of Sullivan's periodical contributions may we identify his chronologically closest articles on relativity.[52] Given Pound's fondness for algebraic metaphors, it is also interesting to find that Sullivan shortly afterwards wrote an article on mathematics and music as objects of aesthetic contemplation.[53] Within this methodology, biographical research is valuable, but only in a strictly factual and anti-humanist form: individuals are understood not in affective terms, but as bearers of texts and metaphors.

These conceptual tools—the generalist periodical and the literary community—provide another means of understanding the relation

[50] Woolf, diary entries for 17 Apr. 1919 and 6 Jul. 1920, *Diary*, i. 264–5, ii. 52; for Sullivan, see Ottoline Morrell, *Ottoline at Garsington* (London: Faber, 1974), 259, and Ida C. Baker, *Katherine Mansfield: The Memories of L. M.* (London: Virago, 1985), 131; Mansfield, letter to Woolf dated 27 Apr. 1919, *The Letters of Katherine Mansfield*, ed. Vincent O'Sullivan and Margaret Scott, 4 vols. to date (Oxford: Oxford University Press, 1984–95), iii. 314.

[51] Pound, letter of 10 Aug. 1922 to John Quinn, *The Selected Letters of Ezra Pound to John Quinn* ed. Timothy Materer (London: Duke University Press, 1991), 216

[52] Sullivan, 'New and Old Ideas' [a review of *Philosophy and the New Physics* by Louis Rougier], *Nation and Athenaeum*, 31 (29 Jul. 1922), 604, 606; for a bibliography, see Whitworth, 'Physics and the Literary Community, 1905–1939', D. Phil. thesis (Oxford, 1994), 320–68.

[53] The article was Sullivan's 'Music and Other Arts', *TLS* (7 Sept. 1922), 561–2, reprinted under the title 'Mathematics and Music' in *Aspects of Science* (London: Cobden Sanderson, 1923), 159–76. For Pound and mathematics, see Ian F. A. Bell, *Critic as Scientist: The Modernist Poetics of Ezra Pound* (London: Methuen, 1981).

between the literal and the metaphorical in scientific writing. This might seem unnecessary, if one accepts the premise that 'all language is metaphorical', but that general premise does not explain how the metaphors we take for granted can become the objects of imaginative manipulation; how, in Black's terms, they can rise from 'dormancy' to a wide-awake state. Moreover, if it is the case that 'all language is metaphorical', one needs to explain how certain communities have been able to maintain their belief in literal truth and work with it so effectively. I would suggest that we may reconcile these problems by reference to Richard Rorty's account of factuality, though in doing so, we need not adopt Rorty's pragmatism in its entirety. On Rorty's account, the 'hardness' of a scientific fact is not an inherent property of that fact, but is simply equivalent to 'the hardness of the previous agreements within a community about the consequences of a certain event'.[54] The kind of event he has in mind would be something like the experimental test of an hypothesis. By analogy, the literalness of a literal statement is due to 'previous agreements' within a speech community to interpret in certain way.

We may associate this, as Rorty does, with Stanley Fish's idea of 'interpretive communities': an interpretive community agrees to certain interpretive strategies; the stability of its interpretations is due not to the inherent stability of the text, but to its stability as a community. Such a stability is, of course, relative: communities 'grow and decline', and individuals 'move from one to another'.[55] As Fish says, one of the most successful interpretive programmes of the last three hundred years has been that which goes by the name of 'ordinary language'; we may add that 'literal meaning' is the dominant strategy within this programme. By implication, the principle that 'all language is metaphorical' must be seen not as the underlying 'truth', but simply as another interpretive programme.

The trouble with the pragmatism of Rorty and Fish is that it provides no means of deciding between interpretive programmes, except retrospectively on the basis of which has been the most 'successful'. Moreover, it offers no account of how institutional power determines the 'agreements within a community'. It implies a community which is a perfect liberal democracy, untroubled by inequalities of wealth,

[54] Richard Rorty, 'Texts and Lumps', *New Literary History*, 17 (1985), 3–16 (p. 3).
[55] Stanley Fish, *Is there a Text in this Class?* (Baltimore: Johns Hopkins University Press, 1980), 170–2.

status, or physical force; it gives no indication of how these inequalities might restrict the ability of individuals and groups to carry out programmes of research. It does not describe something as hierarchical as a scientific research community, a university, or a nation state in the twentieth century. Individuals, in Fish's bland account of communities, simply 'leave': they are never made redundant or forcibly deported. If this pragmatist account of interpretation is to explain such developments, it needs to recognize the materiality of each speech act, its occurring in a particular time and place. Once its materiality is recognized, we can begin to relate it to personal and institutional power.

The advantage of the pragmatist account of interpretation is that it allows us to understand how the same ideas, even the same text, can signify differently according to their context. A non-technical exposition of relativity in a scientific journal would tend to be interpreted within the programme implied by the journal's institutional context; its metaphorical content remains dormant. The same exposition in a generalist journal could be interpreted very differently. The process of juxtaposition in a generalist journal disrupts the agreements that govern the interpretation of articles on history, literature, science, and the arts; furthermore, it implies a programme of comparing ideas between dissimilar disciplines. Such a programme could operate in any period of history, but was particularly important in the early twentieth century, when experiments in visual and textual collage were encouraging similar programmes of generic disruption. The generalist journal allows dormant metaphors to wake, or, volcanically speaking, to erupt. Though such an interpretive programme is most strongly encouraged in relation to the contents of actual journals, it stands a good chance of becoming habitual within the interpretive community, and of being applied elsewhere.

Modernist writers were well aware that metaphor could be found far beyond literature: as Eliot wrote, it 'is not something applied externally for the adornment of style, it is the life of style, of language . . . we are dependent upon metaphor for even the abstractest thinking'.[56] Such abstract thinking included thinking about literary form; the dependency was at times conscious, at other times unconscious. The metaphors were drawn from things familiar and near to

[56] T. S. Eliot, 'Studies in Contemporary Criticism', *The Egoist*, 5/9 (Oct. 1918), 113–14.

hand, but those things were rich and various: they included the contents of the generalist journals; they included the metaphors which shaped the subjectivities of modern city dwellers.

I

The Specialist, the Generalist, and the Populist

THE popularization of science is a symptom of modernity; its relation to modernism is more complex. The verb 'to popularize' originally referred to a political process of gaining favour at court; by the late eighteenth century it had come to imply a division between an elite and a democratic mass; it was first used in relation to technical or abstruse knowledge in 1833, the year before the word 'scientist' entered the language. The noun 'popularizer' was first used in 1848, in collocation with 'science'. 'Popularization' dates from the same period, though the earliest instance cited by the *OED* in collocation with 'science' occurs much later, in 1926. Popularization, in the sense we are interested in, comes into being at the same time as the division of 'reason' into distinct disciplines; this process was itself part of the larger process of the division of labour. According to Habermas's influential account (indebted to Weber), reason was specialized into 'three autonomous spheres', 'science, morality and art', but it is clear that analyses could be made involving four or more spheres, and that further subdivisions took place within each of those named.[1] Modernists acknowledged the process of specialization, though their analyses differed from Weber's as to the cause and the number of parts; most famously Eliot diagnosed a 'dissociation of sensibility' into two parts, wit and emotion, that had taken place in the seventeenth century.[2] If the modernist attitude to specialization implied a nostalgia for a lost unity, it also, for some, implied a programme of reuniting the fragments of sensibility; this programme had some things in common with the impulse to

---

[1] Habermas, 'Modernity—An Incomplete Project' in Thomas Docherty (ed.), *Postmodernism: A Reader* (Hemel Hempstead: Harvester Wheatsheaf, 1993), 98–109 (p. 103). See also Max Weber, *The Protestant Ethic and the Spirit of Capitalism*, trans. Talcott Parsons (London: George Allen and Unwin, 1930), 24–6, on rationalization.

[2] Eliot, 'The Metaphysical Poets' (1921) in *Selected Prose*, ed. Frank Kermode (London: Faber, 1975), 64.

popularize science. However, 'popularization' is an ambiguous concept, describing a movement which could be sideways, between disciplines of equivalent status, but which could also be downwards, from the elite to the mass of the people. This is roughly equivalent to the distinction recognized in the *OED*, between making something 'admired' or 'likeable', and making it 'intelligible'. There is also a religious model behind the ambiguity: whenever the term 'layman' is invoked in descriptions of popular science writing, it implies that there is a corresponding scientific 'clergy'. In so far as modernism defined itself in opposition to the masses, and in so far as popularization appeared to vulgarize the elitist knowledge of science, popular science met with hostility. The *OED*'s instance of 'popularization' in collocation with 'science' comes from Wyndham Lewis's *The Art of Being Ruled*, and in context it is synonymous with 'vulgarization'.[3]

Scientific popularization has only recently emerged as an area of study within the history of science;[4] its treatment as an object of literary criticism is even less well established.[5] None of the dominant models of 'science' grants a significant place to popularization. Realist models demarcate science and non-science very sharply: science is produced 'in esoteric ways by autonomous, exclusive communities'; popularizations are 'science' only in name, and are therefore an inappropriate object of study for historians.[6] In Cambridge University until the 1920s, there was an unwritten rule that Fellows did not write popular books, and this seems to derive from a similar model of science, in which the discipline must remain isolated from

---

[3] Lewis, *The Art of Being Ruled*, ed. Reed Way Dasenbrock (Santa Rosa: Black Sparrow, 1989), 366.

[4] In 1996, Roger Smith described it as having 'hardly been touched': *Popular Physics and Astronomy: An Annotated Bibliography* (Lanham, MD: Scarecrow, 1996), 1–2.

[5] For literary approaches, see Murdo William McRae (ed.), *The Literature of Science: Perspectives on Popular Scientific Writing* (Athens: University of Georgia Press, 1993), and Elizabeth Leane, 'Contemporary Popular Physics: An Interchange between Literature and Science', D. Phil. thesis (Oxford, 1999), 25–9; my account is particularly indebted to Leane.

[6] Richard Whitley, 'Knowledge Producers and Knowledge Acquirers', in Terry Shinn and Richard Whitley (eds.), *Expository Science: Forms and Functions of Popularisation*, Sociology of the Sciences, 9 (Dordrecht: D. Reidel, 1985), 3–28 (pp. 6–7); Michel Cloître and Terry Shinn, 'Expository Practice', ibid., 29–60 (p. 31); see also Roger Cooter and Stephen Pumfrey, 'Separate Spheres and Public Places: Reflections on the History of Science Popularization and Science in Popular Culture', *History of Science*, 32 (1994), 237–67 (pp. 239–40); Leane, 'Contemporary Popular Physics', 25–9.

the 'public' in order to ensure its purity.[7] Constructivist models might at first seem more sympathetic to popular science: they see scientific knowledge not as a reflection of nature, but as a construct of human minds. The truth of science is relative to the socially established norms and procedures of the discipline. However, this approach did not encourage the analysis of popular science: 'it was reasoned', explain Cooter and Pumfrey, 'that if all science was to be regarded as socially permeable, then there was no particular need to study the "popularization" of science to access this sociability.'[8] Indeed, to study it would seem to reinforce the realist model and the distinction it draws between scientist and layman.

Popular accounts of entropy usefully illuminate the ambiguity of 'popularize'. Though entropy is of interest in this book primarily because it rests on themes of fragmentation and probability, it is the theme of heat death which puts 'popularization' under the greatest strain. This theme does not fit the accounts usually offered of popular science. It is usually claimed that popular science attempts to relate pure scientific ideas to practical concerns: new inventions and medical breakthroughs, for example.[9] Though thermodynamics began from the very practical base of steam engines, and though it provided popularizers with many opportunities to relate it to everyday life (heating or steam locomotion, for example), it was more often framed in terms of cosmology than technology. By dwelling on the idea that the sun had a finite life, and that life on earth is doomed to extinction, the popularizers were able to make thermodynamics 'intelligible', but such a gloomy prognosis is not immediately 'admirable' or 'likeable'. We need to recognize, however, that the terrifying prospect of immediate death is in these instances transformed into the sublime contemplation of death many generations in the future. It becomes 'likeable' because it is sensational. We also need to recognize that, fundamentally, popularization works by relating science to something which is familiar to the target audience; practical applications provide one instance of the familiar, but are not the only possibility. Elsewhere, popularizations relate science to less tangible entities, such as familiar metaphors and 'dominant ideological views'.[10]

---

[7] Gary Werskey, *The Visible College* (London: Allen Lane, 1978), 84.

[8] Cooter and Pumfrey, 'Separate Spheres and Public Places', 241.

[9] Whitley, 'Knowledge Producers and Knowledge Acquirers', 22; Peter Broks, *Media Science Before the Great War* (Basingstoke: Macmillan, 1996), 37–8.

[10] Whitley, 'Knowledge Producers and Knowledge Acquirers', 22.

The reasons for framing thermodynamics in cosmological terms are relevant to the other areas of physics we will be examining. As well as conveying the ideas in themselves, the popularizer is also shaping the public image of his science. As several sociological critics have argued, popularizations are addressed not only to the general public, but to other researchers in related areas, and to 'sponsors and legitimators'.[11] In nineteenth-century Germany, popularization seemed to many scientists to be 'the only possible means of overcoming existing (or suspected) prejudices against the sciences and of proving their value for cultural development.'[12] In late nineteenth- and early twentieth-century Britain, where the universities and government were similarly dominated by graduates in the humanities, scientists had a similar interest in presenting their discipline in a philosophical rather than a technological framework. The cosmological frame on thermodynamics allowed them to do this. As we shall see in Chapter 4, the 'practical' frame that was placed on science during the 1914–18 war (by journalists, by classicists, and by scientists themselves) produced a post-war counter-reaction which emphasized the purity of scientific research. In examining the form and style of popular science writing, it is important to note that the motives described above were not necessarily consciously held or unmixed. By the early twentieth century they had become naturalized as an autonomous generic feature of popular science writing. Scientific journalists, who had no interest in the continued survival of any one academic institution, nevertheless wrote books which resembled those of the university professors.

Insofar as historians of science have studied popularization, they have done so within frameworks which, though not incompatible with prevailing modes of literary analysis, do not provide a ready-made methodology for literary study. The more sociologically oriented writers generally employ summaries of texts, and do not engage with local textual detail.[13] They have tended to focus on popularizations in mass-market media: Cloître and Shinn focus on the contemporary French daily press (*Le Monde* and *Libération*)

[11] Ibid., 12–13.

[12] Bayertz, 'Spreading the Spirit of Science', in Shinn and Whitley (eds.), *Expository Science*, 209–27 (p. 216).

[13] In the Shinn and Whitley collection, Steven Yearley's chapter is the exception: 'Representing Geology: Textual Structures in the Pedagogical Presentation of Science', *Expository Science*, 79–101; the essays in McRae (ed.), *The Literature of Science*, are more sympathetic to literary–critical approaches.

and contrast its science coverage with *La Recherche*, a 'semi-professional' monthly similar to *Scientific American*; Peter Broks examines periodicals aimed at the working classes in the period 1890–1914, such as *Cassell's Magazine*, *The Clarion*, *Pearson's Weekly*, and *Tit-Bits*.[14] While the mass-market journals provide a useful point of contrast, the social relations they negotiate are not the same as those in the literary journals which addressed a small, formally educated readership. The reader of the *Fortnightly Review* or of the *Athenaeum* expected to be spoken to as an equal. The model of popularization is here more horizontal in its orientation, making knowledge intelligible across disciplinary boundaries; in addition, the reader may expect to be spoken to as part of an educated elite.

The sociological school of criticism rightly treats popular-scientific texts not as constative utterances, but as perlocutionary ones: though for their original readers they were interesting as descriptions of scientific theory, from a historical perspective they are interesting as attempts to persuade their readers of the relevance of science. Though in later chapters I will be reading the popular texts with close attention to their expository metaphors, here, to grasp popularization as such, it is necessary to pay closer attention to details at the margin of the text. In reading a popular science article, the reader is being told as much about himself as about dissipation, radiation, or the curvature of spacetime. He is being told about his relation to the authority of 'science', and his relation to the fragmented knowledge that characterizes modernity. He is being positioned explicitly, in the use of terms such as 'layman', 'educated layman', and 'intellectual', and implicitly, through the text's use of pronouns, particularly 'we', 'you', and 'they.' In Althusserian terms, the reader is being offered a subject position, interpellated into ideology. Though details of subject position do not affect the scientific content, they are crucial in shaping its reception. Cumulatively, they work to shape the reader's understanding of the relation of science to other modes of knowledge.

Details just outside the text also shape the reader's relation to it. The reader's relation to a popular-scientific text in a generalist periodical is shaped by the general ethos of the periodical, and by comments on and allusions to science in other non-scientific

---

[14] Cloître and Shinn, 'Expository Practice', 47; Broks, *Media Science*, 18–27.

contributions. Advertisements also give clues to the implied reader of the periodical, though the generalist periodicals examined here carried much less advertising than the mass market ones. The marginal signs in a book are harder to pin down, but they range from its physical qualities as a book (the size, the paper, the binding, the jacket) to the identity given to the author through jacket biographies and professional qualifications listed on the title page. The sociological school of analysis has generally paid little attention to the materiality of the text; Peter Broks's study is exceptional in surveying the advertisements that surrounded the popular articles.[15]

The relevant information concerns not the author or the reader in themselves, but the reader's relation to the author. More specifically, it concerns the reader, as someone aware of their incompleteness in a world of specialized knowledge, in relation to the author, as someone who can heal that incompleteness, albeit temporarily. The author, though, does not act alone, but as part of the generalist journal as an ensemble. Though the readers were often addressed as 'laymen', this was not necessarily actually the case: scientists also needed popular accounts of science. Oliver Lodge admitted in private that he, J. J. Thomson, Joseph Larmor, and others of the older generation of scientists found the mathematics of the new physics appallingly difficult.[16] His fear of being left behind in the continual process of innovation was something he shared with lay readers. In public he admitted that he had found one of Sullivan's reviews in the *Times Literary Supplement* helpful in overcoming his objections to relativity.[17] Nor should it be imagined that popular science articles were read only by scientists of an older generation. Eddington wrote in private that he thought highly of Sullivan's writing, and that he thought Sullivan 'quite unique in his combination of qualities'.[18] Several of the physicists who championed relativity had also read Karl Pearson's popular text *The Grammar of Science*: T. Percy Nunn had read it in 1892, and Eddington in 1906.[19]

[15] Ibid., 28–9, 108.

[16] Lodge, letter to Arthur Hill dated 5 Mar. 1928, *Letters from Sir Oliver Lodge*, ed. J. Arthur Hill (London: Cassell, 1932), 223–4.

[17] Lodge, letter to *The Times* (15 Apr. 1922), 13, referring to Sullivan's review of Hermann Weyl's *Space–Time–Matter* in TLS (13 Apr. 1922), 237.

[18] Eddington, letter to Charles Singer dated 14 May 1936, Wellcome Library, Singer Papers, PP/CJS/A.48. Eddington was responding to an appeal on behalf of Sullivan, who was suffering from the incurable nervous disease which killed him in 1937.

[19] Nunn, letter to J. G. Crowther, dated 28 Jun. 1922, University of Sussex, Crowther Papers, box 5; Eddington papers, Trinity College Cambridge, Add MS b. 48, fos. 134–9.

The sense of incompleteness was the crucial motivation behind the collection of essays edited by Joseph Needham, *Science, Religion and Reality* (1925). As an undergraduate Needham had read R. G. Collingwood's *Speculum Mentis*, which had argued that 'the force of human experience could be divided into five forms. These were (a) religion, (b) science, (c) history, (d) philosophy, and (e) artistic creation.'[20] It is interesting to compare this analysis to Weber's: though both feel the effects of specialization, Collingwood finds a five-fold division. More significantly, the mode of '*could be divided*' implies a different analysis of the cause: the division seems less absolute, but also more natural. Needham felt that one could only become 'a perfectly rounded human character' by having 'some feeling' of the role of each of these forms. The collection of essays was intended to facilitate this process of becoming rounded: most essays examined the relations of religion and science in some way, but they did so from a wide variety of perspectives. Contributors included an astronomer (Eddington), an anthropologist (Bronislaw Malinowski), a biochemist (Needham), a historian of medicine (Charles Singer), and the Dean of St Paul's (W. R. Inge). The diverse range of the collection's reviewers gives further indication of its scope: it was reviewed by a scientific journalist (Sullivan), a lawyer (Maurice Amos), a literary critic and philosopher of language (I. A. Richards), and a literary editor (John Middleton Murry).[21]

The generalist periodical has a wider range of formats available to it than the scholarly collection of essays, and the choice of format will create different positions for the reader in relation to science. Open to variation are: the number of scientific contributors employed; the degree of prominence given to the name and status of the authors; the number of scientific articles in the average issue; and the variety of topics covered, both in a given issue and in the periodical over several issues. The usual format for most periodicals was the occasional article. In the 1890s, *The Nineteenth Century* not only ran occasional scientific articles written by specialists, but it also had a column titled 'Recent Science' which usually covered

---

[20] Joseph Needham, letter to the author dated 13 Mar. 1993; see Collingwood, *Speculum Mentis* (Oxford: Clarendon, 1924), 39.

[21] Sullivan, 'Science and Mysticism', *TLS* (12 Nov. 1925), 748; Amos, 'Religion and Science', *New Statesman*, 26 (23 Jan. 1926), 449–50; Richards, 'The Giant Problem', *Nation and Athenaeum*, 38 (23 Jan. 1926), 587; Murry, 'Science and Knowledge', *The Adelphi*, 7 (Dec. 1925), 461–72.

between three and five quite separate topics. Although the column was written by a regular contributor, Prince Kropotkin, he made no attempt to draw topics together, and never ventured to comment on larger trends in science. Thus the reader would find such topics as 'Life in the Moon' alongside 'Animal Psychology', 'Brain Structure' alongside 'The Approach of the Black Death', or 'Biological Chemistry' alongside 'Weather Prediction'.[22] This heterogeneity *within* science gives the science column one of the formal qualities of news, and would have done so even without the emphasis on 'recent' in the title. In this instance the author exerts no unifying influence. There is a positive aspect to this, in that it reinforces the reader's feeling of being up to date, but there is also negative aspect, in that it only exacerbates the sense of fragmentation.

The unusual quality of Kropotkin's column may be clarified by contrast with contemporaneous writing in the *Fortnightly Review*, and with the post–1918 *Athenaeum*. The *Fortnightly* published scientific contributions from a wider range of scientists: Karl Pearson contributed frequently in the 1890s, along with, less frequently, Herbert Spencer, C. Lloyd Morgan, Frederick Harrison and T. H. Huxley, and others who are now less well remembered, such as R. A. Gregory, Robert Ball, and T. E. Thorpe. The range of contributors might have created the formal impression of 'news', though less sharply than a miscellaneous single-author column; however, while some articles emphasized their topicality,[23] generally they took a more philosophical approach. Moreover, the recurrence of certain themes, such as the relation of materialism to morality, provided a continuity of argument, and the themes themselves implied that the review was attempting to negotiate between intellectual spheres, if not to reconcile them.

The Athenaeum's articles under the heading 'Science' were nearly always written by Sullivan, and were usually signed 'S'; on a few occasions Geoffrey Keynes wrote on medicine and A. L. Bacharach on chemistry. Sullivan's columns very rarely addressed the practical applications of science; they addressed topical issues insofar as relativity was topical, but they did not follow the news agenda of new discoveries. Characteristically, they move from a particular scientific

[22] Kropotkin, 'Recent Science', *Nineteenth Century*, 40 (Aug. 1896), 240–59; ibid., 42 (Jul. 1897), 22–43; and ibid., 45 (Mar. 1899), 404–23.

[23] R. A. Gregory, 'The Spectroscope in Recent Chemistry', *Fortnightly*, 64 (Aug. 1895), 289–98.

theory to larger reflections on the philosophical implications of that theory, or to reflections on the relation of science to literature, the arts, or music. The articles in themselves attempt to negotiate the schisms of specialization, and, as we shall see, do so still more effectively when viewed as part of *The Athenaeum* as a whole. Though Sullivan's unifying role as an author was somewhat concealed by the use of an initial, few can have failed to recognize an authorial presence behind the column.

I have suggested that the presentation of science as news tends to reinforce the reader's impression of the heterogeneity of modern culture, but a passage from the short-lived *New Quarterly* (November 1907 to May 1910) opens up the complexity of the issue. *The New Quarterly: A Review of Science and Literature*, edited by Desmond MacCarthy, had a higher proportion of science articles than any generalist periodical. It led its first issue with an article by Lord Rayleigh, and the issue effectively interleaved scientific articles with artistic ones.[24] In his article on the ether, R. J. Strutt reflected on the value of popularizing current research topics:

Readers who take a general interest in current scientific problems may like to gain some idea of the nature of the difficulties to be overcome. It is, perhaps, too much the tendency to limit non-technical exposition to a description of territory which science has conquered. There is often a more living interest in a survey of that border-land where the battle against our ignorance is actually being fought.[25]

The first sentence does not merely define other readers: it defines the reader as he reads it. Of course, such a defining sentence can provide a point of departure as well as a point of interpellation, for the reader who is quite certain that he takes no interest in such things and has no interest in the difficulties. But the following sentences define such a reader negatively, as someone complacent and sheltered. The third sentence, by employing the metaphor of 'science as conquest', makes scientific knowledge appear stable even though it is in a state of continual change. While most analyses, science develops through a process of ramification and increasing specialization, the metaphor of conquering territory implies that science

---

[24] Lord Rayleigh, 'How Do We Perceive the Direction of Sound', *New Quarterly*, 1 (Nov. 1907), 1–16; Bertrand Russell, 'The Study of Mathematics', ibid., 29–44; R. J. Strutt, 'Can We Detect Our Drift Through Space?', ibid., 85–100.

[25] Ibid., 92

maintains the contiguity of the territory it has taken. The passage also illustrates how the presentation of a new theory as news, rather than as something intrinsically interesting, changes the readership's relation to it, reassuring them that they are up-to-date. However, the roundedness that the periodical brings is only temporary: it is soon ruptured by the continuing process of scientific discovery and intellectual specialization.

The relatively low prominence given in these journals to the personal presence of the scientific writer may be defined by contrast with two popular journals of the 1920s and 30s, *John O'London's Weekly* and its offshoot, *The Outline*, which specialized in 'Books, Popular Science and Things of To-Day' in its brief life from 1927 to 1929. Though some of their articles were anonymous, many came with the imprimatur of an acknowledged scientific authority, such as Professor J. Arthur Thomson, or, once his reputation had been established through his popular scientific books, J. W. N. Sullivan.[26] The 'authored' articles generally came with a photograph of their producer, and while there were generally no attempts to include a sentimental 'human angle' on the scientist and his work, the photographs gave the reader a stronger feeling of the author's presence.

The Outline and *John O'London's* also presented its popularizations in the form of 'Talks with the Professor', through the medium of generic figures such as 'The Listener' or 'The Enquiring Layman'. The former developed the idea of the authored scientific column, and allowed the editor to employ unfamiliar scientific journalists, while sustaining his readers' sense of continuity and of a familiar presence. These columns were illustrated with a small drawing of the Professor's book-lined study. While it is unlikely that any but the youngest readers believed in the existence of the Professor, the subliminal effect of continuity remains. The presence of the 'Enquiring Layman' creates a very different relation between reader and journal from that which existed for *The Athenaeum*: while Murry and his contributors inevitably implied their audience in passing, the

---

[26] Harry Roberts, 'The Light that Bends', *John O'London's Weekly* [hereafter *JOLW*], 3 (11 Sept. 1920), 641; Albert Einstein, 'Einstein explains his theory', *JOLW*, 5 (25 June 1921), 325, based on Einstein's Princeton Lectures; J. Arthur Thomson, 'What Relativity Is: Einstein's New Theory of the Universe', *The Outline*, 2 (19 May 1928), 4–5; anon., 'Maeterlinck in Search of the Einstein Blue Bird', *The Outline*, 3 (24 Nov., 1 Dec., and 8 Dec. 1928), 29–30, 50, 66–7, 100–1; anon., 'Is Professor Eddington "On the Side of the Angels?" ', *The Outline*, 3 (15 Dec. 1928), 113–14; J. W. N. Sullivan, 'Time and Space: A Sketch of Einstein's Famous Theory', *The Outline*, 3 (5 Jan. 1929), 202.

reader was never represented to himself so explicitly. On the one hand the inclusion of the 'Enquiring Layman' provided the reader with a recognizable, even flattering, subject-position from which to learn about science, but on the other, it served as a permanent reminder of his distance from learning and its institutions; women readers were doubly distanced.

The instability of the position may be illustrated through Walter Grierson's collection of the articles he wrote as 'The Enquiring Layman', *The Conclusions of Modern Science*. The title itself is significant, emphasizing closure in a period when science was notably turbulent and its conclusions only ever provisional. The preliminary pages are particularly interesting: they feature a Foreword from Sullivan, writing authoritatively as 'Author of *Aspects of Science* etc.', and an Introduction from Grierson, speaking as plainly as possible.[27] Sullivan speaks approachably, but downwards ('the ordinary reader, I take it, will find here a description of his own perplexities'), while Grierson writes of his indebtedness to Sullivan, 'whose mathematical accomplishments, and detailed knowledge of physics and relativity leave me bewildered'.[28] Grierson's pronouns are significantly unstable: scientists, consistently 'they', have spent centuries piercing the thicket of their subject, and now 'they are making very plain to us the net results to date. They are telling enquiring laymen the things that, as laymen, they want to know.' What 'they' want to know, not 'we': Grierson, as mediator, is both inside and outside the group, and the enquiring reader is doubly reminded of his distance from science. The distance is vertical, with the expert scientist located above the layman reader. The process of popularization is here conceived not only in terms of making intelligible, but making likeable. The apotheosis of this conception came in anonymous articles in *John O'London's* which tried to make

---

[27] There is not space for a full consideration of a related theme, the use of the scientist to provide an authorizing preface to a non-scientific text: for examples, see Eddington, 'Foreword', in A. Allen Brockington, *Mysticism and Poetry* (London: Chapman and Hall, 1934), pp. vii–ix, and Sullivan, 'Foreword', in H. A. Overstreet, *The Enduring Quest: A Search for a Philosophy of Life* (London: Jonathan Cape, 1931), 7–13. James Joyce claimed that Sullivan had been approached, and had declined, to write a preface to the *Examination of Work in Progress*. Though Joyce may have been jesting, even an imaginary approach to Sullivan acknowledges the convention of the scientist's authorizing preface: letter to Harriet Shaw Weaver dated 27 May 1929, *Letters of James Joyce*, ed. Stuart Gilbert and Richard Ellmann, 3 vols. (London: Faber, 1966), i. 279.

[28] Walter Grierson, *The Conclusions of Modern Science*, Outline Library, 10 (London: Newnes, 1930), pp. x, xv.

relativity more accessible by making it amusing: one took the form of a speech, purportedly by Einstein, in a mock-German accent; another, in a similar music-hall vein, was a dialogue in which a young man insists on teaching relativity to his mother-in-law.[29]

The majority of the generalist journals responded to relativity by giving authoritative accounts by recognized experts; however, from its inception, relativity had caused dispute over whose authority counted. The first article on the General Theory in Britain was written by the Dutch physicist W. de Sitter in *The Observatory*; it was followed by some correspondence and further articles there, in *Nature*, and in the *Monthly Notices of the Royal Astronomical Society*.[30] However, the world of the scientific journal was not hermetically sealed: ideas about space, time and gravity were being discussed at the Aristotelian Society and in its *Proceedings*, and in the philosophical journal *Mind*.[31] In their debate in *The Observatory*, James Jeans and Eddington were unable to agree whether the metaphysical element in relativity was essential to it or a superficial 'garment'.

The first expositions in popular journals appeared early in 1919, one by a scientist in the relatively specialist pages of *Science Progress*, the other a series of five articles by Sullivan in *The*

[29] Anon., 'Relativity without Tears', *JOLW*, 6 (7 Jan. 1922), 454, reprinted from Aberdeen University's *Alma Mater*; anon., 'Something about Einstein', *JOLW*, 6 (18 Mar. 1922), 782.

[30] W. de Sitter, 'Space, Time and Gravitation', *The Observatory*, 39 (Oct. 1916), 412–19; T. J. J. See, 'Einstein's Theory of Gravitation' [letter], *The Observatory*, 39 (Dec. 1916), 511–12; James Jeans, 'Einstein's Theory of Gravitation', *The Observatory*, 40 (Jan. 1917), 57–8; Arthur Eddington, 'Einstein's Theory of Gravitation', *Monthly Notices of the Royal Astronomical Society*, (Feb. 1917), 377–82; Eddington, 'Einstein's Theory of Gravitation', *The Observatory*, (Feb. 1917), 93–5; Eddington, 'Gravitation and the Principle of Relativity', *Nature*, 101 (7 Mar. 1918), 15–17, and ibid. (14 Mar. 1918), 34–6 (a discourse first delivered at the Royal Institution, Friday 1 Feb. 1918). A full account of the scientific reception of relativity from 1907 to 1919 may be found in José M. Sanchez-Ron, 'The Reception of Special Relativity in Great Britain', in Thomas F. Glick (ed.), *The Comparative Reception of Relativity*, Boston Studies in the Philosophy of Science, 103 (Dordrecht: D. Reidel, 1987), 27–58.

[31] L. J. Russell, 'Space and Mathematical Reasoning', *Mind*, 67 (July 1908), 321–49; C. D. Broad, 'What do we mean by the question: is our space Euclidean?', *Mind*, 96 (Oct. 1915), 464–80; Norman Campbell, 'The Common Sense of Relativity', *Philosophical Magazine*, 6th ser., 21 (Apr. 1911), 502–17; H. W. Carr, 'The Time Difficulty in Realist Theories of Perception', *Proceedings of the Aristotelian Society* [hereafter *PAS*], 12 (1911–12), 124–87; Carr, 'The Principle of Relativity and its Importance For Philosophy', *PAS*, 14 (1913–14), 407–24; A. N. Whitehead, 'Space, Time and Relativity', *PAS*, 16 (1915–16), 104–29.

Athenaeum.[32] However, it was not until the announcement of Eddington's experimental confirmation of the theory, at the Royal Society on 7 November 1919, that the majority of newspaper and journal editors sought out authoritative expositions. Both scientists and philosophers offered non-technical accounts to the generalist journals, with Bertrand Russell contributing to *The Athenaeum* and *The English Review*, Eddington to *The Contemporary Review* and *The Quarterly Review*, and Oliver Lodge to *The Nineteenth Century* and *The Fortnightly Review*.[33] The contributors to other journals included a mixture of scientists (E. N. da C. Andrade, E. Cunningham, F. M. Denton, F. A. Lindemann, A. C. D. Crommelin), philosophers (C. D. Broad, H. Wildon Carr), mathematicians (A. N. Whitehead), and professional journalists: A. E. Randall, who wrote for *The New Age*, was also their theatre critic, though to the reader his two identities were separate.[34]

Some of these disciplinary categories were relatively permeable—one could classify Russell and Whitehead either as mathematicians or as philosophers—and this requires us partially to qualify the Weberian thesis about specialization. Specialization is a gradual process, and in its early years, the boundaries are open to revision. In Kuhn's terms, the creation of a discipline occurs when a scientific group is converted to a new paradigm. In the period of the initial reception of a paradigm, 'the formation of specialized journals, the foundation of specialists' societies, and the claim for a special place in the curriculum' take prominence.[35] However, for a significant period, an individual scientist can belong to several

[32] G. W. De Tunzelman, 'Physical Relativity Hypotheses Old and New', *Science Progress* (January 1919), 475–82; J. W. N. Sullivan, 'A Crucial Phenomenon', *The Athenaeum* (9 May 1919), 303; 'On Relative Motion', ibid., (16 May 1919), 337; 'The Notion of Simultaneity', ibid., (23 May 1919), 369; 'The Union of Space and Time', ibid., (30 May 1919), 402; 'The Equivalence Principle', ibid., (6 June 1919), 433.

[33] For full details, see the bibliography.

[34] For full details, see the bibliography under these names. Randall wrote the theatre column as 'John Francis Hope': see Wallace Martin, *The New Age under Orage* (Manchester: Manchester University Press, 1967), 125. The professional identities of other writers remain obscure, because they wrote anonymously, or because a shortage of biographical information; more importantly, they would have been obscure even to a well-informed contemporary reader: anon., 'Einstein's Reaction on Philosophy', *Saturday Review* (22 Nov. 1919), 481–2; R. W. Western, 'The Principle of Relativity', *New Age*, 25 (27 Nov. 1919), 54–6; Western, 'Relativity and Metaphysics', *New Age*, 25 (1 Jan. 1920) 137–8; ibid. (8 Jan. 1920), 154–5; ibid. (15 Jan. 1920), 171–2.

[35] T. S. Kuhn, *The Structure of Scientific Revolutions* (1962; Chicago: University of Chicago Press, 1970), 18–19.

societies (mathematical, philosophical, physical), and can write in several journals without becoming self-contradictory. At the time of its first arrival, relativity seemed as much to have destroyed the disciplinary boundaries as to have put a new one in place. It created an unusual situation for the educated intellectual who was aware of his specialized narrowness: insofar as he could not comprehend the theory, he remained incomplete; but it appeared that if he could, several fields of intellectual enquiry would be unified. The promised unification was analogous to the 'comprehensiveness' of Einstein's theory, but far exceeded it in scope.

Thus far I have concentrated on the attraction of science to the intellectual reader, in terms of personal wholeness, but it is worth asking why journal editors and publishers found it worthwhile to print. One cannot automatically assume that their motives were financial. Some of the most significant generalist British journals of the period were owned, indirectly, by the Joseph Rowntree Social Service Trust, which was concerned primarily to advance its progressive Liberal ethos, even if it made a loss.[36] It purchased *The Speaker* in 1907, and retitled it *The Nation*; it bought a share in *The Contemporary Review* in 1911, and it started *War and Peace* (later, under Leonard Woolf, *The International Review*) in 1917. It purchased *The Athenaeum* in April 1917. Although during Murry's editorship the Trust owned the title only indirectly, it estimated that between 1917 and 1922 it had lost £22,378; losses of this order of magnitude were considered to be 'heavy'. We can never know whether the *Athenaeum*'s focus on pure science made it a more or a less viable commercial proposition. It appears that publishers placed a value on factors which a narrowly analytic mode of accounting would not take into consideration. When Chatto and Windus accepted a translation of Vasiliev's *Space Time Motion* in 1923, they told the translator that they had accepted it on account of its intellectual rather than its financial value.[37] Just as Joseph Needham was concerned to be a 'fully rounded human character', so the publishers were concerned to maintain a fully rounded list. The value of a good list, they believed, was sufficient to outweigh the risk of losses on individual titles.

---

[36] I am grateful to Elizabeth Jackson, librarian at the Joseph Rowntree Foundation, for supplying me with extracts from 'A Review of the Work of the J.R.S.S.T. 1905–1939 and suggestions regarding future policy' (1942).

[37] Letter from Geoffrey Whitworth to the co-translator, Mrs H. M. Lucas, dated 19 Sept. 1923, Reading University, Chatto and Windus Letterbook, MS 2444/106 f. 522.

More speculatively, one may consider how the intellectual specialization characteristic of modernity relates to the form of the generalist periodical. The mass-market Victorian periodicals had relied on serialized fiction as a means of retaining their readers from one issue to the next. The reader continually desires narrative closure: typically, by the time one serialized story has reached that point of closure, another has begun in parallel. We see the final echo of this mode in *The Egoist*'s serialization of Wyndham Lewis's *Tarr*, but by that date the link between serialization and narrative form had been broken. However, instead of a desire for narrative closure, the generalist periodical creates a desire for intellectual closure. This desire has even less chance of being fulfilled. The generalist periodical continually reminds its reader of the diversity of intellectual life, and allows them to grasp that diversity, momentarily, in a single binding. *The Athenaeum*, for example, advertised itself as being intended not for 'the ordinary man', but for 'the man who thinks, or desires to learn'; it was 'an indispensable instrument of that process of liberal education which should end only with a man's or woman's life'.[38]

I spoke in the introduction of intertextual, cross-disciplinary reading as something made *possible* by the format of the generalist periodicals, but it is important to note that, on occasion, it was actively encouraged by their editors. In *Fortnightly Review* for September 1894, Karl Pearson's 'Politics and Science' was juxtaposed with 'Some Anarchist Portraits' by Charles Malato.[39] Pearson was concerned to defend scientific materialism from the conservative Lord Salisbury's attack on scientific knowledge; he noted in passing that some Liberal journals had associated materialism with anarchist politics. The editor's juxtaposition of Pearson's article with Malato's provided the reader with the basis for speculation on the link between political and scientific materialisms. When St George Mivart, Catholic apologist and Fellow of the Royal Society, came to praise Salisbury and criticize Pearson a year later, he quoted from both articles, and claimed to have found a common factor in the intellects of empirio-critics and anarchists: both were in unconscious slavery to 'the mere faculty of the imagination'.[40] It goes

---

[38] Advertisement in *Times Education Supplement* (11 Dec. 1919), 624, the same text was used in *The Dial* (Jan. 1921), inside rear cover.

[39] Pearson, 'Politics and Science', *Fortnightly Review*, 62 (Sept. 1894), 334–51; Malato, 'Some Anarchist Portraits', ibid., 315–33.

[40] St George Mivart, 'Denominational Science', *Fortnightly Review*, 64 (Sept. 1895), 423–38 (p. 431).

without saying that Mivart's claims are dubious, and that the distance between Pearson's materialism and Marx's is very great, but nevertheless, the heterogeneity of the *Fortnightly* presented Mivart with an apparently panoramic world view. It allowed him to synthesize diverse materials, or, in Bain's ambivalent phrase, to 'forge' the missing links.[41]

The furthest logical extension of this process is to read each issue of a periodical as if it constituted an authored unity, but such a reading requires considerable ingenuity, and is perhaps only an academic exercise.[42] It is more relevant to recognize intertextual constellations containing only two or three adjacent items, as has been done in relation to *The Waste Land*'s context in *The Criterion*.[43] That case is atypical, however, as the poet chose the context himself: other writers were at the mercy of their editors. In 1921, Herbert Read wrote an article for *The New Age* which quoted from Whitehead's *Concept of Nature* to correct what Read considered the 'vanity' of Shaw's Victorian world view: Shaw's humanism was 'narrowly anthropocentric', placing man at 'the centre of space and time'. Orage, the editor, placed the article between a review which criticized Shaw's *Back to Methuselah*, and an article which criticized Einstein's notion of simultaneity.[44] While these three articles do not provide the reader with a consistent world view, they nevertheless suggest that philosophical problems in literature and physics may be discussed within a common discourse.

Generally speaking, editors employed more subtle means to encourage readers to make connections. From April 1919 onwards, *The Athenaeum*'s masthead reminded readers that it was 'A Journal

[41] Quoted by John Tyndall, 'The Scientific Use of the Imagination' (1870), *Fragments of Science* (London: Longmans, Green, 5th edn., 1876), 425.

[42] Mark Turner, 'Gendered Issues: Intertextuality and *The Small House at Allington* in *Cornhill Magazine*', *Victorian Periodicals Review*, 26 (1993), 228–34; the idea of reading journals 'holistically' has also been raised by James A. Davies, 'The Effects of Context', *Yearbook of English Studies*, 16 (1986), 51–62.

[43] The founding texts of this method are by Jerome McGann, particularly *A Critique of Modern Textual Criticism* (Chicago: University of Chicago Press, 1983), and by D. F. McKenzie, particularly *Bibliography and the Sociology of Texts* (1985; Cambridge: Cambridge University Press, 1999). For Eliot, see Edward Bishop, 'Re:Covering Modernism—Format and Function in the Little Magazines', in Ian Willison, Warwick Gould and Warren Chernaik (eds.), *Modernist Writers and the Marketplace* (Basingstoke: Macmillan, 1996), 287–319.

[44] 'John Francis Hope' [A. E. Randall], review of *Back to Methuselah*, *The New Age*, 29 (18 Aug. 1921), 186–7; Herbert Read, 'Readers and Writers', ibid., 187–8; Francis Sedlak, 'Einstein's Theory or Pure Thought', ibid., 188–90.

of Literature, Science, and the Arts'. In his 'Prologue' to the first
issue, Murry used the first person plural frequently, referring inclu-
sively to the writers and readers as a post-war generation; he examined the strain of idealism in the diverse spheres of Christianity,
rationalism and science, and claimed to see a unity in their universality of intention.[45] Though its terminology is vague, Murry's
'Prologue' provided a frame within which the reader could forge
connections between the scientific and the literary content. In the
following week's editorial, Murry alluded again to the identity of
the readership as a post-war generation; he spoke of the war as a
dividing line between two epochs, and of the choice between the life
of the spirit and the life of material ease. These remarks define
rather than describe. The latter remark is more subtle in its process
of definition than the direct use of the first person plural: it implies
that the audience will choose the 'life of the spirit', but allows them
to forget their privilege in being able to choose. In another article,
Bertrand Russell spoke of 'the half-educated public' who misapply
Darwin, implying that the *Athenaeum* reader was a fully educated
person who would do no such thing. In another article, by Paul
Valéry, 'the physicists' and 'us' are quite distinct.[46] The implied
reader of the *Athenaeum* comprehends but does not practice the sciences. Moreover, the reader has a cosmopolitan outlook, apparent
in such details as the presence of Valéry's column, and Murry criticizing a xenophobic letter which had appeared in *The Daily Mail*.
This openness of outlook was important in relation to the journal's
science coverage: as we shall see in Chapter 4, the war years had seen
a resurgence in the idea of science as an imperialist project, and
some scientists objected to Einstein's theory xenophobically.[47]

Having established a readership that was keen to remain up-to-
date with contemporary science, and appointed as deputy editor and
science columnist a man well-equipped to explain the new physics to
that readership, Murry was able to introduce scientific allusions into
his editorials. In the editorial for 9 May 1919, in the midst of a discussion of the post-war flowering of the arts, Murry alluded to 'those
paradoxes which, we are told, lie at the basis of the structure of the

[45] Murry, 'Prologue', *The Athenaeum* (4 Apr. 1921), 130.
[46] Bertrand Russell, 'The Biology of War', *The Athenaeum* (11 Apr. 1919), 172
(unsigned); Paul Valéry, 'Letters from France', ibid., 183.
[47] Murry, 'Vandals and Huns', *The Athenaeum* (6 June 1919), 421–2; the letter in
question, by Mr Boyd Cable, had appeared in *The Daily Mail*, 26 May 1919.

universe'.[48] I am not interested in the paradoxes as such, but in the marginal detail which defines the reader, the casual phrase 'we are told'. The reader who was a complete outsider to *The Athenaeum* and to the culture of science might be troubled by the phrase, wondering not only who 'we' are, but who we are told by. Exactly what Murry meant by the paradoxes in the structure of the universe would not become clear until Sullivan's article two weeks later, 'The Notion of Simultaneity'. The casual nature of the reference suggests to the readers that they should know, and that, if they do not, they should turn to the 'Science' column. Sullivan too, writing the editorial for 19 December 1919, could refer without further explanation to the way that Einstein had unified 'the most disparate phenomena' and disturbed fundamental notions; he lamented the absence of such a figure in the world of the arts. Reviewing Murry's *The Evolution of an Intellectual* in the same issue, he could refer casually to the idea that Euclidean space was not an inherent property of the physical world.[49] Reviewing Eddington's *Space, Time and Gravitation* in July 1920, he could quickly summarize aspects of relativity theory that 'may be taken as more or less familiar', and refer back to his articles of May and June 1919.[50] He could do this because the generalist periodical was more than a fragmented collection of isolated articles: the editor gave it a degree of unity, and the reader was encouraged to read it as a whole. In unifying it, the editor encouraged the reader to remain loyal to the journal, as part of the never-ending process of education.

Murry's achievement as the editor of *The Athenaeum* was greatly admired, even by those who disliked him personally or who disagreed with his literary philosophy. In 1920 Virginia Woolf defended *The Athenaeum*'s 'honesty' and 'high standard' to J. C. Squire. In 1921, after Rowntree had amalgamated it with *The Nation*, and its identity had begun to suffer 'gradual suffocation', T. S. Eliot praised Murry for having had 'higher standards and greater ambitions for literary journalism than any other editor in London'. In 1928 he referred again to its 'brief and brilliant life'.[51] Eliot's remarks are

[48] Murry, 'A Modern Prophet', *The Athenaeum* (9 May 1919), 293–4.

[49] Sullivan, 'Dissolving Views', *The Athenaeum* (19 Dec. 1919), 1361–2, and 'The Dreamer Awakes', ibid., 1364–5.

[50] Sullivan, 'The Unification of the World', *The Athenaeum* (16 July 1920), 85–6.

[51] Woolf, diary entry for 31 Jan. 1920, *The Diary of Virginia Woolf*, ed. Anne Olivier Bell, 5 vols (London: Chatto and Windus, 1977–1984), ii. 15; Eliot, 'London Letter', *The Dial*, 70 (June 1921), 686–91 (p. 689); Eliot, *The Sacred Wood* (1920; London: Methuen, 1928), p. vii.

particularly interesting, because they suggest that once *The Athenaeum* had begun to suffocate, Eliot recognized that there was a potential audience for a generalist journal that included science. *The Criterion* is usually categorized as a literary review, but in planning it, Eliot told Pound that he wanted a review 'as unliterary as possible'; he wanted 'Sir J. Frazer, Trotter, Eddington, Sherrington or people like that'; Eddington did not appear, but Sullivan was certainly due to contribute.[52] Eliot was perhaps thinking of himself as the ideal reader: in a letter to his brother, he regretted that he had no time to fill in the 'innumerable gaps' in his knowledge of past literature and history; there were many things that he felt he 'ought to have read long ago', and 'so much that I should like to know in the various sciences'.[53] In an editorial in 1926, Eliot justified the scope of *The Criterion* by reference to 'literature' rather than the reader, but the programme was the same. If a literary review defined 'literature' too narrowly, it risked destroying 'the life of literature'; ideally a review should include work in history, archaeology, anthropology, and 'even the more technical sciences' when their results were 'of such a nature to be valuable to the man of general culture and when they can be made intelligible to him'.[54] *The Criterion* regularly included reviews of non-technical scientific works, particularly those with philosophical implications.[55] In 1929 I. A. Richards offered to Eliot to look among 'some of the younger physicists and logicians' at Cambridge for 'somebody worth printing'.[56]

It is difficult to find evidence which allows us to determine whether the implied reader corresponded to actual readers and their processes of reading. The evidence we have is fragmentary and anecdotal. The most vivid picture comes in a letter from Jacob Isaacs to Sydney Schiff, written when Sullivan's *Aspects of Science* was published. Isaacs, who had graduated from Oxford with an English

---

[52] T. S. Eliot, letters dated 7 Nov. 1922 and 1 Dec. 1922, *The Letters of T. S. Eliot*, ed. Valerie Eliot, 1 vol. to date (London: Faber, 1988), i. 593 and i. 603. Sullivan was unable to contribute.

[53] Eliot, letter dated 31 Dec. 1922, *Letters*, i. 617.

[54] Eliot, 'The Idea of a Literary Review', *The Criterion* 4 (Jan. 1926), 1–6 (pp. 3–4).

[55] See the reviews and articles listed in the bibliography under Montgomery Belgion, Hugh Sykes Davies, William Empson, H. W. B. Joseph, John Macmurray, Charles Mauron, Frank Morley, Joseph Needham, Herbert Read, Michael Roberts, and Geoffrey Tandy.

[56] Letter conjecturally dated Feb.–July 1929, *Selected Letters of I. A. Richards, CH*, ed. John Constable (Oxford: Clarendon, 1990), 49.

degree in 1921, recalled reading Sullivan in *The Athenaeum* and the *Nation and Athenaeum*

with an interest that was far in advance of my comprehension. I remember the fact—though none of the substance of several discussions his writings have stimulated when a stray copy of the Nation has brightened a continental ramble. I shall certainly try to follow anything that may be unravelled from his collected volume.[57]

Isaacs also recalled a fellow Oxford undergraduate who had been a 'disciple' of Sullivan, and who 'often used to speak of [his] powers'. We cannot be sure how far Isaacs' relation to his older, richer, and more influential correspondent colours his account, particularly his remark about his interest exceeding his comprehension. He may be enthusing artificially about a writer he had found incomprehensible, or he may be paying an ambiguously phrased compliment to Sullivan. Compared to Needham's, Isaacs' programme of reading seems more concerned with entertainment than with creating a rounded self. However, his conscious choice to read works beyond his comprehension indicates a desire to stretch his disciplinary limits. The reference to the awed 'disciple' suggests that, for undergraduates at least, the model of popularization was a vertical one, with the hierarchical model of high-priests and laymen still fully operative.

Isaacs' experience of reading *The Athenaeum* influenced his expectations as a reader of *The Criterion*. In another letter to Schiff, surveying the contents of the first issue, he lamented the recent death of W. H. R. Rivers, 'one of the few men who could have—(& certainly in stimulus did so—) bridged the gap between science & the arts'; in his suggestions for future articles, he insisted that 'the scientific should not be neglected'.[58] Though Isaacs may have overestimated the degree of influence that Schiff had over Eliot, his wish that the scientific writers should give their views 'in their widest and least technical aspects' correctly anticipates Eliot's editorial line.

I have examined the literary periodicals at a length which is disproportionate to their sales because they allow us to demonstrate that science was deeply embedded in literary culture. The popular

[57] Isaacs, letter to Sydney Schiff, dated 18 Mar. 1923, British Library, Schiff MS 52918, fo. 130.

[58] Isaacs, letter to Sydney Schiff, dated 11 Feb. 1923, British Library, Schiff MS 52918, fo. 127.

science books of the 1920s and 1930s sold extraordinarily well: Eddington's *The Nature of the Physical World* sold over 10,000 copies in its first fourteen months; Jeans's *The Mysterious Universe* sold 70,000 copies in its first two months.[59] However, figures alone provide no evidence of whether popular science books reached the literary culture, let alone how they were valued. Evidence that literary writers read popular science may be found in their diaries, but such reading would be idiosyncratic were it not sustained by a larger culture of discussing and reviewing scientific books in the journals. *The Nature of the Physical World* becomes significant not because of its sales, but because it was reviewed in *The Criterion, The Listener, The Nation and Athenaeum, The New Statesman* and the *TLS*. Read appropriately, the books in themselves can reveal much about their intended audience or audiences, as can the surviving archives; but these are worth pursuing only because of the journals.

Eddington recognized the potential for popular expositions of relativity before the results of the eclipse observations had been announced. He wrote to the Secretary to the Syndics of the Cambridge University Press recommending a translation of a short booklet on the subject, saying that 'a most amazing amount of interest' was being taken in the subject, 'not only among mathematicians and physicists, but all classes in England'.[60] 'Classes' is an ambiguous term: though it could refer to social classes, in contrast to 'mathematicians and physicists' it seems to refer to classes of specialized intellectuals; however, 'in England' indicates that Eddington was thinking of intellectuals beyond the confines of his university. He added that he was writing a book 'much more popular in style' than the translated booklet, meaning by this his *Space, Time and Gravitation* (1920).

The problem for the popularizer—a problem of form as well as style—is how to take theories that are unfamiliar, and that seem to defy common sense, and relate them to familiar experiences and ideas. Recent popular science books have, argues Martin Eger, adopted a common structure: the book begins with 'a philosophical

[59] Whitworth, 'The Clothbound Universe', 67, 68.
[60] Eddington, letter to A. R. Waller dated 20 Oct. 1919, Cambridge University Library, CUP archives, CUP UA Pr.A.E.34 (11). The booklet, unnamed, but translated by H. L. A. Brose and recommended by H. H. Turner, was almost certainly Erwin Freundlich's *The Foundations of Einstein's Theory of Gravitation* (Cambridge: Cambridge University Press, 1920).

survey . . . in which certain human or social problems are posed'; it 'often refers to the two-cultures split . . . promising new ideas that might heal the wound'; the relevant science 'is then expounded in a lengthy technical or quasi-technical section'; in conclusion, the work returns to the original philosophical problem, and offers solutions on the basis of the scientific content.[61] The structure applies not to all books, but to those 'with subjects that have philosophical or social or humane implications'.[62] Although Eger claims that this genre has emerged only recently, the structure resembles that of many of the books from the 1920s and 1930s. Though the phrase 'the two cultures' had not been applied to the arts/science divide, many of the books begin by alluding to the schisms created by intellectual specialization.

For the moment, I will overlook the question of where the popular text begins, though it will be necessary to consider the marginal aspects such as jackets, titles, and prefaces in order to reach a full account. Eddington begins *Space, Time and Gravitation* with a dialogue between an experimental physicist, a pure mathematician, and a relativist, who discuss the question 'What is geometry?' The choice of *dramatis personae* seems to emphasize divisions within science rather than those between the two cultures, but, by making the physicist voice common-sense objections to pure mathematics and relativity, Eddington also creates a position for the reader: the physicist admits that he is 'hazy about strict definitions', as there is 'not time for everything'; he claims that non-Euclidean space seems 'contrary to reason', but the mathematician argues that he means 'contrary to common sense, which is a very different thing'.[63] In *The Nature of the Physical World*, Eddington introduces the distinction of two world-views far more directly and vividly with his image of the two tables. In works by other authors, the schism of knowledge is most commonly embodied, be it implicitly or explicitly, in the idea that science can know things that are unavailable to unaided human perceptions.

James Jeans's *The Universe Around Us* (1929) comes to the question of cultural specialization rather more gradually, through a brief

[61] Martin Eger, 'Hermeneutics and the New Epic of Science', in McRae (ed.), *The Literature of Science*, 186–209 (pp. 189–90).

[62] Ibid., 186.

[63] Eddington, *Space, Time and Gravitation* (Cambridge: Cambridge University Press, 1920), 4, 10–11.

history of astronomy, which leads Jeans to ask 'what reward astronomy has to offer'. The contrast here is not with the rewards of literature, philosophy, or common sense, but the 'more mundane sciences', which 'prove their worth by adding to the amenities and pleasures of life'.[64] Not only does this introduction contradict the rule that popular science emphasizes the practical applications of science; it must also lead us to qualify Eger's statement, in that here the initial distinction is between different scientific cultures. The end of Jeans's introduction alludes to further divisions within science: he will, he says, call on the resources of 'physics, chemistry and geology'.

The information we shall obtain will be fragmentary. If it must be compared to anything, let it be to the pieces of a jig-saw puzzle. Could we get hold of all the pieces, they would, we are confident, form a single complete consistent picture, but many of them are still missing. It is too much to hope that the incomplete series of pieces we have already found will disclose the whole picture, but we may at least collect them together, arrange them in some sort of methodical order, fit together pieces which are obviously contiguous, and perhaps hazard a guess as to what the finished picture will prove to be when all its pieces have been found and finally fitted together.[65]

Although the problem that Jeans earlier posed was generally 'the relation of human life to the universe', and specifically 'the beginnings, meaning and destiny of the human race', the passage quoted suggests that a solution to the puzzle will also bring about a unification of knowledge, and an end to specialization.

I do not propose to consider in detail the middle part of Eger's sandwich, the scientific discussion. Eger notes that his texts invariably emphasize the newness of their science: they argue or imply that 'only recently' has a 'scientific' treatment of the philosophical questions become possible. In the case of the relativity books, the newness was implied by the subject matter and was not emphasized. Indeed, at least for Eddington, the newness of quantum mechanics was a reason for treating it cautiously.

The conclusions are more interesting, and mark a point of significant difference from the popular science writing found in

[64] Jeans, *The Universe Around Us* (1929; Cambridge: Cambridge University Press, 2nd edn. 1930), 6–7.

[65] Jeans, *The Universe Around Us*, 15; the image of the jig-saw puzzle may derive from Eddington, *Physical World*, 352.

many of the periodicals. In Eger's account of recent texts, the final section 'includes unabashed *calls for a new morality* or a new "vision" of the world'.[66] Though the texts of the 1920s and 1930s very rarely propose a new ethos, the more religiously minded ones propose a new understanding of the place of 'man' in the universe and his relation to 'God'; the more atheistic propose a new understanding of science. In *Space, Time and Gravitation*, Eddington was content to restrict the final chapter to a discussion of the nature of knowledge, but the title, 'On the Nature of Things', promised more: those readers who assumed that a discussion of the 'nature' of things would reveal their essence must have been disappointed by a theory in which everything is reduced to relations.[67] Bertrand Russell directly took up Eddington's questions about our knowledge of the universe in the concluding paragraph of *The ABC of Atoms*, and superbly subverted the generic pattern of popular science books: 'Is the world "rational", i.e., such as to conform to our intellectual habits? Or is it "irrational", i.e. not such as we should have made it if we had been in the position of the Creator? I do not propose to suggest an answer to this question.'[68]

Other writers felt less able to pass over such questions in silence. Oliver Lodge very boldly announced that the ether of space, far from being made redundant by Einstein's theory, was in fact 'the garment of God'.[69] In *The Nature of the Physical World*, Eddington was required by the terms of the Gifford Lectures to touch on questions of natural theology, and turned in his final proper chapter to the relation of 'Science and Mysticism'.[70] His conclusions were far more cautious than Lodge's: he specifically repudiated the idea that the beliefs of religion could be proved by reference to scientific data or scientific method. Rather, he argued that science was no longer so extensive in its territorial claims as to offer any obstacle to religion.[71] Moreover, the final chapter is followed by a 'Conclusion':

---

[66] Eger, 'Hermeneutics', 191, his emphasis.

[67] Eddington, *Space, Time and Gravitation*, 197.

[68] Russell, *ABC of Atoms* (1923; London: Kegan Paul, Trench, Trubner, 3rd impr., revised, 1925), 170–1.

[69] Lodge, *Ether and Reality* (London: Hodder and Stoughton, 1925), 179.

[70] For the terms of Gifford's will (1885), see Stanley L. Jaki, *Lord Gifford and his Lectures: A Centenary Retrospect* (Edinburgh: Scottish Academic Press, 1986), p. vii.

[71] Sullivan's conclusion to *The Bases of Modern Science* (London: Ernest Benn, 1928) was very similar: 'Our aesthetic and religious experiences need not lose the significance they appear to have merely because they are not taken into account in the scientific scheme' (244).

here Eddington turns to the revolution in science, and its implications for our understanding of knowledge, addressing the question of why the scientist does not 'lose faith' in his work.[72]

Jeans's conclusion to *The Universe Around Us* was unusual in that it derived a 'message' from astronomy, and that it derived an ethos from this message. The message was contradictory, being both one of 'melancholy grandeur and oppressive vastness', but also 'endless possibility and hope'; the ethos was 'responsibility to the individual', 'because we are drawing plans and laying foundations for a longer future than we can well imagine'.[73] In his concern with heat-death and the long-term future of mankind, Jeans was closer than his contemporaries to the Victorian thermodynamic popularizers. *The Mysterious Universe* made similar large claims. Although in his final paragraph, Jeans suggested that science 'should leave off making pronouncements', this was not before he had claimed that 'the Great Architect of the Universe' was 'a pure mathematician', and implied that the atoms of which we consist are thoughts in a mind greater than ours.[74]

The book format demands and facilitates such conclusions. It demands them insofar as readers of books expect some form of closure, and it facilitates them, in that the structure of a book is less tight-knit than that of a short article; claims that would seem illogical or ludicrous in an article seem plausible at the end of a larger and more complex structure. Although the journals published articles claiming that the new physics supported religion, and others that related it to occultism and spiritualism, none appeared in the mainstream generalist titles.[75] Articles there were restricted either to wry commentary on the phenomenon (books, as Sullivan said, that apparently resulted from a collaboration between 'a professor of physics, an archdeacon and a Bond Street crystal-gazer'), or to logical arguments to the effect that the alleged 'problem' of science and

---

[72] Eddington, *Physical World*, 352–3.   [73] Jeans, *Universe Around Us*, 353–4.

[74] Jeans, *The Mysterious Universe* (Cambridge: Cambridge University Press, 1930), 150, 134, 148.

[75] e.g. A. T. Swaine, 'Relativity and the Deity of Jesus Christ', *The Expositor* (Oct. 1920), 273–81; The Revd. James O. Patterson, 'Relativity: Some Metaphysico-Theological Considerations', *The Ecclesiastical Review*, 66 (Mar. 1922), 251–63; W. Kingsland, 'Relativity and Reality', *The Occult Review*, 36 (Aug. 1922), 96–103; Hugh C. McAllister, 'The Aftermath of Relativity: Substrates of Science', *The Quest*, 14 (Oct. 1922), 98–104; H. H. Henson, 'Science and Religion', *JOLW*, 14 (31 Oct. 1925), 171; J. D. Beresford, 'Science and Religion', *The Aryan Path* (July 1930), 460–3.

religion was a distraction from the real problem of unbelief.[76] Of course, not all writers made such large claims as Jeans. For the writers of all books, the presentation of science in a context of philosophical or humanistic questions provided the readers with a familiar point of reference. It was less important for the conclusion to provide a definite answer, or even to address the question implied in the introduction, than it was for the author to modulate into a different discursive key.

Though Eger's schema of the popular science text's structure is a useful starting point, it cannot accommodate features at the margins of the text, and features which are not part of its linear structure: titles, title pages, epigraphs, indexes, and jackets. Such features orientate the reader towards the text, establish the author's scientific authority, and provide further points of connection between scientific discourse and the more familiar literary world. Ultimately, they play their part in confirming the reader's sense of his or her cultural narrowness, and in raising the expectation that the author can help to restore wholeness. Given their marginality, their effects are more variable than those of structure, more open to the whims of the reader's interpretative strategies; to isolate them is to distort the subtle effects of colour they bring, but analysis requires that we isolate specific illustrations. Each of the twelve chapters of *Space, Time and Gravitation* bears an epigraph, and while most come from scientific or philosophical writers (Lucretius, Descartes, Newton, Clifford and Minkowski), one comes from the Bible (Deuteronomy) and four others from literary sources: *Love's Labour's Lost, A Midsummer Night's Dream*, Newman's *Dream of Gerontius*, and H. G. Wells's *The Time Machine*. The epigraphs from Newman and Wells are particularly interesting, in that they construct a literary lineage for the relativistic concepts that follow. That from Wells quotes the Time Traveller himself, explaining that portraits of a man at 8, 15, 17, and 23 years old are sections, 'Three-Dimensional representations of his Four-Dimensional being'.[77] Elsewhere Eddington used Wells to provide an expository analogy: he alluded

---

[76] Sullivan, 'The Entente Cordiale', *Athenaeum* (9 Apr. 1920), 482; Eliot, 'Religion and Science: A Phantom Dilemma', *The Listener*, 7 (23 Mar. 1932), 428–9.

[77] Eddington, *Space, Time and Gravitation*, 45. The novel had previously been alluded to by L. Silberstein, *The Theory of Relativity* (London: Macmillan, 1914), 134, and by Alfred J. Lotka, 'A New Conception of the Universe: Einstein's Theory of Relativity, with illustrative examples', *Harper's Magazine* (Mar. 1920), 477–87.

to Wells's 'The New Accelerator', a story in which the 'accelerator', a drug, accelerates the protagonist's perceptions and movements; the allusion reminds the reader that 'natural' concepts of space and time are constructs of our bodies and our perceptions.[78] However, unlike the expository analogy, the epigraph leaves more room for the reader's interpretation.

Titles are also important. Jeans's correspondence with Cambridge University Press reveals the great care he took to make *The Mysterious Universe* 'popular', in the sense of 'accessible', 'likeable', and 'sensational'.[79] The first title he suggested, 'Religio Physici', was clearly too literary and latinate for the mass market. His later suggestions 'The Wasting Universe' and 'The Shadowland of Modern Physics' show him moving in a more melodramatic direction, suggested perhaps by Eddington's references to the 'borderland' and 'hinterland' of physics; 'The Mysterious Universe' maintains the melodrama, but also creates an intellectual narrative of sorts.[80] The title is reminiscent of Ernst Haeckel's best-seller *The Riddle of the Universe* (1900), and Virginia Woolf certainly responded to these resonances, in recording an evening spent with David Cecil, Lytton Strachey and Clive Bell: 'Talk about the riddle of the universe (Jeans' book) whether it will be known; not by us.'[81]

If titles are important, so too are title pages: they establish the scientific authority of the author. The analysis of scientific authoring given by Foucault in 'What is an Author' needs modification to explain popular texts. Foucault describes how, in the medieval period, literary texts were anonymous, while scientific ones were acceptable only if associated with the name of an authority; in the seventeenth or eighteenth century, a reversal occurred, such that 'Scientific discourses began to be received for themselves, in the anonymity of an established or always redemonstrable truth', while literary discourses 'came to be accepted only when endowed with the author-function'.[82] The popular scientific text, however, requires the support of a name; not only that, but the name, ideally,

[78] Eddington, 'Einstein's Theory of Space and Time', 643; the story is mentioned briefly in *Space, Time and Gravitation*, 160, and also in Edwin Slosson's *Easy Lessons in Einstein* (London: George Routledge and Sons, 1920), 54.

[79] Whitworth, 'The Clothbound Universe', 69.

[80] Eddington, *Physical World*, 349.

[81] Woolf, diary entry dated 17 Dec. 1930, *Diary*, iii. 337.

[82] Foucault, 'What is an Author?', in David Lodge (ed.), *Modern Criticism and Theory: A Reader* (Harlow: Longman, 1988), 196–210 (pp. 202–3).

requires the support of institutional authority. The title page of Lodge's *Ether and Reality* represents the furthest limit of the tendency to bolster the author's authority: beneath the name 'Sir Oliver Lodge' and the affiliation 'F.R.S.' come twelve lines in small italics listing Lodge's qualifications and affiliations: one D.Sc., seven honorary D.Scs., four honorary LL.Ds, and an honorary M.A.; membership of two societies, corresponding and honorary membership of four others; presidency of the Radio Society, and ex-presidency of three other societies; two medals, one former professorship and one former principalship.[83] Few of Lodge's readers would have known what it meant to be 'Corr. Mem. Bataafsch Genoots (Rotterdam)', but the title page does not require them to reason: it requires them to be impressed. The title page, as much as anything that Lodge writes in the Preface or Prologue, establishes the reader's relation to the author.

The first editions of Whitehead's *Science and the Modern World* and Eddington's *The Nature of the Physical World* made similar, though more modest shows of their authors' qualifications, but the principle was the same. However, in the matching 'Cheap Editions' of March 1932, the title pages were reset: unusually, the authors' names appeared above the titles of the books, and they were entirely shorn of qualifications.[84] The authority of the author no longer needs to be protested: it resides in the title itself, and in the status of the author as a household name. It was additionally bolstered by the reviews quoted on the jackets: for Whitehead, Herbert Read's review in *The Criterion*; for Eddington, Lodge's in *The Nineteenth Century*.[85] These titles also had the popular authority of being bestsellers: in the case of Jeans's *The Universe around Us*, Cambridge University Press wrapped yellow bands around the second edition to remind potential purchasers of its popularity.[86]

The displays of scientific authority seen in the popular books are paradoxical, in that ultimately they support arguments that break down disciplinary boundaries, and they allow the authors to make ethical or theological conclusions. At certain points in the period 1919 to 1939, certain scientists, philosophers, and other commentators

[83] Lodge, *Ether and Reality*, p. v.
[84] For a transcription of Eddington's, see Whitworth, 'The Clothbound Universe', 66.
[85] Details from the jacket of *Science and the Modern World*, which advertises Eddington's work on the rear cover with a quotation from Lodge.
[86] Whitworth, 'The Clothbound Universe', 69.

employed their authority to the opposite ends: to reassert disciplinary boundaries, and to reassert the hierarchical distinction between scientist and layman. Oliver Lodge, for example, was deeply committed to the ether hypothesis, particularly because of his interest in psychical research; for Lodge, the ether was home to the spirits, not least that of his son Raymond, killed in the 1914–18 war.[87] While Lodge used his authority to break down the barriers between ether science and spiritualism, he simultaneously used it to cordon off relativity. His article on relativity for *The Nineteenth Century* disorientates the reader by presenting the theory as a list of disconnected premises and conclusions.[88] Having done so, Lodge concludes that 'it is useless to attempt to instruct general readers in its intricacies'.[89] Readers who consider themselves superior to the 'general' reader, or who felt that they would benefit from instruction, may have been alienated by such remarks, but those readers who had been confused by the preceding paragraph would have accepted this remark as a definition; for them, it is a point of interpellation. While for other popularizers, the general reader was someone who could benefit from patient exposition (even if, like Isaacs, his comprehension fell short of his interest), here the general reader is defined in opposition to the expert scientist. If, in *Ether and Reality*, Lodge used his authority to propose a unifying theory that explained things diverse as gravitation and immortality, he was simultaneously using his authority to suppress Einstein.

While Lodge wished to isolate only the school of science he had rejected, others argued for the separation of all science from cultural, philosophical, and theological questions. As, for many readers, such questions were the only point of access to the new theories, the isolation of science implied at the very least a drier style of popularization, and more commonly, implied that science was the preserve of specialists. As *The ABC of Atoms* evinces, Bertrand Russell resisted throughout the 1920s the temptation to confuse quanta with the Creator, without altogether foregoing vivid metaphors and analogies as expository tools. He had also criticized the appropriation of relativity by idealist philosophy; in criticizing Haldane's *The Reign of Relativity* for its idealist interpretation, he also tentatively

---

[87] David B. Wilson, 'The Thought of Late Victorian Physicists: Oliver Lodge's Ethereal Body', *Victorian Studies*, 15 (1971), 29–48 (p. 31).

[88] I examine the relevant paragraph in detail in Chapter 7.

[89] Lodge, 'The New Theory of Gravity', 1196.

criticized Eddington for passages in his popular expositions 'which might seem to people ignorant of physics and mathematics to bear this interpretation'.[90] The important implication of the phrase is that one needs to be properly qualified to read even a popular exposition.

While Eddington's idealism was tolerated by the generalist periodicals, Jeans's less cautious statements were not, and the publication of *The Mysterious Universe* led to the separationist argument becoming the dominant one. The review of Jeans in *The Adelphi* focused entirely on his comments about the 'Great Architect of the Universe', without allowing any praise for his exposition.[91] In *The Nation and Athenaeum* the fallacies of his argument were exposed. 'In vulgar parlance', wrote Sylva Norman, 'he has fairly put his foot in it.'[92] The self-consciousness with which Norman adopts the 'vulgar parlance' indicates her distance from it: the vulgarity belongs to Jeans and his readers. Jeans's fall from grace led to a decline in Eddington's reputation: for the Marxist popular science writer J. G. Crowther, the mysticism of Eddington and Jeans indicated their failure to understand; it was 'the substitute for comprehension', 'the margarine of philosophy'.[93] Though one anonymous writer attempted to distinguish Eddington's subtler arguments, he acknowledged that the two were usually spoken of 'as if their philosophical conclusions were essentially the same'.[94]

Though the success of Lodge and Jeans was due in no small part to their successes as broadcasters on the BBC, by the late 1920s the Corporation's contributors and producers were taking an attitude to science popularization which was fundamentally opposed to their work. The BBC favoured talks which explained scientific method, and discouraged those which detailed scientific conclusions; even more, it discouraged those which extrapolated from scientific conclusions. The position was first articulated in an editorial

---

[90] Russell, 'Relativity, Scientific and Metaphysical', *Nation and Athenaeum*, 31 (16 Sept. 1922), 796–7.

[91] Geoffrey Sainsbury, 'Anthropomorphic Universe', *The Adelphi*, 1 (Jan. 1931), 338–41.

[92] Norman, 'The Universe and its God', *Nation and Athenaeum*, 48 (24 Jan. 1931), 546, 548.

[93] Crowther, *An Outline of the Universe* (London: Kegan Paul, Trench, Trubner, 1931), pp. xiii–xiv.

[94] Anon., [review of] '*The Mysterious Universe* by Sir James Jeans', *The Twentieth Century*, 4/20 (Oct. 1932), 21–3.

in *The Listener* in 1929: 'It is not so easy to collect a group of students to observe, demonstrate and discuss the processes by which scientists reach their conclusions, as it is to find a public ready to devour text-books in its armchair, or to indulge its curiosity by taking in the illustrated fortnightly parts of a serial production.'[95] The writer felt that the interest in conclusions would soon be satisfied, and recommended that scientists popularize scientific method. In this connection, the writer recommended a series of radio talks on biology: the non-mathematical sciences were generally seen as a better means of disseminating the ideal of method. A similar attitude was shared by *The Listener*'s regular writer on chemistry and physics, A. S. Russell. In 1930, Russell outlined his position, in response to a colleague who had complained that, in spite of the work of J. S. Haldane, J. B. S. Haldane, and J. W. N. Sullivan, there were still no popular science books 'for the masses'. Russell agreed, but cautioned that good science books would always be hard, because science itself is hard. His position might seem to support the idea that scientific discourse is independent of its author, but Russell emphasized authorial credentials: the best books were written by 'good scientists', and the bad ones were written by 'unknown people, often American'; though he went on to offer stylistic criteria (such books displayed a 'dreadful light touch, slang, queer analogies and forced breeziness'), these were not enough in themselves. In another article, Russell distinguished science and popular science as 'the substance' and 'the shadow'. It is a position that allows no room for the discursive or social construction of science. By separating pure science from its linguistic forms and from its philosophical implications, Russell made it a wholly unsuitable subject for broadcasting.[96]

The separationist position was shared by Marxists and those on the right. In 1931 the Marxist physicist Hyman Levy responded directly to Jeans's best-seller: although scientific exposition was desirable, the 'public scientist' must clearly demarcate his 'public responsibilities' from the 'private region where science does not operate'; he must not speak privately 'with the confidence of

---

[95] Anon., 'Broadcasting and Popular Science', *The Listener*, 1 (15 May 1929), 676.
[96] Margaret Cole, 'A Petition to Scientists', *The Listener*, 3 (2 Apr. 1930), 602; A. S. Russell, 'Science and its Popularisation', *The Listener*, 3 (23 Apr. 1930), 731; A. S. Russell, 'Dr Lynch and Professor Einstein', *The Listener*, 8 (16 Nov. 1932), 710.

scientific certainty'.[97] In the same year, T. S. Eliot responded to a passage in the Report of the Church of England's Lambeth Conference which had claimed that 'there is much in the scientific and philosophic thinking of our time which provides a climate more favourable to faith in God than has existed for generations'.[98] Eliot argued that, while the writings of Whitehead and Eddington might remove 'prejudices' which were a barrier to faith, they could not confirm anyone in the faith. Unlike continental scientists and thinkers, the 'Anglo-Saxons' enjoyed 'drawing general conclusions from particular disciplines, using our accomplishment in one field as the justification for theorizing about the world in general'. Whatever label we place on Eliot's political position, it was certainly not Marxist, yet he shared with Levy the desire to separate one field from another. The Marxist and the Anglo-Catholic Royalist differ only in the value they accord to science within their hierarchies of knowledge.

The separationist position was consolidated in a series of books in the 1930s: Bertrand Russell's *The Scientific Outlook* (1931), Levy's *The Universe of Science* (1932), C. E. M. Joad's *Philosophical Aspects of Modern Science* (1932), and a book directly critical of Eddington and Jeans, L. Susan Stebbing's *Philosophy and the Physicists* (1937). There were some dissenting voices, and others expressing only qualified approval, but in the 1930s the generalist periodicals increasingly supported the view that disciplinary transgressions were undesirable, both in their own pages and in the books under review.[99] The process of intellectual specialization had by no means ceased, but the prevailing attitude to it had changed. Rather than attempting to regain the authority that came from being a 'perfectly rounded human character', intellectuals of all factions sought to argue for the superior authority of their own particular position.

[97] Levy, 'Is the Universe Mysterious?', *The Listener*, 5 (4 Mar. 1931), 602.

[98] Quoted by Eliot, 'Thoughts after Lambeth', in *Selected Essays* (London: Faber, 1951), 370.

[99] For dissenters, and those qualifying their approval, see, e.g., Needham, 'Science and Metaphysics', *New Statesman and Nation*, 3 (4 Jun. 1932), 737–8; G. F. Brett, 'Science Marking Time', in *New Country* ed. Michael Roberts (London: Hogarth, 1933), 43–61; Michael Roberts, [review of *Philosophy and the Physicists*], *The Criterion*, 17 (Apr. 1938), 542–5.

2

Things Fall Apart: *The Secret Agent* and Literary Entropy

[I]n the language of physics alone we find the rise in the last six decades of terms such as radioactive decay, or decay of particles; displacement law; fission; spallation; nuclear disintegration; discontinuity (as in energy levels of atoms); dislocation (in crystals); indeterminacy, uncertainty; probabilistic (rather than classically deterministic) causality; time reversal . . .[1]

MISSING from Gerald Holton's list of the scientific thema of 'disintegration, violence and derangement' is the theme that is ancestor to them all: dissipation. Though the second law of thermodynamics was developed by Sadi Carnot as early as 1824, drawing on work by Fourier earlier in the century, it anticipated many of the scientific developments of the late nineteenth and early twentieth centuries; it was for Eddington 'so fundamental in physical theory' that he devoted two chapters of *The Nature of the Physical World* to it.[2] At the time of the 'two cultures' debate, Al Alvarez asserted, in response to C. P. Snow's jibe that the 'arts men' could not understand the second law, that in fact the 'whole of modern art' centres on 'the principle of psychic entropy'.[3] Alvarez's assertion was an effective rhetorical gesture, but for a more detailed consideration it is necessary to distinguish the many implications of the second law, and the many means of applying it to literary works.[4] Moreover, one

---

[1] Holton, *Thematic Origins of Scientific Thought*, 95.

[2] Eddington, *The Nature of the Physical World*, 63.

[3] Al Alvarez, 'American After-thoughts', *Encounter*, 24/6 (June 1965), 48–51.

[4] Two of the best accounts of the cultural ramifications of the second law are Greg Myers's 'Nineteenth Century Popularizations of Thermodynamics and the Rhetoric of Social Prophecy', *Victorian Studies*, 29 (1985), 35–66, and Stephen G. Brush's *The Temperature of History* (New York: Burt Franklin, 1978); the best socio-historical account of its genesis is Crosbie Smith's *The Science of Energy* (London: Athlone, 1998). Short accounts may be found in: Karl Beckson, *London in the 1890s: A Cultural History* (New York: Norton, 1992), pp. xii–xiii; Robin Gilmour, *The Victorian Period: The Intellectual and Cultural Context* (London: Longman, 1993), 136–7. Essays considering entropy in more detail include George Levine, '*Little Dorrit* and Three Kinds of Science',

must recognize that the scientific theme itself had social roots. This chapter considers the theme of dissipation in general terms, before turning to consider entropy in Conrad's *The Secret Agent*, a 'tale of the nineteenth century' which bridges the concerns of the *fin de siècle* and modernism.

Following the early thinking of Carnot, and the coining of the term 'entropy' by Clausius in 1850, the second law was generalized by William Thomson (later Lord Kelvin) in 1852, and further elaborated by Herman von Helmholtz in 1854.[5] The theory grew from a consideration of the properties of mechanical engines, and of the fact that the work produced by an engine is always less than the energy put into it. Energy can neither be created nor destroyed (according to the first law of thermodynamics), but the energy not converted into work is lost through friction in the form of heat. These ideas were generalized to cover all inanimate matter, including the sun. Kelvin summarized the theory in popular form in 1862:

The second great law of Thermodynamics involves a certain principle of *irreversible action in nature*. It is thus shown that, although mechanical energy is indestructible, there is a universal tendency to its dissipation, which produces gradual augmentation and diffusion of heat, cessation of motion, and exhaustion of potential energy through the material universe.[6]

The conclusion of this article was bleak: the 'inhabitants of the earth cannot continue to enjoy the light and heat essential to their life . . .'[7]

The second law was slower to grip the popular imagination than Darwinism, perhaps because its initial concerns with engines were less contentious. However, in the 1860s, it became directly relevant to the debates over evolution: it was thought that the age of the earth could be calculated by considering the effect of cooling, and that this would confirm or disprove the time scale required in Darwin's theory. Moreover, 'heat-death', the idea that the sun would eventually cool

in Joanne Shattock (ed.), *Dickens and other Victorians* (Basingstoke: Macmillan, 1988), 3–24, and Gillian Beer, ' "The Death of the Sun": Victorian Solar Physics and Solar Myth', in *Open Fields: Science in Cultural Encounter* (Oxford: Clarendon, 1996), 219–41.

[5] My account derives from Brush, *The Temperature of History*, chapter 3, and the primary sources noted below.

[6] Lord Kelvin, 'On the Age of the Sun's Heat', *Popular Lectures and Addresses* (1889; 2nd edn. in 3 vols., London, 1891 (vols. i and iii), 1894 (vol. ii)), i. 356. First printed in *Macmillan's Magazine*, March 1862.

[7] Kelvin, *Popular Lectures*, i. 375.

down, struck at deep-rooted apocalyptic fears in the popular imagination. Finally, the idea of entropy lent implicit support to the idea
of biological degeneration: 'the second law of thermodynamics was
the most powerful figuration of degeneration that the nineteenth
century proposed'.[8]

Though, as we have seen in Chapter 1, it is possible to make these
bleak prospects 'popular' by making them sensational, one of the
most successful accounts of entropy in the late nineteenth century,
The Unseen Universe by Tait and Stewart, attempted to recover a
more optimistic interpretation. It rested on a misunderstanding.
Tait and Stewart reasoned that if energy were being lost, it must be
going somewhere else. The sun is dissipating its energy, but what,
they asked, is the point of this expenditure? If the image of the sun
is travelling in all directions through the universe, then perhaps its
present energy is being used to preserve the past.[9] Transforming this
dubious idea into a general principle, Tait and Stewart asserted that
there must be an unseen universe where the 'lost' energy goes. This
unseen universe may correspond with the afterlife, in which we will
be able to recover the lost energy and lost thoughts of the past. Thus
the image of universal heat death is turned into a consoling picture
of the afterlife.

Tait and Stewart confuse the second law's idea of energy 'lost' for
all practical purposes, with a common-sense notion of energy lost
absolutely. Several of Kelvin's articles on the subject, both scientific
and popular, hinted at some escape clause whereby the inevitable
process of decay could be reversed. His first article on the subject
concluded that the earth would eventually become: 'unfit for the
habitation of man as at present constituted, unless operations have
been, or are to be performed, which are impossible under the laws
to which the known operations going on at present in the material
world are subject'.[10] This peculiarly equivocal conclusion hints that
some unnamed agent might intervene at the eleventh hour, and
Kelvin's popular article in 1862 concluded more explicitly that life
would cease 'unless sources now unknown to us are prepared in the

[8] J. Edward Chamberlin, 'Images of Degeneration: Turnings and Transformations',
in Chamberlin and Sander L. Gilman (eds.), *Degeneration: The Dark Side of Progress*
(New York: Columbia University Press, 1985), 263–89 (p. 272).

[9] Peter Guthrie Tait and Balfour Stewart, *The Unseen Universe* (London: Macmillan,
1875), 155–6.

[10] Kelvin, 'On a Universal Tendency in Nature to the Dissipation of Mechanical
Energy', *Philosophical Magazine*, 4th ser., 4 (Oct. 1852), 304–6 (p. 306).

great storehouse of creation'; his popular article in the *Fortnightly* in 1892 repeated his 1852 conclusion almost word for word.[11]

Tait and Stewart also drew support for their erroneously optimistic view of the future from James Clerk Maxwell's idea of a 'sorting demon'.[12] Maxwell noted that the second law 'was undoubtedly true so long as we can deal with bodies only in mass, and have no power of perceiving or handling the separate molecules of which they are made up'. His imaginary demon has the power to create an exception to the law: it should be conceived as 'a being whose faculties are so sharpened that he can follow every molecule in its course, such a being, whose attributes are still as essentially finite as our own, would be able to do what is at present impossible to us'.[13] The demon operates a frictionless door in a divided vessel of gas, opening and closing the door to separate swift-moving molecules from slow ones. It thereby raises the temperature in one part of the vessel, and reduces it in the other. Maxwell's demon is an impossibility, as the energy required to sort the molecules would be more than that produced by the sorting process, but it is a peculiar form of thought experiment, in that the exception it creates is more vivid than the reminder of the law's universality. The reader feels unwarrantedly reassured. Tait and Stewart follow their discussion of the demon by saying that particles can be 'rendered capable of doing work by mere *guidance* applied by finite intelligence', as if this guidance required no input of energy.[14] The demon's frictionless door becomes for them the gateway between the seen and the unseen universes.

Kelvin introduced his escape clause not only in the popular presentations of the second law, in *Macmillan's Magazine* and the *Fortnightly Review*, but also in that for the *Philosophical Magazine*. The need to mitigate the theory's consequences is determined not by the exigencies of presenting it to a 'popular' audience, but those of presenting it to any human audience. For writers of fiction, the sensational prospect of the end of civilization was easier to convey,

[11] Kelvin, 'On the Age of the Sun's Heat', 375; 'On the Dissipation of Energy', *Fortnightly Review*, o.s. 57 (Mar. 1892), 321.

[12] The phrase 'sorting demon' apparently originated in Kelvin's 'The Sorting Demon of Maxwell', a lecture of 28 Feb. 1879, abstracted in *Popular Lectures and Addresses*, iii. 137–41. See Edward E. Daub, 'Maxwell's Demon', *History and Philosophy of Science*, 1 (1970), 213–27.

[13] James Clerk Maxwell, *Theory of Heat* (London: Longmans, Green and Co., 1871), 308.

[14] Tait and Stewart, *Unseen*, 89.

particularly as the *fin de siècle* was already predisposed to imagine itself as the end of the world. Camille Flammarion's 'The Last Days of the Earth' (1891) described the earth in AD 2,200,000. The sun has become 'yellower, even reddish'; by the end of the story it shines with a 'reddish and barren light', and eventually becomes an 'enormous invisible black ball'.[15] The last great city on earth, Suntown, has been given over to decadent pleasure:

Leaving far behind it the childish amusements of Babylon, of Rome, and of Paris, it had thrown itself heart and soul into the most exquisite refinements of pleasure and enjoyment; and the results of progress, the achievements of science, art and industry had, during several centuries, been applied to raising all the joys of life to their maximum intensity. Electricity, perfumes, music, kept the senses in a state of over-excitement . . .[16]

The excitement was such that at around the age of twenty-five men and women 'dropped dead of total exhaustion'. Max Nordau, criticizing what he believed to be the similarly decadent culture of 1890s, took heat death as a metaphor for 'a Dusk of the Nations, in which all suns and all stars are gradually waning, and mankind with all its institutions and creations is perishing in the midst of a dying world'.[17] Nordau's later reference to the 'reddened light of the Dusk of Nations' ostensibly referred to the sunsets that followed the Krakatoa eruption, but inevitably carried suggestions of the sun's decay.[18] The title of Oswald Spengler's *Untergang des Abendlandes* (1918–1922) drew on this idea, though its literal meaning, 'the sunset of the western lands' is occluded in the English translation, 'The Decline of the West'. Anatole France had also absorbed the image of the dying sun. His review of Flammarion's *Urania* reached the melancholy conclusion that the stars, far from offering transcendent escape from 'the perpetual vicissitudes of life and death', only reflected human life: 'white in their burning youth, like Sirius, they afterwards grow yellow, like our sun, and before their death assume a deep red tinge'.[19] The most sensational image of the promised end,

[15] Camille Flammarion, 'The Last Days of the Earth', *Contemporary Review*, 59 (1891), 558–69 (pp. 559, 569).

[16] Flammarion, 'Last Days', 560.

[17] Max Nordau, *Degeneration* translated from the 2nd German edn. (London: Heinemann, 'fourth edition' 1895), 2.

[18] Nordau, *Degeneration*, 6.

[19] Anatole France, 'Astronomical Day-Dreams', *On Life and Letters*, 3rd ser., tr. D. B. Stewart (London: John Lane, 1922), 210. The French original was published in *Le Temps*, 24 Nov. 1889.

and perhaps the best known, came in H. G. Wells's *The Time Machine* (1895), where the sun is 'red and very large . . . a vast dome glowing with a dull heat'.[20] The idea of heat-death was accessible through both scientific and literary sources, and, as Katherine Mansfield's familiarity with it shows, through conversation as well.

The second law also became widely known through Herbert Spencer's attempts to incorporate it into a more comprehensive philosophy. The antithetical relations of evolution and dissipation have already been noted; the philosophy advanced by Spencer in *First Principles* attempted to explain the relation in more detail. Spencer saw evolution as a process affecting *matter* (we might nowadays see it as affecting genetic *information*), and dissipation, or dissolution as he preferred to call it, as affecting *energy*:

> The processes thus everywhere in antagonism, and everywhere gaining now a temporary and now a more or less permanent triumph the one over the other, we call Evolution and Dissolution. Evolution under its simplest and most general aspect is the integration of matter and concomitant dissipation of motion; while Dissolution is the absorption of motion and concominant [sic] disintegration of matter.[21]

Spencer aimed to develop these first principles into a comprehensive system that would explain the evolution and dissipation not only of physical systems, but also of biological and social ones; the later chapters 'Equilibration' and 'Dissolution' advance arguments of this type.[22] His works were enormously influential in their time, leading, among other things, to D. H. Lawrence's loss of faith.[23] Much of their persuasive force derived from the way they grant explanatory priority to physical science, a discourse apparently objective and value-free. However, as Greg Myers has shown, the popularization of thermodynamics was from the outset 'intertwined with social thought'.[24] The flow of ideas is not a unidirectional trickling down from the hard to the soft sciences, as Spencer imagined it to be, but a circulatory system. As Myers says, 'the language of social and moral criticism came to permeate the rhetoric of

---

[20] H. G. Wells, *The Time Machine* (1895; London: Dent, 1993), 82–3.
[21] Herbert Spencer, *First Principles* (London: Williams and Norgate, 4th edn. 1880), 285.
[22] Spencer, *First Principles*, 519–22.
[23] D. H. Lawrence, letter to Rev. Robert Reid, 15 Oct. 1907, *Letters of D. H. Lawrence*, ed. James T. Boulton et al., 7 vols. (Cambridge: Cambridge University Press, 1979–93), i. 36–7.
[24] Myers, 'Nineteenth-Century Popularizations', 35.

the nineteenth-century British popularizers of physics, and . . . the language of physics came to be used for social and moral criticism'.[25]

The second law of thermodynamics rests on what Lakoff and Johnson would term a 'container metaphor'.[26] Container metaphors allow us to impose artificial boundaries on physical phenomena. The cylinders and boilers of practical thermodynamics would appear to be quite literally 'containers', but in fact, even with the best insulation available, are radiating heat in all directions: thermodynamically, they are continuous with their environment. The sun may appear to be a discrete entity, but its outline is ragged. Though it may be sharply differentiated from its surroundings, it is continuous with them. The thermodynamic version of the metaphor also rests on the idea that the contents are small, indistinguishable, and able to flow. This second specification allows the concepts of thermodynamics to be transferred to a wide range of human activities. A bank account, for example, is conceptualized as a container; when a unit of currency is put in or taken out of the account, it becomes indistinguishable from all the others.

Unusually, the metaphor often manifests itself with the same vocabulary in a wide range of spheres of application. This is best illustrated with 'dissipation' and its cognates, the word used by Kelvin in the three articles referred to above. Used by Kelvin and other physicists in the OED's meaning 2, 'dissipation' cannot help carrying overtones of other meanings, most obviously 4 ('Wasteful expenditure or consumption of money, means, powers, faculties . . .'), 5 ('Distraction of the mental faculties or energies from concentration on serious subjects . . .') and 6 ('Waste of the moral or physical powers by undue or vicious indulgence in pleasure . . .'). As a student, the young William Thomson was much concerned with meanings 4 and 5, being anxious to set himself apart from the 'dissipated men'.[27] Other terms in Kelvin's 1852 paper also release the semantic potential of 'dissipation'. Kelvin's reference to the possibility of the 'restoration' of energy to its 'primitive condition' suggests a half-formed political or theological myth.[28] The semantic

---

[25] Myers, 'Nineteenth-Century Popularizations', 36.

[26] Lakoff and Johnson, *Metaphors We Live By*, 29–32.

[27] Crosbie Smith and Norton Wise, *Energy and Empire: A Biographical Study of Lord Kelvin* (Cambridge: Cambridge University Press, 1989), 71–2.

[28] Kelvin, 'On a Universal Tendency', 304.

overspill was widespread. Myers quotes the Victorian physicists Stewart and Lockyer, who used a social analogy to explain 'dissipation': 'As in the social world a man may degrade his energy, so in the physical world energy may be degraded; in both worlds, when degradation is once accomplished, a complete recovery would appear to be impossible, unless energy of a superior form be communicated from without.'[29] Though the usual escape clause is present, the insistence on inevitability is important: it seems that as the second law of thermodynamics became more widely known, 'dissipation' and its cognates came to be used increasingly in contexts implying inevitability. The present and future tenses of the verb fall from view, while the past tense, the past participle and the noun become increasingly prominent. When, in 1817, Coleridge described the secondary imagination as something that 'dissolves, diffuses, dissipates, in order to re-create', the process is subject to an active agent.[30] When John Tyndall used the verb in 1870, with reference to the evolution hypothesis, it was not only, grammatically, in the passive—'Under the fierce light of scientific enquiry, it [the hypothesis] is sure to be dissipated if it possesses not a core of truth'—but more importantly, was associated with an inevitable process.[31] Pater's use of it in the 'Conclusion' to *The Renaissance*, where the external objects of experience 'are dissipated' under the influence of 'reflexion', is indebted to Coleridge, but is, like Tyndall's, conspicuously passive.[32]

The verb 'to dissipate' is also divided according to the classes of object it can take. In the examples above, the imagination or other faculty of mind dissipates an illusion in order to penetrate to the real essence of things, but elsewhere the subject dissipates one of the material necessities of life, such as energy, matter, or capital. The verb can carry a positive or a negative moral value. This creates an interesting ambiguity near the beginning of D. H. Lawrence's *The Trespasser*, after Siegmund has left his wife Beatrice: 'In the miles of

[29] Myers, 'Nineteenth-Century Popularizations', 52, quoting from Balfour Stewart and J. Norman Lockyer, 'The Place of Life in a Universe of Energy', *Macmillans*, 20 (Sept. 1868), 322.

[30] S. T. Coleridge, *Biographia Literaria*, ed. James Engell and W. Jackson Bate, in *Collected Works*, ed. Kathleen Coburn (London: RKP, 1969–83), vii (part 1), 304.

[31] John Tyndall, 'The Scientific Use of the Imagination' (1870), *Fragments of Science* (London: Longmans, Green and Co., 5th edn. 1876), 455.

[32] Walter Pater, *The Renaissance*, ed. Donald L. Hill (Berkeley, Ca.: University of California Press, 1980), 187.

morning sunshine, Siegmund's shadows, his children, Beatrice, his sorrow, dissipated like mist, and he was elated as a young man setting forth to travel.'[33] It would seem that his wife and children were the mist of illusions, stripped away to reveal the reality of his love for Helena. Yet when, immediately afterwards, we are told that 'everything had vanished but the old gay world of romance', it seems that the dissipated object is the reliable world of his life in London. That Helena and Siegmund should travel to an island to pursue their affair becomes interesting in the light of thermodynamics and its metaphors: it raises the question of whether a couple, or even an individual, can exist in a perfectly contained system, completely insulated from the outside world. Can the romance world of the Isle of Wight become so self-contained as to constitute a real world for Siegmund and Helena?

The financial sense of 'dissipation' was the one that preoccupied Joseph Conrad in his letters, many of which are concerned with financial worries. In 1902 he wrote to his publisher thanking him for a cheque 'which I found on my return home from a bout of dissipation in London'.[34] It is clear that the primary meaning is OED 4 ('Wasteful expenditure . . .'), though an element of moral self-reproach tinges the reference. Conrad's 1915 letters to his literary agent indicate that he associated this form of 'dissipation' with the metropolis.[35] Woolf had similar feelings during the war, remarking that 'going to a Hall' (the Coliseum Music Hall) was 'an unheard of dissipation'.[36]

The metaphor of energy as money was, as Myers suggests, a readily reversible one. Tait and Stewart remarked that 'the tendency of heat is towards equalization; heat is *par excellence* the communist of our universe, and it will no doubt ultimately bring the system to an end'.[37] The idea of dissipation as redistribution informs Wells's *The Time Machine*, where the Very Young Man speculates that one might 'invest all one's money, leave it to accumulate at interest, and

[33] D. H. Lawrence, *The Trespasser*, ed. Elizabeth Mansfield (Cambridge: Cambridge University Press, 1981), 55.

[34] Conrad, letter to William Blackwood, dated 5 Nov. 1902, *The Collected Letters of Joseph Conrad*, ed. Frederick R. Karl and Laurence Davies, 5 vols. to date (Cambridge: Cambridge University Press, 1983–96), ii. 451.

[35] Conrad, letters to J. B. Pinker, dated 9 Mar. 1915 and [7 Oct. 1915], *Letters*, v. 452, 518.

[36] Woolf, entry for 15 Jan. 1915, *Diary*, i. 19.

[37] Tait and Stewart, *The Unseen Universe*, 90–1.

hurry on ahead'; the narrator quips that having travelled through time, he might well discover a 'strictly communistic' society.[38] The financial metaphor was invoked much later by Einstein, in explaining why the vast quantities of energy contained in matter had gone unnoticed for so long: 'The answer is simple enough: so long as none of the energy is given off externally, it cannot be observed. It is as though a man who is fabulously rich should never spend or give away a cent; no one could tell how rich he was.'[39] The rich man has, in the earlier language of entropy, created a perfectly self-contained system.

Dissipation, and the threat of dissipation, became central to the understanding of the body, the mind, and hence of subjectivity. Though Virginia Woolf in her diaries occasionally used the word in its financial sense, or in relation to wasting the time available for work, she predominantly used it to refer to her mental and physical state: 'dissipated and invalidish', or 'dissipated and rather frittered' are typical.[40] As Freud evolved his model of the self, he had to think it, as Althusser remarks, in 'imported concepts', and its emphasis on 'drives' and 'pressures' identifies it as an essentially thermodynamic conception: the psyche as steam engine.[41] It is clear however, that Woolf's sense of being 'dissipated' differs significantly from the Freudian model, referring not to unconscious or libidinal energies so much as to the total bodily or mental energy. It is closer to the Victorian medical doctrine which declared that the body had a limited reserve of energy which must be drawn upon with great caution. This had been the topic of Michael Foster's 1893 Rede lectures, which saw the problem in economic terms:

Whether the muscle be at rest or be moving, some of the capital of living material is always being spent, changed into dead waste, some of the new food is always being raised into living capital. But when the muscle is called upon to do work, when it is put into movement, the expenditure is quickened, there is a run upon the living capital, the greater, the more urgent the call for action.[42]

[38] Wells, The Time Machine, 7. Compare the plot of When the Sleeper Wakes (1899).

[39] Einstein, Science Illustrated (April 1946), quoted in John Carey (ed.), The Faber Book of Science (London: Faber, 1995), 275.

[40] In relation to work time on 10 Nov. 1917 and 16 Sept. 1929 (Diary, i. 72 and iii. 253), and, as quoted, on 14 Feb. 1922 and 14 Nov. 1934 (Diary, ii. 161 and iv. 261).

[41] Louis Althusser, Lenin and Philosophy (London: New Left Books, 1971), 182; Michel Serres, Hermes: Literature, Science, Philosophy ed. Josue V. Harari and David F. Bell (Baltimore: Johns Hopkins University Press, 1982), 72.

[42] Michael Foster, 'Weariness', The Nineteenth Century, 34 (Sept. 1893), 337–52 (pp. 339–40); a lecture delivered in Cambridge on 14 June 1893.

The Victorian version of this doctrine was gendered, with women's energy being considered particularly vulnerable.[43]

A more elaborate version of this model is advanced in Lawrence's *The Trespasser* and *Aaron's Rod*. In the earlier work, the minor character Hampson holds that death begins 'once we've begun to leak'. Siegmund is puzzled by this vocabulary, though in fact he has already recognized that he has 'lived too intensely' and that his soul 'seems to leak out'; Hampson, in remarking that Siegmund lacks 'reserve'—'You've no dispassionate intellect to control you and economize'—is only restating Siegmund's self-knowledge in more formal terms.[44] His metaphors are drawn from economics, biology, and thermodynamics, and he is indebted to Nietzsche, but the underlying theme is that of dissipation.[45] The model makes gender distinctions, albeit obscurely: the 'ordinary woman' is 'a great potential force, an accumulator, if you like, charged from the source of life', but she cannot convert this energy into a useful form without a man. In the later work the narrator theorizes the difference between Sir William Frank and Aaron Sisson, the one holding life to be 'a storing-up of produce and a conservation of energy', the other seeing it as 'a sheer spending of energy and a storing up of nothing but experience'.[46] Their drives and pressures are only very distantly Freudian.

The process of disintegration can affect not only an individual's bank balance and his mind, but also his nation. The earliest English uses of 'dissipate' and 'dissipation' refer to political contexts: 'Subuersions of empires and kingdoms, skatterings and dissipacions of nations' (*OED*). In late 1887, there was a series of protests and riots in Trafalgar Square and Hyde Park in protest at unemployment, which Roger Fry considered in a letter:

is it a volcano as Wedd would have it which is like to blow Modern Society to smithereens, or is it a penny squib according to the gospel of McTaggart. I for one incline to the volcano theory—society has come to a pass—but any

---

[43] Cynthia Russett, *Sexual Science: The Victorian Construction of Womanhood* (London: Harvard University Press, 1989), 105, 126–8; William Greenslade, *Degeneration, Culture and the Novel 1880–1940* (Cambridge: Cambridge University Press, 1994), 134–5.

[44] Lawrence, *The Trespasser*, 106, 111–12.

[45] On Nietzsche, see Cecilia Björkén, *Into the Isle of Self* (Lund: Lund University Press, 1996), 179.

[46] Lawrence, *Aaron's Rod*, ed. Mara Kalnins (Cambridge: Cambridge University Press, 1988), 155.

way out of the difficulty beats me hollow. I suppose that either we or fate shall find an outlet even if the British nation is dissipated on the way . . .[47]

In fact the idea of dissipation is doubly present, once, silently, in the idea of the crowd as a growing volcanic pressure, and then explicitly in the idea of the nation being dissipated by the consequent explosion. The idea of the crowd as a mass of atoms, or of atoms as a swarming crowd, creates a powerful metaphoric connection between physical and social thinking. Clerk Maxwell in his popular lecture 'Molecules' (1873) compares the mass of atoms firstly to a swarm of bees, and secondly to a messenger with a letter moving through a dense crowd; he borrows a more muted metaphorical description from Clausius: 'in ordinary water the molecules are not only moving, but every now and then striking each other with such violence that the oxygen and hydrogen of the molecules part company, and dance about through the crowd, seeking partners which have become dissociated in the same way'.[48] Here the world of clashing atoms comes to resemble a rowdy, promiscuous and violent gathering of people.

In *The Nature of the Physical World*, Eddington uses the distinction of the individual and the crowd throughout his chapter on the second law: 'this law has no application to the behaviour of a single individual, and as we shall see later its subject matter is the random element in a crowd'.[49] The analogy of crowds is more than an expository image: Maxwell justified the use of the statistical method in the second law by reference to the use of statistics in the study of the population; 'statistics' was originally the science of the state. For the statisticians, 'the number of individuals is far too great to allow of their tracing the history of each separately, so that, in order to reduce their labour within human limits, they concentrate their attention on a small number of artificial groups'.[50] Although there is not an exact correspondence of vocabulary—crowds 'disperse' rather than 'dissipate'—there is an underlying similarity of outlook.

[47] Roger Fry to C. R. Ashbee, dated 22 October 1887, *The Letters of Roger Fry*, ed. Denys Sutton, 2 vols. (London: Chatto and Windus, 1972), i. 115.

[48] Clerk Maxwell 'Molecules' (22 Sept. 1873), *Scientific Papers*, ed. W. D. Niven (Cambridge: Cambridge University Press, 1890), ii. 361–78 (pp. 368, 370).

[49] Eddington, *Physical World*, 67.

[50] Clerk Maxwell, 'Molecules', 373. Theodore Porter discusses the respects in which Clerk Maxwell's emphasis on the uncertainty of the method differed from that of the statisticians: 'A Statistical Survey of Gases: Maxwell's Social Physics', *Historical Studies in the Physical Sciences*, 12 (1981), 77–116.

A similarly circular interchange occurs in thinking about crowds and about bacteria. As David Bodanis has argued, Pasteur's reactionary fears of the swarming mob provided him with a framework within which to hypothesize the existence of bacteria, around 1857, long before he had empirical evidence to support the idea.[51] On the reverse side, when Gustave Le Bon wrote *Psychologie des foules* (1895), and sought a suitable metaphor to describe their destructive effects on civilization, he drew his simile from microbiology: 'crowds act like those microbes which hasten the dissolution of enfeebled or dead bodies'.[52] Here, as in Fry's description, the crowd is not the object of dissipation but its agent. According to this conservative outlook, civilization is organized, and can suffer degradation, but the crowd, though it contains energy, is already highly disorganized.

The mode of describing crowds as faceless, abstract flows of matter was common to late-Victorian and modernist writers. The conservative W. S. Lilly, writing in 1886 against the immorality of 'materialism' in science and literature, saw French democracy as 'the domination of the brute force of numbers', and considered 'the masses' to be 'little more than matter in motion'.[53] The newspaper reports of the Hyde Park protestors in 1887 did little to individualize them. Even their main spokesman could be identified only as 'an Italian', leaving the impression that the reporter observed the events from the safety of a fourth floor window.[54] In her novels, Virginia Woolf's crowds are less threatening, having some aesthetic qualities of form, but are nonetheless presented as abstractions. In *The Voyage Out*, when the musicians strike up for the dance, heads appear in the doorway 'like the rats who followed the piper'. The depersonalization of the dancers goes further. 'Couples' leap into the dance, but are soon transformed into abstract 'eddies', which 'seemed to circle faster and faster, until the music wrought itself into a crash, ceased, and the circles were smashed into little separate bits'.[55] The point of this depersonalization is to emphasize the individuality of Rachel and Helen, for whom the dance represents an

[51] David Bodanis, *Web of Words: The Ideas Behind Politics* (Basingstoke: Macmillan, 1988), 15–21.

[52] Le Bon, *The Crowd* (1896; London: E. Benn, 1952), 18.

[53] W. S. Lilly, 'Materialism and Morality', *Fortnightly Review* o.s. 46 (Nov. 1886), 575–94 (p. 582).

[54] 'The Police and the Mob', *The Times* (21 Oct. 1887), 11.

[55] Woolf, *The Voyage Out* (1917), ed. Jane Wheare (London: Penguin, 1992), 138–9.

infernal torment. Similarly, in *Night and Day*, at a moment of emotional crisis Ralph sees the people in the street as 'only a dissolving and combining pattern of black particles'.[56] Katharine later has a similar perception of the impersonality of city streets, expressed in terms of 'torrents' and 'currents' rather than 'particles'.[57]

In a particularly interesting diary entry from 1919, Woolf describes the crowds on Hampstead Heath on Easter Monday in terms recalling *The Voyage Out*:

> the crowd at close quarters is detestable; it smells; it sticks; it has neither vitality or colour; it is a tepid mass of flesh scarcely organized into human life . . . It was a summer's day—in the sun at least; we could sit on a mound & look at the little distant trickle of human beings eddying round the chief centres of gaiety & filing over the heath & spotted upon its humps.[58]

The point is not simply that Woolf shows a contempt for the crowd—such feelings were, as John Carey has shown, all too widespread—but that her description of them leaves them inanimate and abstract.[59] Her earlier description of humans as rats is the exception, allying her with the disgust of writers who see crowds as swarming bacteria, insects or other animate forms: her general tendency to abstraction mixes her disgust with a sense of abstract beauty. The forces which unite Woolf's groups and crowds will be considered in more detail in Chapter 5.

The association of dissipation with crowds, with money, and with the body and the mind, may be said to be part of the concept's unconscious. Authors and readers conscious of the second law of thermodynamics would have been conscious principally of the dissipation of heat, and the prospect of universal heat death. In this light, the name of Inspector Heat in Conrad's *The Secret Agent* becomes particularly interesting. Though not as Dickensian or as grotesque as some of the other surnames found in Conrad's *oeuvre* (Toodles, Sir Ethelred, Singleton, Kurtz), it would appear to have symbolic overtones, if only because it is unheard of as an actual British surname.[60] In one respect his name is, like the others, part of the 'ironic method' which Conrad applied to his subject ('Author's

[56] Woolf, *Night and Day* (1919), ed. Julia Briggs (London: Penguin, 1992), 193.
[57] Ibid., 374.   [58] Woolf, entry for 24 April 1919, *Diary*, i. 268.
[59] John Carey, *The Intellectuals and the Masses* (London: Faber, 1992).
[60] Cedric Watts, *A Preface to Conrad* (London: Longman, 2nd edn. 1993), 193–7, for symbolic and allegoric names.

Note', 7).[61] However, it may also direct the reader's attention towards the ideas and images outlined above.

Studies of Conrad's work and science have largely overlooked physics, concentrating instead on Darwin, ideas of literary and bio-logical degeneration, or on the 'scientific attitude' in general.[62] Writings on science and *The Secret Agent* have concentrated almost exclusively on degeneration, and Lombroso's criminology.[63] Entropy has been seen largely as a nineteenth-century concern, and those critics who have related it to Conrad's novels have focused largely on *Heart of Darkness*.[64] However, Conrad conceived *The Secret Agent* in the 1890s, after the Greenwich Park bombing of 1894, and the dedication identifies it as a tale 'of the XIX century' ([2]): as I will show, this was a period when the theme of entropy pre-occupied him.

Entropy is not the only meaning that a reader might attach to 'heat' within *The Secret Agent*: some of the other possibilities are significant, others spurious.[65] The most important is that of 'intens-ity of feeling' (*OED* 11), as seen in the contrast that emerges between the cold calculations of the Professor, and the moral com-mitment of the Chief Inspector. Most obviously, when the Professor declares to Ossipon that they as individuals are of no consequence, he is said to speak 'carelessly, without heat, almost without feeling' (60): his coldness is stereotypically that of the scientist.[66] Later, the

---

[61] References in the text are to *The Secret Agent*, ed. Bruce Harkness and S. W. Reid (Cambridge: Cambridge University Press, 1990).

[62] Jacques Berthoud, *Joseph Conrad: The Major Phase* (Cambridge: Cambridge University Press, 1978), 156–8; Allan Hunter, *Joseph Conrad and the Ethics of Darwinism: The Challenges of Science* (London: Croom Helm, 1983); Redmond O'Hanlon, *Joseph Conrad and Charles Darwin* (Edinburgh: Salamander, 1984).

[63] Hunter, *Joseph Conrad*, 182–205; Greenslade, *Degeneration*, 106–19; Martin Ray, 'Conrad, Nordau, and Other Degenerates: The Psychology of *The Secret Agent*', *Conradiana*, 16 (1984), 125–40. Ray (140 n. 4) gives other references.

[64] Daphna Erdinast-Vulcan, *Joseph Conrad and the Modern Temper* (Oxford: Clarendon, 1991), 12; Patrick A. McCarthy, '*Heart of Darkness* and the Early Novels of H. G. Wells: Evolution, Anarchy, Entropy', *Journal of Modern Literature*, 13 (1986), 37–60; Norman Sherry, *Conrad's Western World* (Cambridge: Cambridge University Press, 1971), 274–7; Ian Watt, *Conrad in the Nineteenth Century* (London: Chatto and Windus, 1980), 152–5; Watts, *Preface*, 86–7.

[65] Some readers familiar with crime fiction may take 'the heat' in the sense of 'the police' (*OED* 12b), and therefore picture the Chief Inspector as a stereotypical police-man. Though it is possible that this meaning was in circulation by 1906, this sense emerges clearly only in the 1930s, in America.

[66] On the background to this image of the scientist, see Haynes, *From Faust to Strangelove*, 64–91 and 211–35.

Professor's 'sinister detachment' and 'nerveless gait' are contrasted with the Chief Inspector's sense of moral authority, and his 'purposeful briskness' (77). The Chief Inspector has feelings of warmth towards the planet's 'teeming millions', and his very walk appears to be filled with a moral energy. The narrator also distinguishes the two in the language of vitalism and eugenics: Heat has a 'vigorous, tenacious vitality', while the Professor is 'frail' and 'obviously not fit to live' (75–6). This fundamental contrast between the two characters becomes more interesting when the ideas of thermodynamics are brought into play.

The London of *The Secret Agent* is a peculiarly gloomy one: much of the action takes place in the evening and at night, with gaslights failing to provide much illumination; it seems that the sun has already exhausted itself in its battle against London, 'cruel devourer of the world's light' ('Author's Note', 6). Even when the action takes place in the day, there is little sign of sunlight. Verloc's shop is a place 'where the sun never shone' (194). As Ossipon leaves the Silenus, the day is described as 'gloomy' and the sky as 'grimy', even though the season is 'early spring' (65). Several critics have remarked upon this atmosphere, and Erdinast-Vulcan has related it to images of London as a submarine world.[67] However, the gloominess of the light is attributed at various points to the feebleness of the sun. In Chapter 2, 'a peculiarly London sun' shines on Hyde Park, 'against which nothing could be said except that it looked bloodshot' (11). The image of the sun as a bloodshot eye complements the description of Verloc's eyes as 'heavy-lidded' (11), and the later description of Winnie's as 'dry, enlarged, lightless, burnt out like two black holes in the white, shining globes' (221).[68] Later in Chapter 2, the 'rusty' sunshine is said to be 'struggling clear of the London mist' and to shed a 'lukewarm' brightness into the Embassy (26). The sun is apparently subject to the 'rule of decay affecting all things human and some things divine' (125). Michaelis in his cottage 'could not tell whether the sun still shone on the earth or not' (95): this partly indicates the extent of his isolation, but the narrator does not say that the upstairs room was windowless; the remark reinforces the

---

[67] Avrom Fleishman, 'The Symbolic World of *The Secret Agent*', *ELH*, 32 (1965), 196–219 (pp. 208–9); Daphna Erdinast-Vulcan, ' "Sudden Holes in Space and Time": Conrad's Anarchist Aesthetics in *The Secret Agent*', in Gene M. Moore (ed.), *Conrad's Cities* (Amsterdam: Rodopi, 1992), 207–22.

[68] 'Black hole' would not have carried its present-day cosmological implications, but may nevertheless have suggested an extinguished sun.

general sense of the sun's decay. As Martha Turner notes, the only sign of vitality in this de-energized world, the butcher boy 'driving with the noble recklessness of a charioteer' (17), appears as an incongruous survival from a lost heroic age.[69]

It is clear that Conrad had been familiar with the scientific 'rule of decay' since at least December 1897. In a letter to Cunninghame Graham, explaining that Singleton of the *Narcissus* is an 'elemental force', Conrad wrote that '[n]othing can touch him but the curse of decay—the eternal decree that will extinguish the sun, the stars one by one, and in another instant shall spread a frozen darkness over the whole universe'.[70] A month later, Conrad related the theory to political ideology, implicitly addressing Cunninghame Graham's socialist views: 'The mysteries of a universe made of drops of fire and clods of mud do not concern us.'[71] One recalls that Winnie, 'alone in London', finds that 'the whole town of marvels and mud, with its maze of streets and its mass of lights, was sunk in a hopeless night . . .' (203). Conrad continued:

The fate of a humanity condemned ultimately to perish from cold is not worth troubling about. If you take it to heart it becomes an unendurable tragedy. If you believe in improvement you must weep, for the attained perfection must end in cold, darkness and silence. In a dispassionate view the ardour for reform, improvement for virtue, for knowledge, and even for beauty is only a vain sticking up for appearances as though one were anxious about the cut of one's clothes in a community of blind men.[72]

As Watt, Watts, and McCarthy all note, these images soon found their way into Conrad's fiction, appearing at the start of *Heart of Darkness*, where the sun 'changed to a dull red without rays and without heat, as if about to go out suddenly . . .'[73] But it seems that by the time he was writing *Heart of Darkness*, Conrad had begun to think of *The Secret Agent*, and to associate the Greenwich Park bombing with the idea of entropy.

---

[69] Martha Turner, *Mechanism and the Novel* (Cambridge: Cambridge University Press, 1993), 126.

[70] Letter to Cunninghame Graham dated 14 December 1897, *Letters*, i. 423. O'Hanlon and McCarthy both quote this letter but neither relates it to *The Secret Agent*: McCarthy, 56; O'Hanlon, 19.

[71] Conrad, letter to Cunninghame Graham dated 14 Jan. 1898, *Letters*, ii. 16–17.

[72] Ibid.

[73] Watt, *Conrad in the Nineteenth-Century*, 154; Watts, *Preface*, 86–7; McCarthy, 'Heart of Darkness', 57; Conrad, *Youth, Heart of Darkness, The End of the Tether* (London: Dent, 1946), 46.

Though many sources were available, Wells's *The Time Machine* seems the most likely. Conrad had apparently read it before their friendship began in 1896, and *The Secret Agent* is dedicated to Wells not only as '[t]he chronicler of Mr Lewisham's love' and 'the biographer of Kipps', but also as 'the historian of the ages to come' ([2]). There are similarities not only in his description of the 'rusty' sun, but in his descriptions of London's gloomy light and its 'immensity of greasy slime' (116). Wells's time traveller is appalled not only by the monstrous crabs, but by their claws 'smeared with an algal slime', and by the beach covered in 'the uniform poisonous-looking green of the lichenous plants', and again, a thousand or so years later, by the 'green slime on the rocks'. The crabs crawl 'in the sombre light, among the foliated sheets of intense green'.[74] In *The Secret Agent*, the shades of green silk fitted over the Assistant Commissioner's lights 'imparted to the room something of a forest's deep gloom' (164). Wells's image of the crabs on the desolate beach may also have led, in general terms, to Conrad's image of London at night, 'slumbering monstrously on a carpet of mud' (224). The grotesques who populate *The Secret Agent* are not so strangely mutated as the Morlocks, the Eloi, or the slimy invertebrates of Wells's novel, but their existence is based on a similar assumption that a decaying planet will be peopled by decaying species.

Conrad was aware not only of heat death, but of 'dissipation' in its financial and its moral senses. He was drawing upon the discourse of the body when he wrote to Edward Garnett in 1904, saying that he regretted 'the dissipation of your energy, the waste of vigour and the sound of divine blows lost in an unresonnant [sic] medium'.[75] The appearance of 'dissipated' in *The Secret Agent* is more easily overlooked:

[Verloc] looked up and shook his head. His eyes were bloodshot and his face red. His fingers had ruffled his hair into a dissipated untidiness. Altogether he had a disreputable aspect, expressive of the discomfort, the irritation and the gloom following a heavy debauch (147).

'Dissipated' here is something more than a synonym for 'disreputable': the reference to Verloc's bloodshot eyes refers the reader back to the earlier 'bloodshot' sun (15), and thence to the idea of heat death. Related to Verloc's *dissipation* is the moral *disintegration* of

---

[74] Wells, *The Time Machine*, 84–5.
[75] Conrad, letter of 3 Sept. 1904, *Letters*, iii. 162.

society. The Professor aims to bring about 'the disintegration of the old morality' (60), and Verloc is later said to lack 'moral energy' (167) and to be 'shaken morally to pieces' (174). It seems that Conrad associated 'disintegration' as closely with entropy as he did 'dissipation'. In a letter to Cunninghame Graham in 1898, he complained that he was 'not able to say one cheering word' to his depressed friend; 'It seems to me I am desintegrating [sic] slowly. Cold shadows stand around.'[76] 'Cold shadows' would have referred Cunninghame Graham back to the letter of 14 January 1898, and the idea of a humanity condemned to perish in cold. The association of decaying morals and declining morale with dissipation and disintegration may have had personal meanings for Conrad and Cunninghame Graham, but the cluster of ideas was more widely available.

The moral collapse of Conrad and Verloc suggests Stevie's fate, which leaves his body in a physical 'state of disintegration' (71). His remains are seen by Heat, mixed up with 'small gravel, tiny brown bits of bark, and particles of splintered wood as fine as needles' (71). The description is repeated, with variants, when Verloc is informed of the death (159), and when Winnie remembers the details (195). The Greenwich Park bomber of 1894 had lost a hand and was grotesquely mutilated, but was still alive and conscious when found. Conrad's transformation has the effect, as Sherry argues, of denying sympathy for Stevie, but it also serves to emphasize the novel's theme of disintegration.[77] The Professor threatens to reduce the Inspector and himself to a similar state of disintegration, as thoroughly mixed as Stevie and the gravel. 'I've no doubt', he tells the Inspector, 'the papers would give you an obituary notice.' 'But', he continues, 'you may be exposed to the unpleasantness of being buried together with me, though I suppose your friends would make an effort to sort us out as much as possible' (75). As we have seen, Conrad differentiates the Professor and the Inspector in terms of their emotional temperature. The bomb, if detonated, would reduce them to a homogeneous mixture. The Inspector's friends would be left with the painstaking task of Maxwell's sorting demon, separating the swift from the slow, the cold Professor from Inspector Heat. The city authorities are charged with a similar, if less gruesome task, in sorting the houses that have 'strayed' from their proper place (17). Fragmentation is all pervasive.

[76] Conrad, letter of 9 Dec. 1898, *Letters*, ii. 129.
[77] Sherry, *Conrad's Western World*, 232–3.

The specificity of *The Secret Agent*'s relation to ideas about the second law may be clarified by contrasting another celebrated modernist depiction of decay, the 'Time Passes' section of *To the Lighthouse*. Though the narrator speaks of 'flesh turned to atoms', and although Andrew Ramsay is killed by an exploding shell, in many respects Woolf's vision of dissipation is a gentler one than Conrad's.[78] Woolf's lyrical style relates it to an older tradition of nature poetry about the passage of time and the seasons. Crucially, the process of decay is an active one, not the result of the inevitable ebbing of cosmic energy. The 'profusion of darkness' creeps in 'at keyholes and crevices', rather than waiting for the light to disappear.[79] And in so far as the process is inevitable, it is seen to be the inevitable assertion of a natural order over an artificial one: 'What power could now prevent the fertility, the insensibility of nature?'[80] It is also a gradual process: the 'stray airs' in *To the Lighthouse* 'nibble' at the furniture; Conrad's urban vision of entropy more closely resembles that of *Mrs Dalloway*, where time is a matter of 'shredding' and 'slicing'.[81]

One phrase suggests a possible line of connection to popular scientific writings about entropy, but it is also an exception that proves the rule: 'Night, however, succeeds to night. The winter holds a pack of them in store and deals them equally, evenly, with indefatigable fingers.'[82] This anticipates Eddington's introduction of the topic of entropy through the metaphor of shuffling. The 'original systematic order' of a pack of cards fresh from the maker will disappear with a few minutes of shuffling, but 'will never come back'—at least, its reappearance is highly improbable— 'however long you shuffle'.[83] That Woolf's reference to winter's pack of cards anticipates the publication of Eddington's lectures is not a problem, as the metaphor of shuffling could well have been used in a conversational explanation of entropy. Nor is the fact that shuffling is only implied in Woolf's description: that the survival or destruction of the house is a matter of chance is clear enough. The real difficulty is that the image of entropy as a process of shuffling identical objects seems far more

---

[78] Woolf, *To the Lighthouse* (1927), ed. Stella McNichol (London: Penguin, 1992), 145. Michael Rosenthal sees 'Time Passes' as a battle between chaos and order, though without recruiting the language of thermodynamics: *Virginia Woolf* (London: Routledge and Kegan Paul, 1979), 120–1.

[79] Woolf, *To the Lighthouse*, 137.   [80] Ibid., 150.

[81] Ibid., 140; *Mrs Dalloway* (1925), ed. Stella McNichol (London: Penguin, 1992), 112.

[82] Woolf, *To the Lighthouse*, 139.   [83] Eddington, *Physical World*, 63.

appropriate to Conrad's London, and particularly its strayed houses, than it does to Woolf's Hebrides. The shawl, the skull and the wallpaper retain their individuality in spite of their decay. Stevie loses a great deal of his. Although Mrs McNab's work in restoring order to the Hebridean house resembles in some respects that of Maxwell's demon, the matter she manipulates has not been blown to indistinguishable atoms.

The implications of entropy and dissipation in *The Secret Agent* extend beyond the restricted scientific ideas of heat death and Maxwell's Demon. An interpretation which focuses purely on the scientific may miss the ways in which the 'scientific' image is a displacement of a more controversial social concern. The novel itself suggests this, as the attack on the Greenwich meridian is not an attack on pure mathematics, but a displaced attack on the empire: Greenwich is known to the 'whole civilized world' (32). In what ways does the unconscious of 'dissipation' inform the novel?

The first possibility centres on the metaphor of the sun as a reserve of capital, and the reciprocal metaphor of reserves of capital as hot bodies. Under a free market, money-energy would circulate, dissipating from certain centres, but accumulating in others. However, the second law predicted a universe in which only dissipation reigned. The financial meanings of dissipation were of concern to both the young William Thomson and to Conrad, and are clearly relevant to a novel in which one character at least is committed to 'the annihilation of all capital' (88). In an important early letter, Conrad had depicted socialism as a bringer of 'despoliation and disorder', and this, rather than a concern for social justice, seems to inform Michaelis's desire to dissipate capital.[84] The backdrop of a dying sun may have seemed to Conrad to be simply appropriate to Michaelis's vocation. However, an ironic juxtaposition is more appropriate to the novel's all-pervasive ironies. By this reading, the sun's natural and inevitable depletion of its reserves contrasts with the anarchists' failure to bring about the 'annihilation of all capital' and 'despoliation and disorder'.

Anxieties over national and racial unity also sharpened the Victorian fear of entropy. The fear of slower, weaker bodies that might reduce the average level of energy is common to eugenics and thermodynamics. It is a fear that the essential characteristics of the

---

[84] Conrad, letter to Spiridion Kliszczewski, 19 Dec. 1885, *Letters*, i. 16.

nation might dissipate. In this light Maxwell's demon is an altogether more sinister character, a eugenicist border-guard sorting the strong from the weak. The idea of the demon as the enforcer of social segregation was touched upon by Maxwell in a letter to Strutt, where he characterized it as a 'doorkeeper'.[85] Conrad had touched upon this theme of barriers in his 'despoliation and disorder' letter of 1885. It was too late to stop social-democratic ideas: 'For the sun is set and the last barrier removed. England was the only barrier to the pressure of infernal doctrines born in continental back-slums. Now, there is nothing! The destiny of this nation and of all nations is to be accomplished in darkness . . .'[86] In *The Secret Agent*, the anarchists are meeting in the dark slums of London, and in the eyes of Mr Vladimir, England, with its 'sentimental regard for individual liberty' (28), is the irritating exception to the continental rule of repression. Mr Vladimir as doorkeeper-demon would prefer to keep the anarchists 'under lock and key'.

The theme of the dissipation of national characteristics is best illustrated by the Assistant Commissioner's reflections on the Italian restaurant:

the patrons of the place had lost in the frequentation of fraudulent cookery all their national and private characteristics. And this was strange, since the Italian restaurant is such a peculiarly British institution. But these people were as denationalized as the dishes set before them with every circumstance of unstamped respectability. Neither was their personality stamped in any way, professionally, socially or racially. They seemed created for the Italian restaurant, unless the Italian restaurant had been perchance created for them. But that last hypothesis was unthinkable, since one could not place them anywhere outside those special establishments. (115)

The restaurant is another game, playing a version of 'Italian' that has no relation to any real Italy. But the Assistant Commissioner, a former colonial policeman (89), is uncomfortable with its inauthenticity, and with the sight of his own 'foreign appearance' (115) in a mirror. The strange artificiality of the restaurant removes the outlines of national identity, and plunges him into the colonialist's worst nightmare, the possibility that he might be going native.

[85] Maxwell, letter to Strutt, 6 Dec. 1870, *The Scientific Letters and Papers of James Clerk Maxwell*, ed. P. M. Harman (Cambridge: Cambridge University Press, 1995), ii. 582.
[86] Conrad, *Letters*, i. 16.

We have already seen Roger Fry's fears about the dissipation of the British nation state in the late 1880s. The end of the century also saw growing fears that empires, through their very size and diversity, might reach a point of self-destruction. 'Dissolution' was the favoured word, but as we have seen, in Herbert Spencer's writings this word combined the political and the physical much as 'dissipation' did. In 'A Dissolving Empire', Francis Hirst suggested that the Austrian empire had become too racially, religiously and linguistically diverse to survive; in 'The French Colonial Craze', Gaston Donnet argued that 'A nation cannot dilate itself like a gas, to its thousandth power; limits exist which are not to be overstepped'; in 'The Coming Dissolution', written against the background of the Boer War, F. A. White suggested that the British Empire may have expanded beyond its limits.[87] Charles H. Pearson argued, in his examination of the 'Decay of Character', that man would decay like everything else, and he invoked 'Science, with its record of glacial epochs and its forecast of vanishing heat'.[88] J. A. Cramb warned that 'the spaces of the past are strewn with the wrecks of dead empires, as the abysses where the stars wander are strewn with the dust of vanished systems, sunk without sound in the havoc of the æons'.[89] If these fears of national dissipation are taken as relevant to *The Secret Agent*, then the entropy theme creates a significant irony. The British Empire identifies itself as 'the Empire on which the sun never sets' (162); the anarchists seem congenitally unable to organize any effective action against it but, as they fritter away their time, the Empire's structure is dissolving, and its sun slowly decaying. The sun will not only go down, but go out altogether.

The final framing irony of the entropy theme is concerned with time. The attack on the Greenwich meridian makes time an obvious unifying theme, and several critics have followed Fleishman's lead in exploring it.[90] Clocks are omnipresent, but clock time in *The Secret*

[87] Hirst, 'A Dissolving Empire', *Fortnightly Review*, 70 (July 1898), 56–71; Donnet, 'The French Colonial Craze', *Fortnightly Review*, 70 (Dec. 1898), 864–71, reprinted from *Revue Bleue*, 24 Sept. 1898; White, 'The Coming Dissolution', *Westminster Review*, 154 (Sept. 1900), 237–52.

[88] Charles H. Pearson, *National Life and Character: A Forecast* (London: Macmillan, 1893), 2, 342.

[89] J. A. Cramb, *Reflections on the Origins and Destiny of Imperial Britain* (London: Macmillan, 1900), 304–5.

[90] Fleishman, 'Symbolic World', 211–19; Erdinast-Vulcan, ' "Sudden Holes" ', in Moore (ed.) *Conrad's Cities*; Sue Tyley, 'Time and Space in the Secret Agent', *The Conradian*, 8 (1983), 32–8.

Agent is 'seldom unambiguously objective'.[91] At several crucial moments in the novel, clock time appears to be suspended: as Stevie and Winnie travel through Whitehall in the cab (121); in Heat's imagination, in the instant of Stevie's death (71); and in Ossipon's imagination, in the twenty seconds allowed by the Professor's personal bomb (56). When Winnie stabs Verloc she regresses to 'the age of caverns' (197): when Verloc's blood begins to tick, it appears that evolution has resumed its normal course.

The theme of entropy is directly relevant to the theme of time. In several places Kelvin used the analogy of a clock to describe entropy. In 1862 he tried to deny that the universe could be running down like a clock, arguing instead for 'an endless progress, through an endless space' of the transformation of potential energy into heat.[92] While this followed from the principle of the indestructibility of energy, it evaded the essential point, that the usable, concentrated bodies of heat would dissipate. In 1892 Kelvin took the more pessimistic view: 'The running down of the weight in the clockwork has its perfect analogue, as Helmholtz was, I believe, in reality the first to point out, in the shrinkage of the sun from century to century under the influence of the mutual gravitational attractions between its parts.'[93] In the novel's moments of timelessness, it seems that the universal clockwork has finally run down. As Arthur Eddington was to explain in 1928, our sense of the directionality of time ('time's arrow') is dependent on the process of entropy. When one reaches a point of maximum entropy, or 'thermodynamical equilibrium', 'we lose time's arrow'.[94] Conrad had died before Eddington delivered his Gifford Lectures, but it was possible to infer the idea from the science of the late nineteenth century. Through the idea of timelessness, the entropy theme creates a circumscribing irony. Fleishman claims that the plot to destroy the first meridian 'is symbolically an effort to end history—thereby theoretically achieving the revolutionary goal of a world beyond history and without time'.[95] The irony is, once again, that the universe itself is approaching a timeless

---

[91] Tyley, 'Time and Space', 35.   [92] Kelvin, 'On the Age of the Sun's Heat', 357.

[93] Kelvin, 'On the Dissipation of Energy', 321.

[94] Eddington, *Physical World*, 78. It should be noted that Eddington read *The Secret Agent* in 1927, the year of the Gifford Lectures: Eddington Papers, Trinity College Cambridge, Add. MS b. 48, fols. 134–9. He recorded only the bare fact of having read the novel, and nothing of his response, but it indicates the possibility of literary texts influencing the presentation and content of scientific ideas.

[95] Fleishman, 'Symbolic World', 213.

state of thermodynamical equilibrium, and judging by the gloominess of London, it seems likely to reach equilibrium before the anarchists achieve their revolutionary goal.

The theme of dissipation seems at times so omnipresent that there is little possibility, in the cultural sphere, for its contestation. The container metaphors on which it rests are so deeply ingrained in the language that we are very easily led into the discourse of dissipation. However, it was as a theme locked into conflict with the theme of evolution, figured in literature as self-improvement and the improvement of society. Moreover, there was significant scope for disagreement over the consequences of dissipation, whether it be imagined as cosmic heat-death or social eruption. A conservative might take it as a justification for reinforcing old dogmas, or, like Conrad in his more pessimistic moments, as proof of the futility of all political actions and attempts (like those of Cunninghame Graham) at progressive politics. A liberal or a socialist might take the idea of disintegration as an opportunity to devise new structures, based on a new ideas of order. The idea of unanimism, examined in Chapter 5, is one such structure. The idea that the universe was fragmented and fragmenting was a necessary condition for the idea of literary form as chaos held in shape by a deep underlying field of force. Aspects of this will be considered in the next chapter (Woolf's 'shower of atoms') and in Chapter 5.

The statistical methods of the second law of thermodynamics led, by the 1920s, to an acceptance of statistical methods in quantum mechanics, but even before that period, they led to an altered conception of science's relation to reality, and of the nature of scientific law. Statistical laws could not speak of the impossibility of an event, only its very great improbability.[96] Though Heisenberg's uncertainty principle is often invoked in relation to the formal quality of uncertainty in modernist literature, it is clear that in science the theme was partially established by the late nineteenth century. This development seemed to many to create an escape from the deterministic world view of Newtonian science. Furthermore, under statistical law, science does not aim to explain the operations of nature, merely to describe what has been observed. These developments provided a language in which literary writers could justify the abandonment of the omniscient narrator; they could embrace subjectivism with the full authority of science.

---

[96] Eddington, *Physical World*, 98.

3

Descriptionism:
Consuming Sensations

D OES the external world exist in its own right, or is it merely something constructed by perceiving subjects? This is an old philosophical problem, but the scientific developments of the late-nineteenth and early-twentieth centuries renewed its importance for science, philosophy, and literature. Physical science was increasingly dealing with phenomena inaccessible to unaided human perceptions. Clerk Maxwell's demon, capable of manipulating minute fast-moving particles, would construct the universe quite differently from human perceiving subjects. Animals too, suggested Ernst Mach and Henri Bergson, construct space and time according to their physiology: if their constructions were not the true reality, why should those of human animals be any more accurate?[1] Were scientific laws representations and explanations or nature, or merely a convenient shorthand for recording human perceptions of it? Does reality consist of an 'incessant shower of innumerable atoms' which fall on the mind, as Virginia Woolf famously claimed, or does it possess an intrinsic structure?[2] The idea that reality is, in itself, chaotic was the basis for philosophical, scientific, linguistic, and aesthetic theories in this period. This chapter seeks to trace the connections between these discourses, and to examine how literary writers responded to scientific debate about reality.

The novelty of the modernist idea of reality has been explained on numerous occasions, with many explanations singling out psychoanalysis and the arts as prime causes. This chapter does not seek to

---

[1] Mach, *The Analysis of Sensations*, trans. C. M. Williams, revised from the 5th German edn. by Sydney Waterlow (Chicago: Open Court, 1914), 160; Bergson, *Essai sur les données immédiates de la conscience* (1889; Paris: Presses Universitaires de France, 1993), 71–2; trans. F. L. Pogson as *Time and Free Will* (London: Swan Sonnenschein, 1910), 96–7.

[2] Woolf, 'Modern Novels', *Essays of Virginia Woolf*, ed. Andrew McNeillie, 4 vols. to date (London: Hogarth, 1986–94), iii. 33.

eliminate these explanations, but to suggest that they are only partial accounts. The affinities between the 'impressionism' of modernist writers and that of French painters are often commented on, and 'impressionism' is often used without further explanation.[3] Freud's discovery of the power of the unconscious mind has also been widely taken to explain the breakdown of the 'rational' literary forms of the late nineteenth century, such as the stable subject-position created for narrator and reader, and the ultimate knowability of the fictional world. Freud is important, but literary historians have over-emphasized psychoanalysis at the expense of other areas of psychology in the period.[4] In spite of its title, Bertrand Russell's *The Analysis of Mind* (1921) had surprisingly little to say about Freud, pursuing instead the questions raised by William James, Bergson, and Mach. Questions about the nature of perception, straddling psychology and the philosophy of science, were just as important. In Bloomsbury, though we find the Hogarth Press publishing Freud in English, we also find Sydney Waterlow co-translating Ernst Mach's *The Analysis of Sensations*, and Karin Stephen writing an exposition of Bergson.

The debate about perception frequently involves 'the linguistic turn' or something closely resembling it, a 'conceptual turn' that does not specifically mention language; however, this turn is itself dependent upon the idea of reality as a chaos. The most common metaphor is of language as a net which catches chaotic reality. For Nietzsche, the Platonic mode of thinking consisted of 'pale, cold, grey conceptual nets thrown over the motley whirl of the senses'; this metaphor recapitulates the larger, mythic distinction of *The Birth of Tragedy* between Apollonian form and unruly Dionysian energy.[5] For Bergson too, reality is in flux, and the 'Heraclitean'

---

[3] Clive Scott's detailed survey uses Impressionism to displace Psychology, claiming that the stream of consciousness technique was 'as much a result of Impressionism as of advances in psychology': 'Symbolism, Decadence and Impressionism', in Malcolm Bradbury and James McFarlane (eds.), *Modernism 1890–1930* (Harmondsworth: Penguin, 1990), 222.

[4] For example, Peter Faulkner, *Modernism* (London: Methuen, 1977), 14. Freud's dominance is noted in one of the few studies to examine the topic in detail, Judith Ryan's *The Vanishing Subject: Early Psychology and Literary Modernism* (Chicago: University of Chicago Press, 1991). One reason for the neglect of Mach may be the difficulty in naming his school of philosophy: for Ryan, it is 'empiricist psychology'; for others it was 'empirio-criticism'; here I follow J. L. Heilbron in terming it 'descriptionism'.

[5] Nietzsche, *Beyond Good and Evil* (1886), trans. R. J. Hollingdale (Harmondsworth: Penguin, 1990), 45.

aspect of his philosophy was emphasized by at least one popular exposition.[6] In his first major work Bergson wrote that 'La conscience, tourmentée d'un insatiable désir de distinguer, substitue le symbole à la réalité, ou n'aperçoit la réalité qu'a travers le symbole.'[7] Bergson shared with Nietzsche a pragmatic and Darwinian perspective, one that insisted on mind as a practical organ which facilitates survival. Concepts correspond to reality only in so far as they contribute to this end. Saussure kept reality at one remove, stating that *thought* rather than the external world was a 'swirling cloud' subdivided by linguistic categories; nonetheless he adopted a position very similar to that of Nietzsche and Bergson.[8]

Nietzsche is often spoken of as if he were the originator of these ideas, but it is clear from *Beyond Good and Evil* that developments in the philosophy of science formed part of their background, however aloof his tone:

It is perhaps just dawning on five or six minds that physics too is only an interpretation and arrangement of the world (according to our own requirements, if I may say so!) and *not* an explanation of the world . . .[9]

Nietzsche gives no clues about the identity of these five or six, but it seems likely that one of them was Ernst Mach, who as recently as 1882 had introduced the idea that science was the 'economy of thought'.[10] Underlying this idea is the thermodynamic and Darwinistic notion that any animal has a limited quantity of energy available to it, and that any action, including thought, causes the expenditure of this energy. The human mind cannot store all the sense impressions it receives, and so summarizes these impressions into the generalizations of language. Science is only a more advanced form of this common mental operation. As Karl Pearson put it, a scientific law or formula can replace in our minds 'a wide range of relationships between isolated phenomena', relieve our memory 'from the burden of individual sequences', and reduce

[6] Joseph Solomon, 'The Philosophy of Bergson', *Fortnightly Review*, 96 (1911), 1014–31 (p. 1015).

[7] Bergson, *Essai*, 95–6 (*Time and Free Will*, 128).

[8] Saussure, *Course in General Linguistics*, trans. Roy Harris (London: Duckworth, 1983), 110.

[9] Nietzsche, *Beyond Good and Evil*, 44.

[10] Mach, 'Ueber die oekonomische Natur der physikalischen Forschung', *Almanach der Wiener Akademie* (1882), translated as 'The Economical Nature of Physical Enquiry' in *Popular Scientific Lectures*, trans. Thomas J. McCormack (Chicago: Open Court, 1898), 186–213.

'intellectual fatigue'.[11] Karl Pearson's version of the 'net' metaphor was the metaphor of the human perceptive faculty as a machine for sifting and sorting stones: 'Sensations of all kinds and magnitudes may flow into it, some to be rejected at once, others to be sorted all orderly, and arranged in place and time'.[12] These mental arrangements of raw experience form the basis of scientific theories.

The Machian school of science rejected the idea that science *explained* the universe, preferring instead the more modest claim that it provided economic descriptions—hence its appellation as the 'descriptionist' school.[13] Though Nietzsche characterizes the new mode of science as one of 'interpretation', it is clear that for some descriptionists, this was too close to 'explanation': Pearson wrote that the goal of science was 'the complete interpretation of the universe', but added that this was an ideal goal, 'the *direction* in which we move and strive, but never a stage we shall actually reach'.[14]

Though Pearson's *The Grammar of Science* appears not to have attracted wide popular attention on its first appearance in 1892, by the mid 1890s its author was creating controversy with his essays for the *Fortnightly*, and the book began to have an impact.[15] Some elements of his thinking had already been advanced in Britain by W. K. Clifford, whose *The Common Sense of the Exact Sciences* (1885) Pearson had posthumously completed, but the *Grammar* gave most readers their first introduction to these ideas.[16] Remembering it in 1906, Henry Adams wrote that the book had 'a historical value out of all proportion to its science', and claimed that 'Pearson shut out of science everything which the nineteenth century

[11] Pearson, *The Grammar of Science* (London: Walter Scott, 1892), 37–8.

[12] Pearson, *Grammar*, 128.

[13] See Pearson's preface to the Second Edition of *The Grammar of Science* (London: A. and C. Black, 1900), p. vii.

[14] Pearson, *Grammar*, 17.

[15] The reviews that appeared were largely in the scientific and philosophical journals; those by Bentley, Caillard, Dixon, Mivart, and Singer, and those that appeared anonymously in *Mind*, *The Monist*, and *The Pall Mall Gazette*, are listed in the bibliography. It was used by Einstein himself, teaching science in Berne in 1902: see Ronald W. Clark, *Einstein: The Life and Times* (London: Hodder and Stoughton, 1973), 65. As we saw in Chapter 1 (n.19), it was read by at least two early champions of Einstein's work, T. Percy Nunn and Arthur Eddington.

[16] Pearson acknowledges Mach's influence in the elimination of terms such as 'matter' and 'force' in his preface to W. K. Clifford and K. Pearson, *The Common Sense of the Exact Sciences* (London: Kegan Paul, Trench and Co, 1885), pp. viii–ix. H. V. Routh, *English Literature and Ideas in the Twentieth Century* (London: Methuen, 1946), 119, is one of the few critics to note the importance of *The Grammar of Science* as a pioneering text; Pearson's later involvement in eugenics may have had a deterrent effect.

had brought into it.'[17] Adams's judgement implies that the book inverted the values of nineteenth-century science, but its effect was more complex, particularly as regards the debate between material-ism and idealism.

In August 1894 Lord Salisbury had made a controversial Presidential address to the British Association, which had strongly emphasized the extent of scientific ignorance. Pearson responded in the *Fortnightly* in September, associating Salisbury's political and scientific conservatism, and describing his address as a 'a message of despair and ignorance'.[18] In rebutting Salisbury, Pearson referred the reader to the *Grammar*, and marshalled arguments that he had first rehearsed there. Salisbury had noted that science was ignorant in three crucial areas: the nature of the atom; the nature of the ether; and the problem of biogenesis. Pearson agreed that scientists were ignorant concerning these things, but argued that Salisbury had mistaken the nature of the problem. The question was not 'what is the atom' or 'what is the ether', but 'what concepts can my mind invent which will describe in brief shorthand the main characteris-tics of certain physical sensations'.[19] The problem, in short, is one of description, not explanation. Salisbury had attempted to dimin-ish the claims of science by noting that the process of evolution involved 'pure chance', and that much science was a matter of 'mere conjecture': 'no certain knowledge can be obtained'.[20] Pearson, who since the first publication of the *Grammar* had been turning his attention increasingly to statistical work on evolution, was able confidently to turn Salisbury's argument against him, arguing that the theory of evolution was 'likely to become a branch of the theory of chance', and stating that all knowledge 'is only knowledge of a greater or lesser degree of probability'.[21]

Pearson's contemporaries found his philosophy difficult to catego-rize. When he argued that science should confine itself to sense-data, he seemed to be a tenacious empiricist, yet when he wrote of science as the process of inventing mental concepts, or wrote that 'the laws of science are products of the human mind rather than factors of the

---

[17] Adams, *The Education of Henry Adams*, ed. Jean Gooder (London: Penguin, 1995), 426.

[18] Pearson, 'Politics and Science', 336.   [19] Ibid., 341.

[20] Quoted by Pearson, ibid., 349, 351.

[21] E. S. Pearson, 'Karl Pearson: An Appreciation of Some Aspects of His Life and Work', *Biometrika*, 28/3–4 (Dec. 1936), 193–257 (pp. 217–18); quotations from Karl Pearson, 'Politics and Science', 349, 351.

external world', he seemed much closer to an idealist position.[22] In his response to Pearson's article, St George Mivart allied himself with Salisbury, stating that the world of science owed him a debt for drawing attention to its ignorance. His argument against Pearson drew attention to the problem of categorizing his philosophy; he noted Pearson's doctrine that 'we can know nothing but feelings', but claimed that, despite his contempt for metaphysics, Pearson was a metaphysician.[23] Pearson responded to Mivart in the preface to the second edition of the *Grammar*, arguing that 'a sound idealism' was replacing 'the crude materialism of the older physicists', and noting with amusement Mivart's mistaken attack on the *Grammar* as 'essentially materialistic'.[24]

The inadequacy of terms such as 'materialism' and 'idealism' to categorize the new physics was to persist as a problem into the era of Eddington and Jeans. Pearson noted that the new outlook was 'agnostic as to the supersensuous', and the supersensuous world was taken to include both physical and religious concepts.[25] To some this agnosticism implied that such concepts were superfluous, while to others it seemed as if science had relented from its atheistic and materialistic assaults. The ambivalence of the new outlook was also a political and ideological ambivalence. Its reliance on the evidence of the senses placed it in a position of radical individualism, antagonistic both to conservatives such as Lord Salisbury, and, as Lenin's lengthy philosophical assault on Mach evinces, to Marxists.[26] As Herbert Samuel was to note many years later, in response to Eddington, a world in which cause and effect are merely mental constructs is a world in which one's political actions have been rendered ineffective.[27]

If this individualist subject-position offered liberation from the deterministic world-view of Victorian science, it also threatened new forms of confinement. The senses are conventionally spoken of as windows onto the world, yet Pearson wrote of the *Dinge an sich* 'lying behind the impenetrable veil of sensations'.[28] Whereas sensations conventionally fall *through* a veil before reaching the senses, in

---

[22] Pearson, *Grammar*, 44.   [23] Mivart, 'Denominational Science', 433.

[24] Pearson, *Grammar* (1900), p. viii.   [25] Ibid., p. vii.

[26] V. I. Lenin, *Materialism and Empirio-Criticism*, trans. David Kvitko (1908, 1920; London: Martin Lawrence, [1927]).

[27] Herbert Samuel, 'Cause, Effect, and Professor Eddington', *Nineteenth Century*, 113 (Apr. 1933), 469–78.

[28] Pearson, 'Politics and Science', 341.

this picture, the sensations, like the Indian *maya*, are the veil itself. In the *Grammar* Pearson introduces a more contemporary version of this idea in the conceit of the mind as a human telephone exchange. The conceit is first introduced to explain the way that certain sense-impressions can lead directly to reactions without the intervention of conscious thought, just as certain telephone lines are routed through the exchange, but are permanently connected between two subscribers. However, Pearson later returns to the metaphor when considering the larger issue of our relation to the external world. Pearson notes that we 'are accustomed to talk of the "external world", of the "reality" outside us', yet if a sensory nerve is cut 'anywhere short of the brain', we lose the sense-impressions associated with it:

How close can we then actually get to this supposed world outside our-selves? Just as near but no nearer than the brain terminals of the sensory nerves. We are like the clerk in the central telephone exchange who cannot get nearer to his customers than his end of the telephone wires. We are, indeed, worse off than the clerk, for to carry out the analogy properly we must suppose him *never to have been outside the telephone exchange, never to have seen a customer or any one like a customer—in short, never, except through the telephone wire, to have come in contact with the out-side universe.*[29]

The 'conscious ego' is placed in a similar position, inferring things about the external universe from its sense impressions, but never coming into contact with the 'things-in-themselves'. Eddington was later to give Pearson's tragically isolated clerk a more comical cousin: a college Bursar who 'dwelt secluded in his rooms devoting himself entirely to accounts', and who 'realised the intellectual and other activities of the college only as they presented themselves in the bills'.[30] The bursar's understanding of the college corresponded to that of the scientist who knows the universe only through pointer-readings.

Pearson's clerk also has important literary predecessors and rela-tives. The telegram clerk in Henry James's 'In the Cage' (1898) is the most pertinent example, not only because of the connection with

[29] Pearson, *Grammar*, 74. The passage was quoted by Emma Marie Caillard in an article that drew extensively on Pearson's book: 'The Human Telephonic Exchange', *Contemporary Review*, 87 (Mar. 1905), 393–401.

[30] Eddington, *Physical World*, 237–8. Eddington first used the parable of the Bursar in 'The Philosophical Aspect of the Theory of Relativity', *Mind*, 29 (Oct. 1920), 421–2.

communications technology, but because her isolated consciousness provides the epitome of those in James's longer works.[31] James is only an isolated instance: in more general terms, the descriptionist outlook on the relation of sense impressions and knowledge may be described as an aestheticist one. As J. Edward Chamberlin has noted, Walter Pater's conclusion to *The Renaissance* bears a striking resemblance to the thinking of Mach and Pearson.[32] Pater signals the fundamental idea of flux with his epigraph from Heraclitus, before offering a more modern scientific description of 'physical life' as being composed of nothing more than 'a combination of natural elements'.[33] The mind is a sorting machine, sifting the 'ten thousand resultant combinations' of the flux: 'That clear, perpetual outline of face and limb is but an image of ours, under which we group them—a design in a web, the actual threads of which pass out beyond it' (186–7). Language invests objects with 'solidity', but beyond these linguistic categories are 'impressions, unstable, flickering, inconsistent' (187). However, once the socially unifying bonds of language are removed, 'the whole scope of observation is dwarfed into the narrow chamber of the individual mind', and the sensitive aesthete finds himself in the same position as Pearson's telephone operator: 'each mind keeping as a solitary prisoner its own dream of a world' (188).

Pater expanded his ideas about this 'anti-metaphysical metaphysic' in *Marius the Epicurean* (1885).[34] In Chapter 8, Marius discovers the writings of Heraclitus, from whom he learns that 'Men are subject to an illusion . . . regarding matters apparent to sense. What the uncorrected sense gives was a false impression of permanence or fixity in things, which have really changed their nature in the very moment in which we see and touch them' (108). This mode of thinking 'attributes to the phenomena of experience a durability which does not really belong to them' (108). Pater acknowledges again the problem of solipsism posed by this philosophy, introducing it in the guise of 'the famous doctrine of the sophist Protagoras',

---

[31] *The Complete Tales of Henry James*, ed. Leon Edel, 12 vols. (London: Hart-Davis, 1962–4), x. 139–242.

[32] J. Edward Chamberlin, 'Whose Spirit is this? Some Questions about Beginnings and Endings', in John Stokes (ed.), *Fin de Siècle / Fin du Globe* (Basingstoke: Macmillan, 1992), 228–32.

[33] Pater, *The Renaissance*, 186. Subsequent references in the text.

[34] Pater, *Marius the Epicurean*, ed. Michael Levey (Harmondsworth: Penguin, 1985), 115. Subsequent references in the text.

that 'the momentary, sensible apprehension of the individual was the only standard of what is or is not, and each one the measure of all things to himself' (109). While Pater recognizes that this might lead to 'despair of knowledge' (109), he also suggests two more complex responses. Having learned that he is the only measure of all things, Marius feels that to move 'in that outer world of other people, as though taking it at their estimate, would be possible henceforth only as a kind of irony' (110). However, Pater also suggests that Marius's discovery of nature's flux leads to a more positive change in his principle of subjectivity, in which he decides to 'maintain a harmony with that soul of motion in things, by constantly renewed mobility of character' (113). This flexibility of self promises a form of empathy that might overcome the ironic detachment.

The problem of solipsism posed by descriptionism was one to which scientific commentators were alive both at the end of the nineteenth century and into the Einstein era. Many British scientists subscribed to Kelvin's belief that a scientific theory was inadequate unless it could provide a mechanical model of the phenomena it purported to explain. Only such models could guarantee the existence of a reality external to the perceiving subject. Continental physicists, whether followers of Mach or not, too often adopted forms of mathematical explanation which gave 'shorthand' descriptions without a physical model. Robert Ball, F. R. S., a traditionalist mocked by Pearson in the *Grammar*, typified the British approach when he wrote in 1893 that the 'genuine student of nature loves to get to the heart of a problem' not through the 'mere formulae or abstract principles' of someone like Helmholtz, but 'so as to be able to visualise its truth and feel its certainty'.[35] The position of Kelvin, unable to grasp a theory unless he could make a mechanical model of it, was very similar, but with the triumph of formalist description in Einstein's theory and in quantum mechanics, such philosophies appeared as relics of the Industrial Revolution.

The turn-of-the-century anxieties concerning scientific investigation and scientific law are neatly paralleled by Conrad in *The Secret Agent*, where the certainty of criminal investigation and law has

---

[35] Robert Ball, 'Atoms and Sunbeams', *Fortnightly Review*, 60 (Oct. 1893), 464–77; Pearson, *Grammar*, 188.

been similarly undermined. As the Professor comments, revolution and legality are 'counter moves in the same game'.[36] Similarly, Heat understands the burglar, because his mind and instincts are the same as those of a police officer: both 'recognise the same conventions' (74). Like Marius, they can move in each other's worlds only as a kind of irony. To think of the burglar and detective following 'conventions' removes the moral content of the law; their relationship is as much of a 'game' as Heat's relationship to the Professor. Heat, however, finds the minds of the anarchists incomprehensible: he is uncomfortable with the rules of the anarchists' game, which are continually being revised. When Heat and the Professor meet, each may or may not carry a secret which will destroy the other: Heat may know of the Professor's involvement in Stevie's death, and the Professor may be carrying his bomb. Each plays his cards close to his chest, operating with 'atrocious allusiveness'. The artificiality of the game is revealed when Heat advises the Professor to 'Give it up— whatever it is' (77): 'it' is suddenly exposed as a blank card, a pronoun without a referent. Heat's dealings with his superiors are characterized by the same artificiality. His reassurance that there will be 'no outbreak of anarchist activity' was sincere, but was satisfying for other reasons, 'because it was clear that the high official desired greatly to hear that very thing' (69). Not surprisingly, his superiors are bound by the same rules: the Assistant Commissioner lingers in Brett Street, 'as though he were a member of the criminal classes' (116).

The correlate of this game playing is that 'real' knowledge, knowledge of the depths of nature, is impossible. Several of the characters in *The Secret Agent* appear to be of this opinion. Ossipon comes to the Professor after the explosion, hoping that he would know 'the inside of this confounded affair', but the Professor's response is evasive, and philosophical in its form: 'what one of us may or may not know as to any given fact can't be a matter of inquiry to the others' (52). There can only be knowledge of appearances, of sense-impressions. Similarly, the narrator says that Winnie's curiosity does not affect 'the inwardness of things' but merely 'the methods' (119). Traditional realism characterizes knowledge with metaphors of depth; these are very often combined with container metaphors. For the descriptionists, there is no content, only surfaces: the surfaces of objects that are

---

[36] Conrad, *The Secret Agent*, 58. Subsequent references in the text.

available to the senses, or, taking the theory to its logical extreme, simply the surface formed by nerve endings on the retina and the skin.

In a universe consisting only of sense-impressions, the detective and scientist lose the distinction between 'fact' and 'information', for there is no external world in which the facts may exist. The Assistant Commissioner recognizes that this is conveniently open to abuse, and tells the Home Secretary that not only does the spy 'fabricate his information', but that he will sometimes 'fabricate the very facts themselves' (108). The obverse of this situation emerges when Verloc agrees with Heat that his defence will be 'practically a full confession', that he will tell 'the whole story': Heat responds that 'You won't be believed as much as you fancy you will' (159). The implication seems to be that the perceived world of terrorism is a construct, and that if the true facts of Verloc's confession do not correspond to that construct, they will appear to be mere stories. This explains Heat's reflection that the 'disclosure' will mean 'the laying waste of fields of knowledge' (159): 'knowledge' is a self-enclosed system for which new facts can often be troublingly inconvenient.

At certain points *The Secret Agent* seems to hint that its 'descriptionist' outlook is due to the expansion of newspaper journalism rather than the philosophy of science. Mr Vladimir comments on 'the ingenuity of journalists' (31); later we learn that journalists have 'written up' Michaelis and 'would be ready to write him down' (96); in the novel's closing phase, Winnie is haunted by journalistic phrases, as is Ossipon after her death. Norman Sherry's methodology implies that Conrad drew as much on journalistic accounts of anarchists and Fenians as he did on the events 'in themselves'.

However, while the rise of the news media provides a significant cultural background to Conrad's 'descriptionism', his letters suggest that science may have been equally important. In a letter of 1913, Conrad compared the truths of art and science. He argued 'that form is the artist's (and the scientist's) province that it is all we can understand (and interpret or represent) and that we can't tell what is behind'.[37] Art was superior, however, because it could 'call on us with authority to behold! to feel!', while science was limited to descriptions of appearances: 'science at best can only tell us—it seems so!'[38] These remarks, which suggest some acquaintance with

---

[37] Conrad to Warrington Dawson, 20 June 1913, *Letters*, v. 237.   [38] Ibid., v. 238.

contemporary debates about scientific realism, lapse into a vaguer Conradian pessimism:

It [science] talks to us of Laws of Nature. But thats only one of its little jokes. It has never discovered anything of the sort. It has made out with much worrying and blundering certain sequences of facts beginning in the dark and leading god only knows where. And it has built various theories to fit the form of activity it has perceived.[39]

The worrying and blundering of the scientist could well be those of the detective out of his depth.

For those who accepted descriptionism, not only the laws of science but even its fundamental concepts such as 'matter' were human constructs. This idea was brought to prominence by Eddington in 1920:

Mind filters out matter from the meaningless jumble of qualities, as the prism filters out the colours of the rainbow from the chaotic pulsations of white light. Mind exalts the permanent and ignores the transitory; and it appears from the mathematical study of relations that the only way in which mind can achieve her object is by picking out one particular quality as the permanent substance of the perceptual world, partitioning a perceptual time and space for it to be permanent in, and, as a necessary consequence of this Hobson's choice, the laws of gravitation and mechanics and geometry have to be obeyed. Is it too much to say that the mind's search for permanence has created the world of physics?[40]

The theory of relativity had made great advances, and yet our knowledge of nature was 'only an empty shell—a form of symbols'. The mind 'has but regained from nature that which the mind has put into nature'. This was a curiously ambivalent form of popular conclusion, one that apparently summarized the new outlook of physics, but that undermined the basis of science's prestige. In conclusion, Eddington offered a memorable image:

We have found a strange foot-print on the shores of the unknown. We have devised profound theories, one after another, to account for its origin. At last, we have succeeded in reconstructing the creature that made the foot-print. And Lo! it is our own.[41]

The concluding pages of *Space, Time and Gravitation* were widely quoted: Herbert Read drew attention to them in his review of

[39] Conrad to Warrington Dawson, 20 June 1913, *Letters*, v. 238.
[40] Eddington, *Space, Time and Gravitation*, 198.   [41] Ibid., 201.

Eddington, and used them for an epigraph to his poem 'The Retreat'; J. W. N. Sullivan used them in a private letter to Middleton Murry, to support his claims for the significance of modern science.[42] The appeal of the image of the footprint lay not only in its concision, but in its playful relation to both literary and scientific ancestors. Its revision of the famous image in *Robinson Crusoe* is clear enough, but it also borrows from Newton's image of himself as 'a boy playing on the sea-shore', diverting himself with 'a smoother pebble or a prettier shell than ordinary, whilst the great ocean of truth lay all undiscovered before me'. Eddington had used this quotation as a chapter epigraph in *Space, Time and Gravitation*, and it was generally well known: *The Times*'s editorial on *The Mysterious Universe* referred to it quite familiarly, as did Yeats in 'At Algeciras—A Meditation upon Death'.[43]

This parentage makes Huxley's use of the footprint in *Crome Yellow* (1921) somewhat ambiguous. As David Bradshaw has written, 'the relativity uproar is the first target of Huxley's broadscale iconoclasm', and the topic is mentioned explicitly in chapter 10, when Priscilla Wimbush voices her anxieties about its impact on her horoscopes. In chapter 24, Denis Stone, an outsider in the Garsington-like world of Crome, discovers a 'familiar but mysterious object'—Jenny Mullion's large red notebook of caricatures, in which he and the others at Crome are represented unflatteringly. It forces Stone to realize that Jenny has hidden depths, and that not only Jenny, but the 'vast conscious world of men outside himself' are every bit 'as elaborate and complete' as he:

periodically he would make some painful discovery about the external world and the horrible reality of its consciousness and its intelligence. The red notebook was one of these discoveries, a footprint in the sand. It put beyond a doubt the fact that the outer world really existed.[44]

[42] Herbert Read, 'Readers and Writers', *The New Age*, 30 (8 Dec. 1921), 67–8; *Mutations of the Phoenix* (London: Hogarth, 1922), 25; Sullivan, quoted in Bradshaw, 'The Best of Companions', 200. It was also included in *Cambridge Readings in the Literature of Science*, ed. W. C. Dampier Whetham and M. Dampier Whetham (Cambridge: Cambridge University Press, 1924), 68, in J. St. Loe Strachey's review of the *Cambridge Readings*, 'Literature and Science', *The Spectator* (12 Jul. 1924), 59–60, and in Maurice Maeterlinck, *The Life of Space*, trans. Bernard Miall (London: Allen and Unwin, 1928), 31.

[43] *The Times* (5 Nov. 1930), 15.

[44] Huxley, *Crome Yellow* (1921; London: Flamingo, 1994), 134.

It is curious that for Stone the footprint should represent Crusoe's conclusion rather than Eddington's. Both Huxley and his audience would have been familiar with both versions, and it is possible that Huxley intends to undercut Stone's conclusion with the unspoken Eddingtonian interpretation. From the moment when Stone first sees Mr Scogan ('like one of those extinct bird-lizards of the Tertiary') his mode of perception itself consists of satirical caricatures; in one respect then, when he discovers the red book he has not discovered an outer world, but a reflection of his own mode of perception—and, of course, that of Huxley.

The idea that consciousness wrongly attributes its own constructs to the world of nature was taken up by A. N. Whitehead in *Science and the Modern World* (1926). Whitehead highlighted the illogicality of classical physics, which saw the primary qualities of matter and motion as the only real features of nature, regarding the secondary qualities of colour, taste, sound and scent as illusory projections of the mind. For Descartes and Locke:

bodies are perceived as with qualities which in reality do not belong to them, qualities which in fact are purely the offspring of the mind. Thus nature gets credit which should in truth be reserved for ourselves: the rose for its scent: the nightingale for his song: and the sun for his radiance. The poets are entirely mistaken. They should address their lyrics to themselves, and should turn them into odes of self-congratulation on the excellency of the human mind. Nature is a dull affair, soundless, scentless, colourless; merely the hurrying of material, endlessly, meaningless.[45]

Like Eddington's conclusion to *Space, Time and Gravitation*, Whitehead's passionate attack on classical physics was widely admired, quoted, and paraphrased.[46] The echo of Pater, who had written that the mind 'attributes to the phenomena of experience a durability which does not really belong to them', may be only accidental, but is interesting; in describing a scientific philosophy in which durability was considered an objective fact, Whitehead ironically echoes a writer who recognized it to be a mental construct.

---

[45] A. N. Whitehead, *Science and the Modern World* (1926; Cambridge: Cambridge University Press, 1927), 68–9.

[46] For example, by J. W. N. Sullivan in *Gallio, or the Future of Science* (London: Routledge, 1927), 76–7: 'Men who must have been theory-mad soberly maintained that little particles of matter wandering purposelessly in space and time produced our minds, our hopes, our fears, the scent of the rose, the colours of the sunset, the songs of the birds, and our knowledge of the little particles themselves.' Though Sullivan alters the content, the phrasing is unmistakable; this passage was plagiarized in turn by C. E. M. Joad, *A Guide to Modern Thought* (1933; London: Faber, 1942), 37–8.

Though the new philosophy of science prompted ambivalent responses such as Eddington's, or bitter assaults on classical physics such as Whitehead's, it also produced more positive responses. Just as Bergson wrote not only of the fixed, spatialized forms of knowledge, but also of intuition's ability to recover a more vital form of reality, so writings on descriptionism attempted to reproduce a pre-conceptualized world, a world described but not explained. Whitehead's account of the meaningless, colourless world of classical physics promised implicitly that the new world of science would acknowledge the lyrical, aesthetic aspect of nature. Mach in his own work frequently adopted a child's eye view, in order to illustrate the processes through which sense-impressions are assimilated to existing conceptual frameworks. He implies that science could adopt a child-like openness to vivid experience. In *The Analysis of Sensations* he describes how a boy, visiting the country for the first time, 'strays, for instance, into a large meadow, looks about, and says wonderingly: "We are in a ball. The world is a blue ball."'[47] More generally, Mach's rejection of metaphysics manifested itself in a habit of looking at the world, as Einstein put it in 1916, 'with the inquisitive eyes of a child, delighting in the understanding of connections'.[48]

The adoption of the 'innocent eye' becomes a regular philosophical trope in this period. Bertrand Russell very nearly adopts the trope in the first chapter of *The Problems of Philosophy*, describing a table:

To the eye it is oblong, brown, and shiny, to the touch it is smooth and cool and hard; when I tap it, it gives out a wooden sound.[49]

Though my quotation has the character of a riddle, reading in context we are never in doubt as to what Russell is talking about. Karin Stephen, in her exposition of Bergson, denied the reader the abstract term, and began with the sense impressions:

Suppose in a dark room which you expected to find empty you stumble against something, the natural thing to do is to begin at once to try to fit your experience into some class already familiar to you. You find it has a

---

[47] Mach, *Analysis of Sensations*, 317.
[48] Einstein, quoted by Martin Klein, 'Introduction' to Mach, *Principles of the Theory of Heat*, Vienna Circle Collection, 17 (Dordrecht: D. Reidel, 1986), p. xii.
[49] Russell, *The Problems of Philosophy* (1912; Oxford: Oxford University Press, 1980), 2.

certain texture which you class as rather rough, a temperature which you class as warm, a size which you class as about two feet high, a peculiar smell which you recognise, and you finally jump to the answer to your question: it is 'a dog'.[50]

While this is ultimately philosophical discourse, it features a strong inheritance from impressionistic narrative. Herbert Dingle's *Relativity for All* is ostensibly an exposition of Einstein but, as the Preface makes clear, is strongly influenced by A. N. Whitehead, and beyond him, by Mach and Bergson. Dingle's second chapter takes everyday concepts of space, time and matter and attempts to render them strange by adopting the 'innocent eye' trope:

Suppose a being, endowed with full human intelligence, but without any experience or knowledge of the world, were suddenly created and placed, say, on Hampstead Heath: what would he perceive?[51]

Classical physics would have said that he saw matter moving in time and space, but the relativist says that he would see a number of 'happenings, occurrences, events', and that 'matter' is an interpretation that would occur later. In this exposition, Dingle is imagining a moment before mind has, in Eddington's terms, filtered out 'matter' from the meaningless jumble of qualities. For the purposes of exposition, however, Dingle introduces the abstractions 'wasp' and 'flower', before re-imagining the wasp as visual sense impressions:

Suppose our visitor sees a wasp alight on a flower. That is an event. Next, suppose the wasp alights on his hand. That is another event. We have here, then, two events, and to the man they would at first be merely two events and nothing more. But now, suppose he begins to use his intelligence and tries to impose some order or arrangement on the circumstances in which he finds himself. He notices that there is something in common to the two events, with which we need not concern ourselves. He has an impression of an 'object' with black and yellow bands, which characterizes the whole series of events from the wasp on the flower to the wasp on the hand. This 'character' of the events he calls 'matter' and the particular example with which we are dealing, 'a wasp'.[52]

To adopt the terminology of Pater's conclusion, the 'cohesive force' of the abstraction 'wasp' is suspended, and the wasp 'is loosed into a group of impressions—colour, odour, texture—in the mind of the

[50] Stephen, *The Misuse of Mind* (London: Kegan Paul, Trench, Trubner, 1922), 15–16.
[51] Dingle, *Relativity for All* (London: Methuen, 1922), 10.   [52] Ibid.

observer'.[53] There are many similar passages in philosophical and popular scientific literature—for example, in Haldane's *The Reign of Relativity*, or the often-discussed 'threshold scene' in Eddington's *The Nature of the Physical World*.[54] Some, such as Eddington's, are 'innocent' precisely because they adopt sophisticated scientific explanations that run counter to 'common sense', but they share many of the qualities of the 'innocent eye' passages.

Impressionism in science and literature was viewed in the 1890s as both a symptom and a cause of degeneracy, but descriptionism occupied an ambiguous position in this debate. In some respects, it seemed to make concessions to humanists by limiting the domain of science, and this concession was important when humanists controlled the money needed for new university science buildings.[55] It seemed less threatening to civilization than earlier, more aggressive forms of science. In other respects, this very reduction and limitation of science's claims made descriptionism seem a threat to manly and disciplined activity. The contempt reserved for materialism and literary naturalism in the 1880s was now directed at descriptionism, while the science that guaranteed knowledge about an external, objective world now earned grudging respect. When W. S. Lilly wrote of 'Materialism and Morality' in 1886, he noted that W. K. Clifford's 'sensism' had seemed to offer an alternative to the 'coarse and vulgar theory' of materialism, but concluded that as Clifford and other empiricists still rejected 'as unverifiable, everything which the senses cannot verify', they too were essentially materialist.[56] For Lilly there were only two schools of thought:

[53] Pater, *Renaissance*, 187.

[54] Haldane, *The Reign of Relativity* (London: John Murray, 1921), 147–9; Eddington, *Physical World*, 342. Eddington produced a first sketch of this alienated first-person narrative in 1918, where it was cast in the first person plural, and another in 1925, where it was cast in the third person singular: in 'Gravitation and the Principle of Relativity', 15, and in 'The Domain of Physical Science', in Needham (ed.), *Science, Religion and Reality*, 189. It has been discussed by Walter Benjamin, 'Max Brod's Book on Kafka' (1938) in *Illuminations*, trans. Harry Zohn (1970; London: Fontana, 1992), 140, and by Gillian Beer, 'Problems of Description in the Language of Discovery', in *Open Fields*, 149–72, and 'Eddington and the Idiom of Modernism', in Henry Krips, J. E. McGuire, and Trevor Melia (eds.), *Science, Reason and Rhetoric* (Pittsburgh: University of Pittsburgh Press, 1995), 295–315.

[55] J. L. Heilbron, 'Fin-de-Siècle Physics', in Carl Gustaf Bernhard, Elisabeth Crawford, and Per Sörbom (eds.), *Science, Technology and Society in the Time of Alfred Nobel*, Nobel Symposium, 52 (Oxford: Pergamon, 1982), 51–73.

[56] W. S. Lilly, 'Materialism and Morality', 575–8. Lilly's arguments were countered and gently ridiculed by T. H. Huxley in the following month's issue: 'Science and Morals', *Fortnightly*, o.s. 46 (Dec. 1886), 788–802.

'spiritualism' (by which he meant a form of Kantian idealism) and 'materialism'. Materialism inculcated 'sensism of the grossest kind', and, by undermining the ideal of duty, could turn a woman into a monster: 'the very type of ruthless cynicism, of all engrossing selfishness, of unbridled passion'.[57] Its literary equivalent was to be found in French naturalism, above all, in Zola.

By the mid 1890s, the terms of the debate had changed considerably. Lilly's binary division, schematic even in 1886, was no longer plausible. And although 'selfishness' was considered one of the symptoms of the new degeneracy, the sense of activity that Lilly found so threatening in the materialist woman had been supplanted by a passive receptivity in both sexes. In a piece strongly influenced by Nordau's newly published *Degeneration*, Janet Hogarth identified a new school of 'impressionist' stories by women, typified by George Egerton's (Mary Dunne's) collection *Keynotes*. This school's 'marked predilection for sensual accessories of colour and perfume' mark them out as aestheticist, as does their ability to 'seize the pictorial moment', and their doubtful capacity for 'sustained effort'.[58] Hogarth noted the influence of Pater on their 'Hellenism', and in the following year the *Fortnightly* carried a two-part article by Russell Jacobus on Pater and Maurice Barrès, titled significantly 'The Blessedness of Egoism'.[59] Jacobus attempted to explain the phenomenon of the aesthete 'scientifically' by reference to 'the lack of nerve energy' which resulted in 'excessive delicacy and extreme sensitiveness to impressions', but he raises issues which were also pertinent to descriptionist science. If each individual, like Pater's Marius, 'constructs for himself a world more or less peculiar, according to the quality of his sensibility and imagination', then how can communication be possible?[60] Jacobus can only explain that there is 'a convenient sameness' about the worlds they construct that allows communication. Pearson had already tackled this problem in the *Grammar*. Although heredity, health, and other factors affected the ability of each individual brain, 'speaking generally'

The same type of physical organ receives the same sense-impressions and forms the same 'constructs.' Two normal perceptive faculties construct

[57] Lilly, 'Materialism', 589.
[58] Janet E. Hogarth, 'Literary Degenerates', *Fortnightly*, o.s. 63 (Apr. 1895), 586–92.
[59] Jacobus, 'The Blessedness of Egoism', *Fortnightly*, o.s. 65 (Jan. 1896), 40–57, and (Mar. 1896), 384–96.
[60] Ibid., 390.

practically the same universe. Were this not true, the results of thinking in one mind would have no validity for a second mind. The universal validity of science depends on the similarity of the perceptive and reasoning faculties in normal civilized men.[61]

The ability of scientists to communicate depends not on the verifiable existence of an external world, but instead on their physiological and cultural 'normality'. Jacobus seems to have acknowledged this with regard to the aesthetes, but his ironic reference to the 'convenient sameness' of their worlds suggests that he could not allow it; given that 'impressionist' writers were considered 'degenerate', the possibility of their making meaningful communication seems to have been excluded from the outset.

Though Pearson did not turn to eugenics until around 1906, he was already aware of Weismann's *Essays on Heredity*, and devoted a long section in the *Grammar* to the notion that society's suspension of the 'stern processes of natural law' might benefit 'degenerate stocks' in the human species; he would have been equally aware of the possibility of science becoming 'degenerate'.[62] Pearson's account of the aesthetic element in theory-formation, while disposing of the argument that science was 'destroying the beauty and poetry of life', simultaneously anticipated the accusation that the involvement of the imagination in science left it weaker.[63] The laws of science satisfied the aesthetic judgement in their ability to concentrate a wide variety of phenomena into a simple statement. The man who could devise such statements was more than a 'mere cataloguer', but was 'endowed with creative imagination'.[64] But Pearson repeatedly emphasized that 'this imagination has to be a *disciplined* one' (his italics), taking into account the facts, and complementing rather than displacing reason. The rhetoric of 'discipline' and 'stern processes' serves to distance Pearson's descriptionism from degenerate aestheticism.

The idea of perceiving the world with an 'innocent eye' reaches its most interesting development in Virginia Woolf's work from 'The Mark on the Wall' (1917) onwards, but elements of it can be seen in more traditional realists much earlier. Many writers noted the paradox that realism, in the form of naturalism, devoted so much attention to minute particulars that representation seemed to become atomized. Thomas Hardy had written in 'The Science of Fiction' of

---

[61] Pearson, *Grammar*, 57.   [62] Ibid., 32–3.   [63] Ibid., 43.   [64] Ibid., 37.

naturalism giving way to 'infinite and atomic truth'.[65] This was also the burden of H. D. Traill's influential article on Stephen Crane and Arthur Morrison in 1897, but Jacobus had remarked on something very similar in the very different context of Pater's *Marius*: it consisted of 'wonderful phrases' which were 'curiously heaped together into sentences whose construction is frequently hideous'.[66]

Virginia Woolf's first experimental prose pieces take the idea of impressionism much further. Though 'The Mark on the Wall' (1917) is concerned principally with psychological associations, its opening plays with the relations of sense impressions and knowledge:

Perhaps it was the middle of January in the present year that I first looked up and saw the mark on the wall. In order to fix a date it is necessary to remember what one saw. So now I think of the fire; the steady film of yellow light upon the page of my book; the three chrysanthemums in the round glass bowl on the mantelpiece. Yes, it must have been winter time, and we had just finished our tea . . .[67]

The initial attempt to establish a definite date for the events requires the narrator to turn to the events themselves. Time, an abstraction, must be derived from sense impressions, some of them as imprecise as the quality of the light. The narrator recalls how 'my eye lodged for a moment upon the burning coals', and the fancies which she derives from them, a 'crimson flag' and 'red knights', suggest again that her narrative begins with pure retinal sense impressions, from which she infers actual and fanciful objects. At the end of the paragraph the narrator returns to a more 'objective' mode of description—'The mark was a small round mark, black upon the white wall, about six or seven inches above the mantelpiece'—but even this description does not identify the mark.

The title of 'Solid Objects' (1920) suggests that the objectivity of external reality will be questioned further, and the opening paragraphs more than fulfil this expectation. Woolf begins again with a small black spot:

---

[65] Hardy, 'The Science of Fiction' (1891), in *Thomas Hardy's Personal Writings*, ed. Harold Orel (London: Macmillan, 1967), 135.

[66] Traill, 'The New Realism', *Fortnightly*, 67 (Jan. 1897), 63–73; Jacobus, 'Blessedness', 384.

[67] Woolf, *Collected Shorter Fiction*, ed. Susan Dick (London: Hogarth, revised edn. 1989), 83.

The only thing that moved upon this vast semicircle of the beach was a small black spot. As it came nearer to the ribs and spine of the stranded pilchard boat, it became apparent from a certain tenuity in its blackness that this spot possessed four legs; and moment by moment it became more unmistakable that it was composed of the persons of two young men.[68]

Here, even the species of the four-legged black spot is momentarily in question. The narrator resembles Dingle's alien on Hampstead Heath, though like Dingle, Woolf does not impose limitations consistently—while the narrator has trouble recognizing two men, the 'stranded pilchard boat' is inferred without difficulty. As the men approach they are perceived to be arguing, but Woolf's narrator can only state this indirectly:

Even thus in outline against the sand there was an unmistakable vitality in them; an indescribable vigour in the approach and withdrawal of the bodies, slight though it was, which proclaimed some violent argument issuing from the tiny mouths of the little round heads.

The narrator 'corroborate[s]' this interpretation by reference to the movement of their walking sticks. It is only in the second paragraph that the cluster of sense impressions are gathered together to form solid objects:

the mouths, noses, chins, little moustaches, tweed caps, rough boots, shooting coats, and check stockings of the two speakers became clearer and clearer; the smoke of their pipes went up into the air; nothing was so solid, so living, so hard, red, hirsute and virile as these two bodies for miles and miles of sea and sandhill.

As in 'The Mark on the Wall', this virtuoso game with perceptual solidity leads into a dramatization of ideological solidity. In the earlier story, the narrator had been torn between three different definitions of 'reality': the reality of immediate perceptions; the reality of her own thought associations; and the metaphysical and ideological reality of patriarchal society, symbolized by 'Whitaker's Table of Precedency'. In 'Solid Objects', John's dilemma has two horns: the deferred reality of a possible 'brilliant career' in politics, or the immediate perceptual reality of the 'full drop of solid matter', the lump of glass that he uncovers on the beach. To the dismay of his friend, he rejects the abstract world of politics, and establishes a 'career' collecting other curious objects. There is an echo in the story's opening scene of Newton on the sea-shore, collecting 'a smoother pebble or a prettier shell than ordinary', but for John the 'great ocean of truth' holds few attractions.

The technique developed in these first experimental stories underlies Woolf's descriptive technique in the novels that followed. The alienated perspective given to Peter Walsh, returning to London after many years abroad, is common to many of Woolf's characters: 'things stand out as if one had never seen them before'.[69] Though Clarissa Dalloway has lived in London for many years, her perceptions are comparable:

For Heaven only knows why one loves it so, how one sees it so, making it up, building it round one, tumbling it, creating it every moment afresh . . .[70]

The perceptive faculty, 'making it up', is a creative one, and lacking the 'metaphysical' notion of the continuity of the self, it recreates the world moment by moment. Septimus shares with Peter and Clarissa the ability to create every moment afresh, sometimes with alarming originality, and this ability distinguishes them as a group from the likes of Bradshaw and Holmes, who seek to impose a rigid metaphysical dogma ('proportion') onto reality.

The process of defamiliarization forms the general background to Woolf's continuing use of the visually 'impressionist' descriptions throughout her work. There is a hint of this at the start of the dinner party in *To the Lighthouse* where Mrs Ramsay takes her place at the head of the table 'looking at all the plates making white circles on it', though here the 'white circles' are identified; she later contemplates Rose's arrangement of fruits with a similar painterly eye, 'putting a yellow against a purple, a curved shape against a round shape', in anticipation of Lily's later work.[71]

A similar abstract contemplation of colour and form occurs before another dinner party, in *The Waves*. As Neville waits for Percival to arrive, it seems to him that 'this knife-blade is only a flash of light, not a thing to cut with'; only when Percival arrives does the retinal sense impression become an object, for 'without Percival there is no solidity'.[72] The centrality of dinner parties to both *To the Lighthouse* and *The Waves* has a philosophical precedent in Russell's discussion of the relation of sense-data to physical objects.

[69] Woolf, *Mrs Dalloway*, 77.   [70] Ibid., 4.
[71] Woolf, *To the Lighthouse*, 90, 118.
[72] Woolf, *The Waves* (1931), ed. Kate Flint (London: Penguin, 1992), 89, 91.

'When ten people are sitting round a dinner-table, it seems prepos-
terous to maintain that they are not seeing the same tablecloth, the
same knives and forks and spoons and glasses. But the sense-data
are private to each separate person; what is immediately present to
the sight of one is not immediately present to the sight of another.'[73]
In both novels, the narrative tension of the dinner-party scenes
emerges from the problem of resolving this philosophical question.
Will the 'seven-sided flower', 'a whole flower to which every eye
brings its own contribution', resolve itself into a public neutral
object?[74]

Neville's mode of perception characterizes the very first utterances
of the children in *The Waves*, who, like Dingle's alien or Mach's children, describe their sense-impressions as purely as possible, without
attributing them to anything so metaphysical as a cause:

'I see a ring,' said Bernard, 'hanging above me. It quivers and hangs in a
loop of light.'

'I see a slab of pale yellow,' said Susan, 'spreading away until it meets a
purple stripe.'

'I hear a sound,' said Rhoda, 'cheep, chirp; cheep, chirp; going up and
down.'

'I see a globe,' said Neville, ' hanging down in a drop against the enormous flanks of some hill.'[75]

As their vocabularies develop, some of these sights and sound are
identified—Susan attributes Rhoda's 'cheep, chirp' to birds, while
Bernard refers to a spider's web that is probably his quivering ring—
but the opening pages are characterized throughout by an emphasis
on direct sensations, at the expense of 'abstractions'. Only gradually do the children discover temporal sequentiality, the first hints
coming from Louis ('When the smoke rises, sleep curls off the roof
like a mist'), and further ones from Rhoda and Jinny ('Bubbles form
on the floor of the saucepan . . . Then they rise, quicker and
quicker'), before Louis's discovery of clock time: 'That is the first
stroke of the church bell . . . Then the others follow; one, two; one,
two; one, two.'[76] Throughout the novel there is a tension between
two modes of perception and existence: the one being of the world
seen 'after the eclipse', 'without a self', 'unable to speak save in a

---

[73] Russell, *The Problems of Philosophy*, 9.   [74] Woolf, *Waves*, 95.
[75] Ibid., 5.   [76] Ibid., 6–7.

child's words of one syllable'; the other being symbolized by the 'boasting boys' and by Bernard's 'phrase making'.

What brought about the simultaneous undermining of 'realism' in both science and literature? It is possible, in certain cases, that literary writers were aware of debates about descriptionism and the philosophy of science. It is known that the young T. E. Hulme argued with his school headmaster about Pearson.[77] Virginia Woolf seems to have known about 'Japanese Dancing Mice', one of the physiological oddities raised by both Mach and Poincaré in discussing the metaphysical nature of space.[78] A general feeling that science would support her idea of perception may have informed her description of the 'shower of innumerable atoms' in 'Modern Novels'—her use of 'atoms' rather than 'perceptions' is merely rhetorical pseudo-science, but her general idea of perception has a basis in descriptionism as well as Pater's 'Conclusion'. It is clear that Conrad was familiar with the idea of scientific theories as economical shorthands, and likely that Huxley knew Eddington's conclusion to *Space Time and Gravitation*. However, such isolated instances become more significant when considered against the larger background.

The metaphors of the scientific expositors provide some clues to the general background, though not all are equally helpful. Pearson's comparison of the perceiving subject to a telephone clerk might be taken to identify telecommunications as a possible cause. Certainly the experience of speaking immediately to a person who was physically distant disturbed ideas of absence and presence, and may have led to larger speculations about the 'presence' of other perceived objects. However, reading Pearson's analogy alongside James's 'In the Cage' suggests that the social referent of the analogy is not telephony but social division. Pearson's telephone clerk, like James's heroine, is divided from the 'real' world of the upper classes by the 'cage' of social distinctions. In an era when the ideal of democratic equality was growing (though the practice lagged behind), thinkers could not help but be increasingly aware of the disparity of perceptions. The part of descriptionism that draws attention to the relativity of perception is rooted not simply in a society of inequalities—those had existed for centuries—but in a society in

---

[77] Alun Jones, *The Life and Opinons of T. E. Hulme* (London: Gollancz, 1960), 19.

[78] See Michael Whitworth, 'Virginia Woolf and "the mouse which turns for ever" ', *Notes and Queries*, n.s. 43 (1996), 56–7.

which the ideal of equality co-existed with the actuality of vast social divides.

There are, however, other aspects to descriptionism, most importantly the idea that the perceiving subject exists in a chaos of sensations from which it abstracts the essential persistent entities. It seems possible that the idea of taste and choice in an increasingly consumerist economy may be of relevance here.[79] Bertrand Russell's argument in *The Problems of Philosophy* unconsciously suggests this possibility. Tackling the problem of whether a table continues to exist when we go out of the room, whether, in other words, there is 'something not a sense-datum', he replies that 'Common sense unhesitatingly answers that there is.' This is unsurprising, but the way he chooses to illustrate 'common sense' criteria is interesting: 'What can be bought and sold and pushed about and have a cloth laid on it, and so on, cannot be a *mere* collection of sense-data' (Russell's emphasis). Were it not for the fourth criterion (suitability as a surface for table cloths), Russell's definition would seem to define not objects, but commodities. The rhetorical form of his statement also invites the suggestion that the purchaser is buying not a table, but a collection of sense-data, and Russell quite rightly follows up this possibility two paragraphs later:

I bought my table from the former occupant of my room; I could not buy *his* sense-data, which died when he went away, but I could and did buy the confident expectation of more or less similar sense-data.[80]

This description sounds less confident than that provided by 'common sense': it seems as if Russell is dealing not in tangible commodities, but in shares, and as if the sense-data he receives are the dividends due to him for buying a perceptual stake in the table. The value of sense-data can fall as well as rise; his perceptual investments are not secure.

Pearson in the *Grammar* aligns descriptionism with the world of the consumer, when, varying his metaphor of the mind as a sorting machine, he says that human minds resemble 'automatic sweetmeat-boxes which if well constructed refuse to act for any coin but a penny'.[81] The human perceptive faculty is here reduced to a machine that, on receiving the sense impression of a penny, tells the mind that it has perceived a chocolate bar. This is trivial, but the analogy of

---

[79] Regenia Gagnier, 'Is Market Society the *fin* of History', in Sally Ledger and Scott McCracken (eds.). *Cultural Politics at the* fin de siècle (Cambridge: Cambridge University Press, 1995), 290–310.

[80] Russell, *Problems*, 9.   [81] Pearson, *Grammar*, 121.

perception with consumerism runs deeper. Pearson repeatedly emphasizes that we can know only sense-impressions, and not the external world. He ventures that the only thing that can be known of 'things-in-themselves' is that they have 'a capacity for producing sense-impressions', but concludes that if the external world is unknowable, 'to talk of its contents as *producing* sense-impressions is an unwarranted inference'.[82] We can know ourselves, and know the 'impenetrable wall' of sense impressions that surrounds us, but there is 'no necessity' to conjecture the existence of something that 'cannot be part of the mind's contents'. In this model, the sense impressions take on the role not of money, or dividends, but of commodities themselves, presented to the consumer with all traces of productive labour removed.

Contemporary accounts of shops and shopping lend their support to this reading, and among the most interesting is Lady M. Jeune's 'The Ethics of Shopping'.[83] Jeune contrasts the shops of 1895 with those seen twenty-five years previously, noting particularly the elaborate and tempting window displays of modern shops; the new department stores of the late nineteenth century made maximum use of glass and illumination to attract the attention of the shopper.[84] Twenty-five years previously, there had been 'little or no display in the windows'; purchases had been made according to need, and although consumers exercised some choice in relation to 'colour, price, and material', purchases were essentially determined by the season and by tradition—'Jones sold the best silks, Smith the best gloves', and we 'dutifully followed in the steps of our forefathers'.[85] The settling of accounts annually further limited the pace of transactions. Against this slow-moving established order, Jeune contrasts the modern shops, with 'endless profusion of goods' and their immense variety of colours, their 'overwhelming temptations to buy which besiege us at every turn' in their 'Paradise of ribbons, flowers, and chiffons'.[86] Though Jeune dislikes the 'noise, heat, and overcrowding' of the shops, she finds these counterbalanced by 'the brightness of the electric light and the brilliancy of colour, and the endless variety on every side'.[87] Jeune may be overemphasizing these

---

[82] Pearson, *Grammar*, 81–2.

[83] Jeune, 'The Ethics of Shopping', *Fortnightly*, 63 (Jan. 1895), 123–32.

[84] Rachel Bowlby, *Just Looking: Consumer Culture in Dreiser, Gissing and Zola* (London: Methuen, 1985), 3.

[85] Jeune, 'Ethics', 123–4.   [86] Ibid., 124.   [87] Ibid., 125.

features—she wishes to contrast, polemically, the low wages and cramped quarters of the shop girls—but other accounts suggest that her sense of profusion was entirely typical. The range of impulse purchases resembles nothing more than Woolf's incessant shower of innumerable atoms, 'trivial, fantastic, evanescent, or engraved with the sharpness of steel'.[88] The modern consumer, overwhelmed by the brightness of the new displays, had little more sense of the labour behind the products than Pearson's perceiving subject has of sense-impressions being produced. The selective work of the mind in perception resembles the task of the consumer in the new department stores, picking out the necessary from the unnecessary.

Jeune's polemical article depicts not only the overwhelming world of sensations that confronts the shopper, but the living conditions of the shop girls, ensuring that her reader cannot mistake the new world of consumerism for a universal condition. Pearson's *The Grammar of Science*, while remaining cautious about the 'ultimate' nature of anything, proposes a world of chaotic sensations as the fundamental condition of perception; Pater's 'Conclusion' and Woolf's 'Modern Novels', by employing the language of 'elements' and 'atoms', invoke the authority of science to validate and universalize their aesthetic theories.

However, in *Marius the Epicurean*, Pater suggested that the attraction of the philosophy of flux was rooted in historical conditions, in 'an age still materially so brilliant, so expert in the artistic handling of material things', in which 'there was more than eye or ear could well take in', it seemed 'natural' to rely 'on the phenomena of the senses'.[89] Here, as elsewhere, Pater's description of the historical conditions could apply equally well to the era of Marcus Aurelius or that of Victoria. Woolf too, in her novels acknowledges that the philosophy of 'Modern Fiction' is only a partial picture. This is true even in the most aesthetic of them, *The Waves*. At one point Bernard expresses the philosophy of languid impressionism, as he travels on the train with hurried commuters:

For myself, I have no aim. I have no ambition. I will let myself be carried on by the general impulse. The surface of my mind slips along like a pale-grey stream reflecting what passes. I cannot remember my past, my nose, or the colour of my eyes, or what my general opinion of myself is.[90]

---

[88] Woolf, *Essays*, iii. 33.   [89] Pater, *Marius*, 113.   [90] Woolf, *Waves*, 84.

However, he acknowledges that this philosophy has its limits: 'Only in moments of emergency, at a crossing, at a kerb, the wish to preserve my body springs out and seizes me and stops me, here, before this omnibus. We insist, it seems, on living'.[91] Momentarily the mind selects out the important material detail, and reinstates the notion of cause and effect. While for Bernard such moments of emergency are only temporary, his acknowledgement of the fact punctures his philosophy's claims to universality, admitting the possibility that for some people, life is a succession of 'emergencies'.

A more direct acknowledgement comes in the 1913 section of *The Years*. Eleanor is selling Abercorn Terrace, and Crosby, the housekeeper of forty years, is to be pensioned off. Eleanor reflects that for Crosby, 'it was the end of everything':

> She had known every cupboard, flagstone, chair and table in that large rambling house, not from five or six feet of distance as they had known it; but from her knees, as she scrubbed and polished; she had known every groove, stain, fork, knife, napkin and cupboard.[92]

While there remains here an element of patronizing hyperbole, one that reduces Crosby's circle of acquaintances to cutlery and cupboards, Woolf (or Eleanor) essentially recognizes that distant, retinal knowledge, such as Neville's knowledge of his knife, is not the only possible form, and that practically oriented forms of knowledge such as Crosby's may be more intimate and more real.

Descriptionism provided a 'scientific' sanction for the idea that representations of reality were selective shorthands, artificial constructs aiming to preserve mental energy. There is evidence that Mach's ideas directly influenced Einstein, but, as importantly from a British perspective, Pearson's work prepared the ground for the popularization of relativity, creating a minority at least who were prepared to consider novel descriptions of gravitation. For the literary world, the idea that scientific theories were only ever hypotheses, and that matter and the idea of cause and effect were merely convenient shorthands, seemed to undermine the determinism of Victorian scientific culture which had been so antipathetic to literature. Moreover, it seemed to promise some form of reconciliation.

---

91 Woolf, *Waves*, 84–5.
92 Woolf, *The Years* (1937; London: Penguin, 1968), 206.

4

An Entente Cordiale?
The New Relations of Literature and Science

LITERARY responses to new scientific theories and methods are framed by the literary culture's construction of 'science' in general. Even when particular scientific innovations are warmly received within the literary culture, the warmth is tempered by an underlying belief that science is antipathetic to literature: that science prefers quantities to qualities, length and mass to colour and scent, mechanism to organicism, reason to imagination. The contradiction between literature's assimilation of scientific concepts, and its rejection of science thus conceived, is so strong as almost to make the two processes seem entirely separate areas of study. However, in a time of highly publicized scientific innovation, such as occurred in the wake of the experimental confirmation of Einstein's theories, the literary image of science is affected by the particular conceptual innovations, and the reception of particular concepts is influenced by the general idea. Though there were thematic continuities between late-Victorian science and the new physics, popularizers encouraged the literary culture of the 1920s to understand the revolution in physics as a dramatic rupture, what we would now term a 'paradigm shift'. As we have seen, certain literary authors had taken cognisance of ideas such as entropy and empirio-criticism, both of which anticipated certain aspects of the new physics, but only with the later revolution did the fundamental nature of the change become apparent.

The change in literary culture was by no means uniform nor complete. Matthew Arnold had left a particularly complex legacy. While for some, his quarrel with T. H. Huxley justified a polarization of literature and science, for others, the ideal of 'culture' as 'a harmonious expansion of *all* the powers which make the beauty and worth of human nature' implied that culture could and should include science.[1] For many poets and critics, the paradigm shift suggested the possibility of a new metaphysical poetry; for T. S. Eliot, the process of conservative revolution in the sciences offered a model for tradition in literary culture.

The prevailing set of expectations about science in the 1920s ultimately derived from the Romantics, but it had been reshaped by the Victorian sages, and, as I shall show, was reshaped again during the First World War. Even those modernists who were interested in science still wrote occasionally as if scientific method could be summarized in Wordsworth's phrase 'we murder to dissect', or in Keats's image of 'cold philosophy' unweaving the rainbow; although *Nature* bore an epigraph from Wordsworth on its title page, the receptive aspects of Romantic attitudes to science remained hidden until the 1930s.[2] The Romantic attitude had been reinforced in 1829 by Carlyle's diagnosis of his age as 'the Age of Machinery, in every inward and outward sense of that word'.[3] Machinery stood here not only for the visible machines of the industrial revolution, but for all intellectual processes of analysis or mental 'dissection'. Carlyle's fundamental opposition between 'mechanism' and a less easily definable 'organicism' was subsequently adopted by Ruskin, and reinterpreted by Arnold as the opposition between 'mechanism' and 'culture', 'Hebraism' and 'Hellenism'. The non-mechanical nature of Einstein's theory of gravitation and the non-mechanical aspects of quantum mechanics were received within this framework of expectations.

Public and literary concepts of science are closely allied to public images of the scientist. Romantic writers had established the image of the scientist as the isolated genius, and hence of science as an essentially individualist enterprise. Individualism was the defining characteristic both of heroic and demonic scientist figures: Mary Shelley's Frankenstein is the prototype; Lydgate and Fitzpiers in

---

[1] Arnold, *Culture and Anarchy*, ed. R. H. Super (Ann Arbor: University of Michigan Press, 1965), 94; Park Honan, *Matthew Arnold: A Life* (London: Weidenfeld and Nicholson, 1981), 416, is sympathetic to the latter view.

[2] See, e.g., Carl Grabo's *A Newton Among Poets: Shelley's Use of Science in Prometheus Unbound* (Chapel Hill: University of North Carolina Press, 1930), the title, epigraph (p. xiv), and theme of which were derived from Whitehead's *Science and the Modern World*.

[3] Carlyle, *Selected Writings*, ed. Alan Shelston (Harmondsworth: Penguin, 1971), 64. The seminal study of the ramifications of Carlyle's definition is Raymond Williams's *Culture and Society* (London: Chatto and Windus, 1958), 72–9, 138.

Middlemarch and *The Woodlanders* respectively are more psychologically rounded descendants of the type.[4] However, in the public sphere the image of the scientist changed during the nineteenth century, there being, according to Frank Turner, three distinct periods.[5] In the first, from 1800 to around the Great Exhibition of 1851, science was seen as 'a mode of useful knowledge' and 'an aid to profitable, rational, and usually individualistic economic activity'. This period correlates broadly with the portraits of the scientist as individualist. In the second period, the great scientific publicists used the successes of scientific theorization in evolution and thermodynamics as a basis on which to forge a scientific *community*, often in opposition to the Church of England establishment. (The popular notion that science was opposed to 'religion' is an oversimplification, as many Victorian scientists came from Nonconformist Christian backgrounds: the real opposition was between science and Anglicanism.)[6] The frustrations of the 1860s, a decade in which scientists found that the public influence they had hoped for had not materialized, led to the repositioning of science in the 1870s in support of 'the values of collectivism, nationalism, military preparedness, patriotism, political elitism, and social imperialism'.[7]

In each of the periods outlined by Turner, the position of science is related to ideas of individual and national identity: whether as a nation of individualists in the first period, as a nation of threatened Anglicans and threatening Nonconformists during the second period, or as an imperial nation in the third. The relation of science to national identity is crucial to its reputation during the First World War; developments in this period were in turn significant for the later reception of Einstein.

The First World War saw a recapitulation of these arguments, with the identity of science being strongly contested. For some, it was identified with utilitarian and mechanistic thought; for others, with high-minded seeking after truth. It was represented both as corrosive of national character, and as the only cure for governmental inefficiency. In the first months of the war, debates about science tended towards propagandistic comparisons of the scientific

[4] Haynes, *From Faust to Strangelove*, 113, 126.
[5] Frank Turner, *Contesting Cultural Authority* (Cambridge: Cambridge University Press, 1993), 203–5.
[6] Adrian Desmond and James Moore, *Darwin* (London: Michael Joseph, 1991), 293, 331; Smith, *The Science of Energy*, 15–30.
[7] Turner, *Contesting*, 205.

strengths of Britain and Germany. Many commentators addressed the anxiety that Germany had been industrially and commercially stronger than Britain before the war and that, in terms of military technology, it was superior. Few writers attempted to deny the material truth of these anxieties, but sought instead to recover a sense of national moral superiority from the situation. William Ramsay argued that Germany had risen to a position of strength only by exploiting the inventions of other nations, or of the 'Hebrews resident among them'; in doing so it relied on the German (or Prussian) talent for organization. Although the British lacked organizational abilities they excelled in imagination.[8] Many writers recognized that Britain needed to adopt some aspects of German organization, without sacrificing imagination. In these debates the idea of the scientist as an anti-corporate individualist, usually amateur and eccentric, was weighed against the belief that individuals must submit to national organization. Some writers wholeheartedly endorsed the Prussian willingness to become 'a cog in the machine', while others argued that scientific discovery could not be directed from above. Others still attempted to resolve the two ideas: Ronald Ross argued that while some work ('major discovery') was best done by gifted amateurs, other work ('minor research') could beneficially be organized.[9]

Discussions of the organization of science also touched on the role of the expert. It was frequently noted that German industrial companies appointed scientists to their boards of management. British companies had either neglected to do so, or had actively resisted the idea, on the grounds that other members of the board would be unable to refute their technical arguments.[10] While the concept of the expert was more easily assimilated to the ideal of individual creativity than was the concept of organization, it implied a deliberate cultivation of knowledge which threatened to

[8] William Ramsay, 'Germany's Aims and Ambitions', Nature, 94 (8 Oct. 1914), 137–9; see also anon., 'The War', Nature, 94 (14 Jan. 1915), 527–8.

[9] Ramsay, 'The Place of Science in Industry', Nature, 94 (12 Nov. 1914), 275–6; Ronald Ross, 'Attempts to Manufacture Scientific Discovery', Nature, 94 (7 Jan. 1915), 512; Ramsay, 'Science and the State', Nature, 95 (20 May 1915), 309–11. Ross's article was occasioned by Ray Lankester's 'Science from an Easy Chair: Attempts to Manufacture Scientific Discovery', Daily Telegraph (15 Dec. 1914), 5.

[10] William Ramsay, 'The Place of Science in Industry', 275–6; anon., 'Science and Industry', Nature, 95 (18 Mar. 1915), 57–9; anon., 'The War and British Chemical Industry', Nature, 95 (1 Apr. 1915), 119–20.

sever the association of individuality and amateurism. To dissociate the two qualities was to undermine the basis of 'gentlemanly' conduct.

In seeking to find a place for science within the state, scientists did not at first emphasize the distinction between pure and applied science, though as the war continued, the relations between the two were repeatedly reconceptualized and debated. In January 1915, an editorial in *Nature* was more concerned to distinguish 'science' in general from 'war', equating the former with British decency and the latter with German barbarity. The distinction of pure and applied science was secondary: in the right hands, both were worthy ideals: 'The aims of science are the antitheses of those of war. It is the object of pure science to attempt to know and correlate natural phenomena, and its devotees are inspired by an insatiable curiosity; it is the object of applied science to make use of that knowledge for the benefit of mankind.'[11] Those who gave the distinction more prominence did so, in the early years of the war, in order to draw attention to the potential of applied science in the war effort: they noted the importance of chemical, engineering, and medical science in general, or drew attention to specific applications such as range-finding for guns, or wireless telegraphy.[12] However, the association of applied science with the machine gun and poison gas soon became a cause for embarrassment or regret. One writer tried to preserve the moral integrity of applied science by distinguishing it from the 'misapplied' science of the enemy, but such a manoeuvre only begged the question of whether British science was not equally misapplied.[13] Moreover, without criticizing the effects of the war machine, some scientists expressed concern that applied science's success in obtaining government funding during the war would lead to a neglect of pure science afterwards.[14] In 1917, several articles began by remarking that 'materialistic' or 'utilitarian' science had become dominant, and went on to offer discussions of scientific method or of pure science by way

---

[11] Anon., 'The War', *Nature*, 94 (14 Jan. 1915), 528.
[12] F. G. Donnan, 'Science in the Service of the State', *Nature*, 95 (8 Jul. 1915), 509–10; Prof. J. A. Fleming, 'Science in the War and After the War', *Nature*, 96 (14 Oct. 1915), 180–5.
[13] D. Fraser Harris, 'The Man of Science in the Community of To-day', *Nature*, 99 (17 May 1917), 236–8. An address delivered 13 Nov. 1916.
[14] Rt. Hon. Lord Moulton, 'Introduction', in A. C. Seward (ed.), *Science and the Nation* (Cambridge: Cambridge University Press, 1917), pp. viii–ix.

of redress.[15] Though Einstein's extraordinarily 'pure' theory met some hostility in Britain in 1919, the sympathetic attitude of those scientists who championed it was shaped in no small part by these wartime debates.

The contestation of 'science' in the respects described above exposed its relations to 'literature' to processes of redefinition. To define British science as a disinterested search for truth was to make claims for the discipline which had formerly been reserved for the humanities. To define it as a pragmatic and utilitarian discipline essential to the survival and well-being of the nation was to challenge the centrality of literature. These were not abstract intellectual disputes: they were fought out on the material and institutional territory of education. While the numerous studies of the 'rise of English' have acknowledged its conflicted relations to the classics, and its relation to questions of national identity, discussions of the relation of the discipline to science have focused on Arnold's relation to it, or on the later scientistic criticism of I. A. Richards.[16] The most important single event was the publication on 2 February 1916 of the memorandum of the 'Committee on the Neglect of Science'.[17] The memorandum criticized the government and civil service for its ignorance of scientific facts, which had in several cases led to serious policy errors in relation to the war.[18] As the most senior ministers and civil servants were recruited from Oxford and Cambridge, the ignorance was attributed to the failings of the ancient universities

[15] Anon., 'National Reconstruction', *Nature*, 98 (11 Jan. 1917), 307–72; Alexander Findlay, 'The Reality of Atoms', *New Statesman*, 9 (16 Jun. 1917), 250–1. Findlay was himself the author of a book of 'utilitarian' science, *Chemistry in the Service of Man* (London: Longmans, 1916).

[16] Chris Baldick, *The Social Mission of English Criticism* (Oxford: Clarendon, 1983), 40–1, 199–203.

[17] 'Neglect of Science: A Cause of Failures in War', *The Times* (2 Feb. 1916), 10; 'University and Educational Intelligence', *Nature*, 96 (3 Feb. 1916), 640. The name and identity of the Committee was ill-defined: it was formed by the Association of Public School Science Masters, but leading scientific men from the universities subscribed to its memorandum; it was referred to in some reports as the Reorganization Committee, and, after it convened a meeting in the rooms of the Linnaean Society at Burlington House on 3 May 1916, as the Linnaean Society Committee.

[18] Most notoriously, the government had allowed lard to be exported to Germany, unaware that it could be used in the manufacture of explosives; the Home Secretary attempted to excuse the export policy on the grounds that he could not be expected to know such a recent scientific discovery; as scientists were quick to point out, the discovery was not at all recent. The incident is referred to in 'Neglect of Science', *The Times* (2 Feb. 1916), 10, and in A. C. Benson (ed.), *Cambridge Essays on Education* (Cambridge: Cambridge University Press, 1917), 127.

and the public schools from which they recruited the majority of their students. The memorandum noted that at Cambridge only four of the colleges were presided over by men of scientific training, and at Oxford, none; it noted that of the thirty-five largest and best-known public schools, the heads of thirty-four were classically trained men; and it noted that although Civil Service examinations had recently been reformed to allow candidates to be tested in science, the system of grading was biased towards classicists. After the publication of the memorandum, several commentators also criticized the preponderance of classical scholarships at the older universities, which distorted the priorities of study at schools.[19] The Committee's criticisms were not altogether new: John Perry's *England's Neglect of Science* and Norman Lockyer's British Association address of 1903 were often cited; however, Lockyer had focused his argument on a comparison of university funding in Britain, Germany, and America, and had not directly compared the prestige of science and classics.[20] More recently, one week before the Committee's memorandum appeared, William Ramsay had contrasted the mentality of the classically trained politician from that of the scientist; the former was ruled by 'precedent', while the latter required factual 'proof'.[21] Although it did not break completely new ground, the Committee's memorandum crystallized several existing debates, and emboldened other critics. Some followed Ramsay's lead in criticizing politicians not only for their ignorance of particular facts, but for their inability to reason from facts in general.[22] Scientific method as well as scientific knowledge were essential to good government.

The meeting convened by the Committee at Burlington House on 3 May 1916 proposed and discussed two main resolutions: 'That the natural sciences should be made an integral part of the educational

[19] Anon., 'Science in the Public Schools and the Civil Service', *Nature*, 96 (17 Feb. 1916), 671–3. Prior to 2 Feb. 1916, there had been some correspondence on the topic in *The Observer*. See particularly: P. W. Robertson, 'Science and Industry', *The Observer* (9 Jan. 1916), 3; the pseudonymous 'Converted Classic', 'The Teaching of Science', *The Observer* (30 Jan. 1916), 17; and ensuing correspondence.

[20] John Perry, *England's Neglect of Science* (London: T. Fisher Unwin, 1900); Norman Lockyer, 'The Influence of Brain-Power on History', *Nature*, 68 (10 Sept. 1903), 439–47 (inaugural address to the British Association at Southport, 9 Sept. 1903).

[21] Ramsay, 'Germany's Aims and Methods', *Nature*, 96 (27 Jan. 1916), 587–9; and see Frank Turner, *Contesting Cultural Authority*, 211–12, 215.

[22] Rt. Hon. Lord Sydenham, 'Education, Science and Leadership', *Nature*, 101 (27 Jun. 1918), 335–6. An address delivered 19 Jun. 1918.

course in all the great schools of the country, and should form part of the entrance examination at all the universities', and that science should be given 'capital importance' in the examinations for the higher branches of the Civil Service and for Sandhurst.[23] Though the Committee's criticism was directed specifically at the classics, in the following months discutants frequently elided the classics with literature, and referred to classicists as 'literary men'. The Committee's resolutions implicitly criticized literary study as an intellectual training and as a basis for public responsibility.

The first significant response to the Committee's resolutions came in a public letter from Lord Bryce and others.[24] Several counter-arguments emerge from the letter. The authors draw upon the established characterization of German science as 'materialistic', and argue that if the nation were to emphasize science, it would be fostering 'that very spirit against which we are fighting to-day'. They argue that the proposed reforms would create 'early specialization' which would be 'injurious' to the intellect. They characterize the study of literature, language, and history as giving 'width of view and flexibility of intellect'; science, by implication, is narrow and inflexible. These are all straightforward oppositional strategies which merely work within the established system of values. As *Nature* noted somewhat bitterly, Bryce's group considered early specialization to be injurious only when it referred to 'elementary science teaching', and not when 'as at present, it signifies classical languages and literature'.[25] More interestingly, the authors attempt to steal some of science's own territory. They assert that 'scientific method' and 'mental training' are necessary to the nation, even more than 'physical science'. 'Scientific method' they gloss as the acquisition of knowledge through 'independent reflection', a process that involves 'the power of selecting, combining and testing the essential facts of the subject in hand'. This sounds at first like the position of a scientist who wishes to emphasize method over results.

[23] Anon., 'Science in Education and the Civil Services', *Nature*, 97 (11 May 1916), 230–1. This report gives the date of the meeting as 4 May 1916; for another account, see 'Science and Greek: The Claim of Modern Subjects', *The Times* (4 May 1916), 6, and for one of the speeches, Sir Edward Schäfer, 'Science and Classics in Modern Education', *Nature*, 97 (18 May 1916), 251–2. See also Sullivan, 'The True Case for Science', *The New Witness*, 8 (24 Aug. 1916), 522.

[24] Bryce, et al., 'Limitations of Science: A Plea for Tradition', *The Times* (4 May 1916), 6.

[25] Anon., 'University and Educational Notes', *Nature*, 97 (11 May 1916), 234.

However, the authors go on to claim that the capacity for independent reflection is common to all branches of knowledge, and not at all unique to science. It could therefore be taught as effectively through the study of classics as through science. This territorial manoeuvre, while not depriving science of 'scientific method' altogether, deprives science of any unique claim to it. Without scientific method, science is little more than 'Prussian' materialism.

Claims about the role of imagination in science have a similar ambiguous function, according to who utters them. A scientist who emphasizes the role of imagination in the formation of theories may be attempting to create a rapprochement between the disciplines, attempting to persuade 'literary men' that they may find science of interest, or attempting to obtain funding from a classically trained Vice Chancellor. A literary writer who emphasizes the role of the imagination may likewise be attempting to create a rapprochement, but he may also be building up to the argument that modern science is merely the latest manifestation of an ancient quest ('the search for truth'), and that the young student is best advised to begin that quest with the tried and tested tools ('imagination' and 'poetry'). The conservative poet and critic Henry Newbolt was paraphrased as having said to the British Science Guild that ultimately there was no antagonism between 'humanistic and scientific study'. It sounds as if he is building to a rapprochement, but he bases the rapprochement on the claim that in both there is 'a search after truth': the claim is not only so vague as to be worthless, but is vague in terms that favour literary culture. Science's ability to find truth in the form of testable hypotheses and quantitative data are entirely ignored.[26]

A fuller response to the meeting of 3 May 1916 came later, in the form of a collection of essays; Lord Bryce provided an introduction.[27] The arguments presented are various, but they are united by a rejection of philological and grammatical approaches to the teaching of literature, and they either argue or imply that literature, approached in the new spirit, should remain at the centre of education. *Nature* characterized the collection as 'an appreciation and defence of a classical education'.[28] It is true that for some of the contributors, science

---

[26] Anon., 'The British Science Guild', *Nature*, 101 (27 Jun. 1918), 333–4.

[27] A. C. Benson (ed.), *Cambridge Essays on Education* (Cambridge: Cambridge University Press, 1917). The meeting is specifically referred to by W. Bateson in 'The Place of Science in Education', in *Cambridge Essays*, 130, 135.

[28] Anon., 'Cambridge Standards of Value', *Nature*, 101 (7 Mar. 1918), 1–2.

was nothing more than materialism, directed towards the acquisition of wealth,[29] but others, while disdaining its tendency to 'utility', attempted at least to accommodate it within their philosophy of education. Most felt that the teaching of science should be governed by the same considerations as the teaching of the classics: it should avoid dry facts, and aim for something more invigorating. For William Bateson, it should aim to develop and exploit the 'inborn curiosity of youth', something to which biology was particularly well suited.[30] A. C. Benson also felt that education should address the faculties of 'curiosity, interest, imagination and sympathy', but was more evasive about how science teaching might achieve these goals. So far as *Nature* was concerned, his essay on 'The Training of the Imagination' dealt only with the 'literary imagination'.[31] Benson accepted, blandly, that 'all connected knowledge is stimulating', and claimed that he 'fully subscribe[d]' to the belief that 'a general knowledge of science is essential'.[32] However, he argued that there was simply more scientific knowledge than could be taught without sacrificing its 'vivid life': 'The thing, frankly, is too big to attempt; and we must henceforth set our faces against the attainment of mere knowledge.'[33] Benson commended instead 'a series of biographies of great men' and the study 'of high literature'.[34]

Dean Inge also set himself against an examination system which valued 'crude information' over the spirit of a subject, though the value of science lay not in the stimulation of curiosity or the refinement of discriminatory powers:

as an instrument of mind-training, and even of liberal education, it [science] seems to me to have a far higher value than is usually conceded to it by humanists. To direct the imagination to the infinitely great and the infinitely small, to vistas of time in which a thousand years are as one day; to the tremendous forces imprisoned in minute particles of matter; . . . —such studies cannot fail to elevate the mind, and only prejudice will disparage them.[35]

However, there were distinct limits to Inge's enthusiasm. This was a concessionary paragraph from one who admitted he was 'not

---

[29] J. L. Paton, 'The Aim of Educational Reform', in Benson (ed.), *Cambridge Essays*, 4.
[30] Bateson, 'The Place of Science in Education', in Benson (ed.), *Cambridge Essays*, 139.
[31] Anon., 'Cambridge Standards of Value', *Nature*, 101 (7 Mar. 1918), 2.
[32] Benson, 'The Training of the Imagination', in Benson (ed.), *Cambridge Essays*, 48–9.
[33] Ibid., 49.   [34] Ibid., 48, 50.
[35] Inge, 'The Training of the Reason', in Benson (ed.), *Cambridge Essays*, 25.

competent to speak' of science teaching, and he followed it by one criticizing science for explaining everything 'in terms of its origin' rather than 'its full development'. Moreover, he went on to recommend English literature as a basis for education, in terms which necessarily excluded science: scientific studies 'include the earlier phases of the earth', but risked cutting off the 'modern Englishman' from his national cultural tradition.[36] Moreover, Inge's conception of the imagination in the quoted passage is of a limited and passive faculty. The science he describes resembles the form of Victorian popular science writing criticized by J. W. N. Sullivan:

The 'Marvels of Science' became a familiar heading, and the unsophisticated public were stunned by figures: the distances of the stars, the number of molecules in a cubic centimetre of water, the weight, in tons, of the earth, the incredible minuteness of light-waves, and so on, the whole object of such discourses being, as Maxwell unkindly put it, to prevent the audience realising that intellectual exhaustion had set in until the hour had elapsed.[37]

As we shall see, there were other ways of appealing to the imagination in the course of a scientific education.

The debates of the war years set the terms not only for the reception of Einstein, but also for the justification of modernist literature in the post-war period. Those who were hostile to Einstein spoke against him in political terms as well as scientific ones: it is impossible to determine which was the motivating factor. Oliver Lodge argued that 'Revolutionary changes' such as Einstein's theory 'ought to be the result of long pondering and much experience, they should not be the outcome of a revolutionary period or be born among the harassments of war'.[38] Lodge reassured his readers that in university courses Galilean and Newtonian dynamics would reign, 'perhaps no longer supreme, but as a limited monarchy'. Using the political metaphor elsewhere, he was less temperate, suggesting that supporters of relativity who had 'complicated the universe unduly' ought to be 'regarded as Bolsheviks and pulled up'. His remarks occasioned playful consideration of the 'aristocratic'

[36] Ibid., 31.
[37] Sullivan, 'Popular Science', *The Athenaeum* (1 Oct. 1920), 444–5.
[38] Lodge, 'The New Theory of Gravity', 1197.

nature of Newtonian mechanics, particularly its preference for those 'at rest'.[39]

Lodge also attempted to capitalize on anti-German feeling. He remarked that he could not accept relativity in spite of 'the admirable audacity of Einstein in the *Weltmacht oder Niedergang* sort of attitude which he takes up about his predicted shift of spectral lines'.[40] The phrase 'Weltmacht oder Niedergang' ('World-power or Decline') had been popularized in Germany before the war by General Friedrich von Bernhardi through his book *Deutschland und der nächste Krieg* (1911). The book had gone through six printings by 1914, and Lodge's readers would have associated Bernhardi's phrase, and hence Einstein's physics, with German war aims.[41] The brief biography of Einstein that appeared in *The Times*, two days after the Royal Society meeting, went to some lengths to emphasize that he was Swiss, that he was Jewish, and that he had opposed the war: a less likely German nationalist is hard to imagine.[42]

Lodge's reception of Einstein in metaphors of kingship and government was undoubtedly due to the late nineteenth-century alignment of science with imperial identity and its revival in the war. However, this very factor is one that may have encouraged post-war modernist writers to construct Einstein as a kindred spirit, in so far as they rejected nationalistic and imperial identities, and perceived themselves as either European, transatlantic, or transnational.[43] The claims made for the role of imagination in science may have arisen as a means of differentiating pure from applied science, but they became territory for contestation and potentially for reconciliation in the conflict between science and literature. Einstein was received in these terms, as a solitary genius, working independently

[39] Lodge, 'The New Theory of Gravity', 1201; Lodge, 'Popular Relativity and the Velocity of Light', *Nature*, 106 (4 November 1920), 325–6; anon, 'Doubting the Obvious' [review of Einstein and Eddington], *Nation*, 27 (25 Sept. 1920), 792, 794. The *Nation's* reviewer was responding to similar remarks that Lodge had made at the British Association meeting in Cardiff, 27 Aug. 1920; Lodge's article in *Nature* was based on this speech.

[40] Lodge, 'The Geometrisation of Physics', *Nature*, 106 (17 Feb. 1921), 795–800 (p. 800).

[41] Fritz Fischer, *World Power or Decline* (1965), tr. L. L. Farrar, Robert Kimber and Rita Kimber (London: Weidenfeld and Nicolson, 1975), 4.

[42] 'Dr Albert Einstein', *The Times* (8 Nov. 1919), 12. The marked copies of *The Times* indicate that the article was provided by the Zionist Press Bureau.

[43] Though, as Paul Peppis has argued in *Literature, Politics and the English Avant-Garde*, the English avant-garde aligned itself to some extent with national and imperial aims in the period 1900–18, the post-war period saw significant readjustment in this respect.

of established institutions. This idea was more readily assimilable to literary ideas of individual creativity than had been the late-Victorian idea of science as a collective endeavour.

In fiction before the war, and before the Einsteinian revolution, science was frequently viewed antipathetically, in terms of mechanism and materialism. Joseph Conrad, though happy to play with ideas of entropy in *The Secret Agent*, simultaneously adopted a hostile view of science. The anti-mechanical rhetoric of the Sages emerges in his often-cited letter to Cunninghame Graham: the universe is a grotesque 'knitting machine', knitting 'time, space, pain, death, corruption, despair and all the illusions', remorselessly; however much one expresses contempt for it, 'the machine will run on all the same'.[44] In *The Secret Agent*, Mr Vladimir establishes the centrality of science early on, when he tells Mr Verloc that 'the sacro-sanct fetish of to-day is science'.[45] It is unclear whether Mr Vladimir's contempt is directed towards science in itself, or towards those who fetishize it, and the proposed attack on the Greenwich meridian does not clarify the issue. However, the novel's animus appears to be directed towards science in itself. The anarchists are characterized by their adherence to science: the Professor's coldness is stereotypically that of the scientist, while Ossipon's adherence to the doctrines of Lombroso is satirized throughout.[46] As no alternative doctrines are given space, one can assume that Lombroso is intended to represent not only bad science, but all science.

Towards the conclusion of the novel, the narrator qualifies many of Ossipon's feelings and actions with the adverb 'scientifically': he was 'terrified scientifically' (217), he 'gazed scientifically' (222), and he 'spoke scientifically in his secret fear' (222). A larger version of the same qualification, carrying the same negative connotations, occurs in the final meeting of Winnie and Verloc. Unable to communicate with Winnie, Verloc declares 'from the fulness of his heart' that he wishes he had never seen Greenwich Park. But the heartfelt expression makes no impact:

The veiled sound filled the small room with its moderate volume, well adapted to the modest nature of the wish. The waves of air of the proper length, propagated in accordance with correct mathematical formulas,

---

[44] Conrad, letters to R. B. Cunninghame Graham dated 20 Dec. 1897 and 14 Jan. 1898, *Letters*, i. 425, ii. 16.
[45] Conrad, *The Secret Agent*, ed. Harkness and Reid, 29.
[46] Haynes, *From Faust to Strangelove*, 64–91, 211–35.

flowed around all the inanimate things in the room, lapped against Mrs
Verloc's head as if it had been a head of stone. (195)

Like Ossipon, he 'spoke scientifically', but Conrad implies that a
scientific description of the world cannot account for the ability of
one person's words to move another.

D. H. Lawrence had also defined his attitude to 'science' before
the popularization of relativity. He resembles Conrad in combining
a negative valuation of science with an enthusiasm for the new
physics and its philosophical consequences, but both his antipathy
and his enthusiasm are more accentuated than Conrad's.
Nonetheless, the critical tradition has tended unquestioningly to
emphasize Lawrence's antipathy. Even N. K. Hayles, who describes
Lawrence's attitude to science as 'ambivalent', writes that he was
'essentially ignorant of post-Newtonian physics', and argues that in
consequence he saw in modern science 'merely the tendency to
objectify reality'.[47] Hayles's assertion has since been repeated by
several critics, while Lawrence's letter to Koteliansky, requesting a
copy of a 'simple book on Einstein's relativity' has generally been
overlooked.[48] That Lawrence took an interest in the new physics
does not necessarily overturn the charges of ignorance, though it
certainly indicates that ignorance needs to be more carefully
defined. Moreover, to assume that Einstein's popular account gave
him some comprehension of post-Newtonian physics does not dis-
solve his very clear antipathy to science as mechanism: rather, it
forces us to acknowledge that an antipathy to science can co-exist
with various scientific interests.

Lawrence establishes his antipathy to mechanism by contrast with
a form of vitalism. This is apparent in Paul Morel's desire to capture
the shimmering protoplasmic nature of his subjects in *Sons and
Lovers*, and is extended into Ursula's image of the unicellular organism in *The Rainbow*, which, under the microscope, is surrounded by
a 'bright mist'.[49] As Krasner has shown, Lawrence's interest in fields

[47] N. Katherine Hayles, *The Cosmic Web* (Ithaca: Cornell University Press, 1984), 86,
110.

[48] Repeated by Martha Turner, *Mechanism and the Novel*, 152, and Michael Wutz,
'The Thermodynamics of Gender: Lawrence, Science and Sexism', *Mosaic*, 28 (1995),
83–108 (p. 84); see Lawrence, letter to S. S. Koteliansky, dated 4 June 1921, *Letters*, iv. 23.

[49] Lawrence, *Sons and Lovers*, ed. Helen Baron and Carl Baron (Cambridge:
Cambridge University Press, 1992), 183; *The Rainbow*, ed. Mark Kinkead-Weekes
(Cambridge: Cambridge University Press, 1989), 408.

of force manifests itself in imagery of vital, shimmering outlines.[50]
For the moment, the significant point is that Ursula's idea of the cell
forms part of a dialogue with the 'woman doctor of physics',
Dr Frankstone. The mechanistic Dr Frankstone, who maintains that
'life' is merely 'a complexity of physical and chemical activities', is
clearly named after Mary Shelley's Dr Frankenstein. But although
Lawrence appears to be identifying science with one of the most
hackneyed images of the scientist, it should be noted that
Dr Frankstone advances her argument as a series of questions:

'I don't see why we should attribute some special mystery to life—do you?
We don't understand it as we understand electricity, even, but that doesn't
warrant our saying it is something special, something different in kind and
distinct from everything else in the universe—do you think it does? . . . I
don't see, really, why we should imagine there is a special order of life, and
life alone—'[51]

Frankstone's tone is difficult to read: it could be that her questions
are coercive, rhetorical, and unanswerable; or that she is encouraging Ursula to look harder, in the hope that she might find the something that gives life its special mystery; or even that she actually
lacks confidence in her own opinions, and is genuinely deferring to
Ursula's authority. The only clue Lawrence gives is that the conversation 'ended on a note of uncertainty, indefinite, wistful'. Ursula
goes on to ask whether she herself is merely 'an impersonal force'.
While the phrase might suggest mechanistic materialism, in
Lawrence's work impersonality is an ambivalent attribute: it can be
both the superficial impersonality of machinery, but also a deeper
impersonality, one that goes beyond the conscious, rational ego.
That Ursula continues to explore these questions, and reaches her
own answer, suggests that Dr Frankstone is not as dogmatic a
materialist as her name might imply.

Lawrence's antipathy to the mechanistic viewpoint is far more
pronounced when he is discussing the social sphere; in this, he
adopts the discourse of the Victorian sages. In Chapter 12 of *The
Rainbow*, both Uncle Tom and Winifred Inger 'worshipped' the
machinery of the colliery, 'the impure abstraction, the mechanisms
of matter'.[52] In the following chapter, the school is characterized in

[50] James Krasner, *The Entangled Eye* (Cambridge: Cambridge University Press,
1992), 157.
[51] Lawrence, *The Rainbow*, 408.   [52] Ibid., 325.

similar terms: it imposes itself on Ursula as a 'hard, stark reality'; its desks have 'an abstract angularity'; Mr Brunt is a 'machine', and the children are in the process of becoming 'one disciplined, mechanical set'.[53] Though Lawrence is continuing in the tradition of the sages, he also relates the mechanical organization to immediately contemporary concerns: the 'rapid firing' of Mr Brunt's questions would immediately have recalled the machine gun.[54]

After the war, scientists and popularizers used the stereotype of science as mechanistic materialism in order to differentiate the new physics from Victorian science. Although the stereotype had a basis in the actuality of mid-Victorian scientific practice, it obscured some of the subtleties of late Victorian science. Sullivan wrote of the 'crude materialists of Huxley's day', and of the Victorian universe as one which was 'objective, indifferent, tracing a purposeless pattern in obedience to "iron" laws'; he rarely acknowledged scientist-philosophers like Pearson, nor indicated that, by the late nineteenth century, the iron laws had become severely fatigued.[55] Whitehead, writing in 1919, aligned himself with Lytton Strachey, describing the pre-Einsteinian ether hypothesis as an 'eminent Victorian' with no place in the modern world. In *Science and the Modern World* he was more subtle, attributing the mechanistic outlook to the seventeenth century, and arguing that by the nineteenth 'the adequacy of scientific materialism . . . was endangered' from several angles.[56] However, even here Whitehead overlooks the philosophical developments of Poincaré, Mach, and others in the descriptionist and conventionalist schools.

Though it was the conservative critics of Einstein who first aligned his 'revolution' with that of the Bolsheviks, this association was one which the supporters of Einstein's theory were willing to accept. When Eddington commented on the 'Bolshevism' of the new physics, it was not to refute the charge in favour of a gradualist picture of theoretical change, but light-heartedly to re-designate 'Rutherford, not Einstein' as 'the real villain of the piece'.[57] Presenting Einstein's theory as a clean break with the physics of the past simplified popular exposition, and raised the prestige of

[53] Lawrence, *The Rainbow*, 346, 347, 350, 355.   [54] Ibid., 349.

[55] Sullivan, *Aspects of Science* (London: Cobden-Sanderson, 1923), 77, 140.

[56] Whitehead, 'A Revolution of Science', *The Nation*, 26 (15 Nov. 1919), 232–3; *Science and the Modern World*, 127.

[57] Eddington, *Physical World*, 1.

physics.[58] The stark antitheses generated in this atmosphere did little to encourage a detailed understanding of the development of Victorian science; the demarcation of distinct periods and modes in Victorian science has become possible only with the lapse of time.

Virginia Woolf's post-war work combines hostility to science with a curiosity about the ideas, images, and vocabularies of physics. Like Lawrence, she characterizes powerful institutions in terms that imply a criticism of science; however, unless we recognize that such terms were, at least in part, metonyms for Victorianism, her apparent antipathy to 'science' may conceal her curiosity. Compared to Lawrence, Woolf more often identifies science with cataloguing and measurement than with mechanism. Her influential criticism of Arnold Bennett is co-ordinated around the idea of 'materialism', which for Woolf implies the unreflective reproduction of superficial material details. Woolf writes that Bennett would have noticed 'how Mrs Brown wore a brooch which had cost three-and-ten'.[59] She implies that such a perceiving consciousness pays attention to the quantifiable at the expense of the qualitative aspects of the brooch, and, more importantly, of Mrs Brown herself. The specification of small financial details invariably signals such a satirical intent on Woolf's part: in *Night and Day*, Mary Datchet needlessly frowns over the account of Mrs Hipsley's bazaar ('five pounds eight shillings and twopence halfpenny'); in *Orlando* the narrator threatens to present the reader with the entire contents of Orlando's ledger books.[60] That such material details are in fact revealing, and that Bennett manipulates them skilfully, has been argued vigorously by John Carey; the satire on 'materialism', in the narrative sense, is one that is very easily made from a materially secure social position.[61]

Woolf's rejection of Bennett's narrative materialism draws on a discourse of materialism which was simultaneously being constructed by the advocates of the new physics. Sullivan's comment on Bennett, saying that he would have made 'a good stodgy scientist of

---

[58] Similarly, the German physicists of the 1920s were willing to use 'crisis' rhetoric in order to gain acceptance for their work: Paul Forman, 'Weimar Culture, Causality and Quantum Theory 1918–1927', *Historical Studies in the Physical Sciences*, 3 (1971), 1–115 (p. 58).

[59] Woolf, *Essays*, iii. 428.

[60] Woolf, *Night and Day*, 137; *Orlando* (1928), ed. Brenda Lyons (London: Penguin, 1992), 74–5.

[61] Carey, *The Intellectuals and the Masses*, 175–9.

the "materialistic" school, for he reports facts accurately and never wonders about them', strikingly re-locates Woolf's comments within the framework of popular science; the ease with which they can be accommodated within the new framework indicates the degree of convergence.[62] Herbert Dingle's *Relativity for All* provides another useful point of reference. In his concluding remarks, Dingle reassured his readers that the new theory was relevant only to objects beyond the human scale, such as atoms and planets:

Everything that we come across in our daily life is left untouched. Space, time and matter have an absolute meaning for observers relatively at rest. For them there is a real and definite meaning in the statements that a man is 6 feet high, that it is nine o'clock, and that sugar is 8d. a pound.[63]

Dingle's specimens of quotidian reality are curiously close to the objects of Woolf's satire, and though one must assume the coincidence to be quite unintentional, this passage allows one to draw certain implications out of Woolf's writing. Her designation of Bennett as a 'materialist' draws on the polarization that occurred in physics, in the public sphere at least, and locates her on the progressive side of the equation.

Aldous Huxley's attitude to science in his novels of the 1920s is significantly different from the attitudes of Lawrence and Woolf; this may reflect a difference in generations, though it may also be an idiosyncrasy. In this as in other matters, Huxley cultivates a detached attitude: he does not vilify 'mechanical' science, and perhaps in consequence, he treats the new physics more coolly. He was 'mischievously unreceptive to Sullivan's claims for the new physics in the early 1920s' and apparently found the scientific mind 'unsympathetic'.[64] Though his interest grew in the middle part of the decade, he employed the new ideas rather as the markers of social and intellectual pretensions than as powerful means of explaining man's place in the universe: in *Antic Hay*, Gumbril's dream of understanding 'perfectly and without effort the quantum theory' is interchangeable with the other elements of his fantasy

[62] Sullivan, letter to S. S. Koteliansky dated 3 March 1928, British Library MS 48973, fo. 54. Sullivan's remarks may also owe something to Middleton Murry's criticisms of Bennett in *The Problem of Style* (London: Humphrey Milford / Oxford University Press, 1922), 102.

[63] Dingle, *Relativity for All*, 67.

[64] Bradshaw, 'The Best of Companions', 191, 195

life; 'quantum theory' is, like 'Einstein' for other writers, little more than a synonym for 'difficult'.[65]

Where Huxley makes more sustained reference to scientific theories, it is often to the mechanistic theories of the nineteenth century. His description of sound in *Point Counter Point* has much in common with Conrad's in *The Secret Agent*, though their ultimate aims are divergent:

Pongileoni's blowing and the scraping of the anonymous fiddle players had shaken the air in the great hall, had set the glass of the windows looking on to it vibrating; and this in turn had shaken the air in Lord Edward's apartment on the further side. The shaking air rattled Lord Edward's *membrana tympani*; the interlocked *malleus*, *incus* and stirrup bones were set in motion so as to agitate the membrane of the oval window and raise an infinitesimal storm in the fluid of the labyrinth. The hairy endings of the auditory nerve shuddered like weeds in a rough sea; a vast number of obscure miracles were performed in the brain, and Lord Edward ecstatically whispered 'Bach!'[66]

Huxley not only characterizes Lord Edward's outlook as scientific, but, by decelerating the process of hearing, and so defamiliarizing it, he conveys a sense of the physiologist's complete detachment from events in Tantamount House. While Conrad uses the 'scientific' mode of description with a savage ironic intent, Huxley's irony here is gentler. Huxley's description differs from Conrad's in other ways: he not only outdoes Conrad in his use of technical, anatomical terminology, but places a much stronger emphasis on the causal sequence of events. This interest in causality again aligns him with his Victorian forebears. Huxley is characteristically interested in intricate casual sequences, and particularly those which lead to unforeseen conclusions: the essay 'Science and Civilization', for example, claims that Besant's and Bradlaugh's proselytizing for birth control led indirectly to the construction of 'tall blocks of five-roomed flats' and a quartering in the average weight of prize bulls.[67] Such an interest in causality could have sustained intricately plotted melodrama, as it had done for Hardy, but in Huxley's case such sequences are more localized in their effect, being the matter of paragraphs, not plots.

Although the modernists' unsympathetic representations of science are significant, they are only half of the story. It is a half-story

[65] Huxley, *Antic Hay* (1923; London: Flamingo, 1994), 10.
[66] Huxley, *Point Counter Point* (1928; London: Chatto and Windus, 1935), 44.

that has been re-told many times since the 1920s. The critical tradition surrounding modernism was informed from its inception by a general post-Romantic antipathy to science, and more particularly by the cultural conservatism of the New Criticism. While the attitudes of Conrad, Lawrence, Woolf, and Huxley were often complex, as were those of other contemporaries, the critical tradition has tended to emphasize their hostility to mechanistic and materialist science, and to neglect the more receptive aspects of the relationship. In the case of high modernism, it has long been taken for granted that the modernist fascination with primitivism was necessarily exclusive of an interest in science; the modernists' irreducible hostility to 'bourgeois modernity'—the technology of urban life—has been taken to include hostility to pure science.[68] Not only was the modernist relation to technology less hostile than has often been argued, but a hostile relation to it need not imply hostility to pure science.

Not only were the consequences of the new theories apparently irrelevant to ordinary mundane concerns, but the form they took was radically new, and harder for many to conceive. The Victorian preference for mechanisms that could be easily visualized and made into mechanical models appeared old-fashioned.[69] It was immediately recognized that the new physics favoured 'a more abstract class of theories altogether—theories which tell us nothing about the mechanism of a process, but tell us the principles the process must obey'.[70] Though the later quantum theories differed from relativity as regards determinacy, they shared its orientation towards formal rather than materialistic themata.[71]

The formal qualities of relativity were said to give it an aesthetic appeal. In 1918 Eddington argued that, regardless of whether it was right or wrong, Einstein's theory was 'beautiful'.[72] Bertrand Russell echoed this in his first exposition in 1919, declaring that, on account of its aesthetic merit, 'every lover of the beautiful must wish it to be true'.[73] That Einstein was led by aesthetic considerations has been

[67] Huxley, *The Hidden Huxley*, ed. David Bradshaw (London: Faber, 1994), 113–14.

[68] Calinescu, *Five Faces of Modernity* (Durham [USA]: Duke University Press, 1987), 41.

[69] See Kelvin's Baltimore Lectures (1884), quoted in Crosbie Smith, *The Science of Energy*, 297.

[70] Sullivan, 'A Scientific Explanation', *Athenaeum* (9 Jan. 1920), 50–1.

[71] Holton, *The Advancement of Science*, 175.

[72] Eddington, *Report on the Relativity Theory of Gravitation* (London: Physical Society of London, 1918), p. v.

[73] Russell, 'Einstein's Theory of Gravitation', *The Athenaeum* (14 Nov. 1919), 1189.

supported by more recent commentators: Holton has argued that Einstein's Special Theory of Relativity was precipitated not by the failure of the Michelson experiment to detect the ether, though this 'experimenticist' story is the one most frequently told in popularizations; rather, it began with Einstein's fundamentally aesthetic dissatisfaction with the *ad hoc* hypotheses of the ether theory.[74] The ugliness of the ether theory was apparent even to amateur commentators: as early as 1901, the lawyer Allen Upward had described it as a 'dustbin into which Science throws her breakages'.[75] The modernist debt to late nineteenth-century aestheticism prepared the ground for the favourable reception of relativity: for modernist writers, all arts could as easily aspire to the condition of mathematics as to that of music. Mathematics, like music, was conceived of as an autonomous, internally consistent system for which referentiality was unimportant. Eddington's suggestion that the truth value of relativity was of secondary importance to its beauty follows in the aestheticist line of critical judgement.

Heisenberg's Uncertainty Principle is frequently alluded to as a scientific point of comparison for the 'subjective' element in modernist literature, but several years previously, relativity theory had given credence to the idea that everything is relative. Einstein's theory of relativity appeared at the end of several decades of philosophical discussion of 'relativity', meaning, most frequently, the historical or social relativity of truth. By 1911, the topic seemed to have been exhausted: one philosopher and physicist apologized for writing on a subject 'discussed so often'; it seemed 'presumptuous to attempt to add anything'.[76] Although 'relativity' was not new, when Einstein's theory arrived, it seemed to give a philosophical concept the sanction of empirical science. Writing in *The Times* in 1920, Middleton Murry suggested that 'for the first time the metaphysical doctrine of subjective idealism has been backed by a scientific proof'.[77]

[74] Holton, *Thematic Origins*, 275–80, 304–16.

[75] Upward, *The New Word* (London: A.C. Fifield, 1908), 120. Upward claims in the preface that he wrote the book in 1901.

[76] Norman Campbell, 'The Common Sense of Relativity', *Philosophical Magazine*, 6th ser., 21 (Apr. 1911), 502–17. 'Relativity' continued to be used in the sense of 'historicism': e.g. in Murry's review ('Shakespeare and "Relativity" ') of a critical study of Shakespeare (*Nation and Athenaeum*, 31 (29 July 1922), 597–8).

[77] Murry, 'Literature and Science', *The Times* (26 May 1922), 16. Murry's discussion was prompted by a private letter from Sullivan: see Bradshaw, 'The Best of Companions', 199–202.

D. H. Lawrence's enthusiastic response to Einstein rests on this misconception: he told Koteliansky that he liked Einstein 'for taking out the pin which fixed down our fluttering little physical universe'.[78] He reproduced these remarks almost exactly in *Fantasia of the Unconscious*, where the theory supported his denial 'of any one absolute principle', and his belief that life 'was always a matter of relationships'.[79] However, by the time he came to write the 'Swan' sequence of poems, his position had subtly changed.[80] Firstly, he no longer associates the image of the universe as a 'cloud of bees' with relativity, but rather with atomic theory: it takes the form of 'Mists /where the electron behaves and misbehaves at will'.[81] Lawrence conflates a wide range of theories, presenting them as 'a mist of atoms / electrons and energies, quantums and relativities' in which 'the father of all things', the new god, swims. It is momentarily unclear whether this 'father' or the mists is 'like a wild swan'. This is the nub of Lawrence's ambivalence: the swan gods resemble the laws of the new physics, but they simultaneously fly through them, they seem more solid, more alive, and, 'treading our women', more crudely masculine. The very call to 'Give us Gods' indicates a need to return to some form of absolute, but it must be the absolute of a relativistic science which has unpinned the universe, or the absolute of plural gods rather than a single God who, in 'Spiral Flame', has ruled the universe 'with rods of iron and rulers and strong men'.

Einstein had originally referred to relativity theory as 'invariantentheorie', and not every philosophy interpreted it as supporting subjective idealism. Bertrand Russell voiced his scepticism about the coupling of relativity and idealism, first in his review of Haldane's *The Philosophy of Humanism*, and later in his popular exposition, *ABC of Relativity*, where he warned that the 'subjectivity' of relativity is a '*physical* subjectivity, which would exist equally if there were no such things as minds or senses in the world . . . The theory

---

[78] Lawrence, letter to S. S. Koteliansky dated 16 June 1921, *Letters*, iv. 37.

[79] Mark Kinkead-Weekes, *D. H. Lawrence: Triumph to Exile, 1912–1922* (Cambridge: Cambridge University Press, 1996), 659; and see Lawrence, *Fantasia of the Unconscious* (1923) in *Fantasia of the Unconscious, Psychoanalysis and the Unconscious* (London: Heinemann, 1963), 19–21

[80] The linked poems are 'Swan', 'Give Us Gods', and 'Spiral Flame' (dated by Christopher Pollnitz to 2–15 Dec. 1928), 'Leda', 'Relativity' and 'Won't It Be Strange' (*c.* 20 Dec. 1928–7 Jan. 1929): see Pollnitz, Appendix II, in David Ellis, *D. H. Lawrence: Dying Game, 1922–1930* (Cambridge: Cambridge University Press, 1998), 589, 592–3.

[81] Lawrence, *The Complete Poems*, ed. Vivian de Sola Pinto and F. Warren Roberts (Harmondsworth: Penguin, 1977), 436–8.

does not say that *everything* is relative; on the contrary, it gives a technique for distinguishing what is relative from what belongs to a physical occurrence in its own right.'[82]

However, had the idealist interpretations of relativity not gained prominence, the consequent renewal of interest in epistemological questions would have lent support to the idea that scientific theories themselves were 'subjective'. As we have seen, Eddington's image of the footprint in the sand was widely influential.[83] Moreover, the feeling that science had become unstable and unreliable, through its very act of self-criticism and development, stirred others who knew little of the latest epistemological thinking. A poem by Edward Shanks typifies one form of response. Shortly after the Royal Society's meeting, J. C. Squire had asked in *The New Statesman* why recent scientific discoveries had not appealed more to the poets. In the same week's issue, E. N. da C. Andrade had given an exposition of Einstein's theories, and expressed regret that they seemed contrary to our intuitions; unlike Kelvin's ideal, they were too abstract and mathematical. Andrade had also expressed the hope that Einstein's theory was merely a preliminary to another theory which would present 'a picture of nature more physical and more easily grasped'.[84] In the following week, the journal printed verses by Edward Shanks which answered Squire's question and incorporated Andrade's idea of theory as a 'picture of nature'. Part of the verses referred to:

> Pythagoras, Heraclitus, Newton, Einstein,
> Grasping the intangible, the inviolate secret,
>
> As children seize their images in water
> Which, though they touch, remain not in their hands
> But still eluding them still mock their purpose
> And shine unmoving in the quiet flood.[85]

Though undistinguished as poetry, Shanks's lines are significant as a popular appropriation of the new epistemology. Combining

---

[82] Russell, 'Relativity, Scientific and Metaphysical', 786–7; *ABC of Relativity* (1925; London: Routledge, 1993), 148.

[83] Eddington, *Space, Time and Gravitation*, 201.

[84] E. N. da C. Andrade, 'The Theory of Relativity', *The New Statesman*, 14 (22 Nov. 1919), 215–16.

[85] J. C. Squire (as 'Solomon Eagle'), 'Books in General', *The New Statesman*, 14 (22 Nov. 1919), 223, and Edward Shanks, 'Astronomy', *The New Statesman*, 14 (29 Nov. 1919), 248.

Andrade's presentation of the new theory as an ungraspable object with a selective reading of conventionalist epistemology, Shanks produces a conservative rejection of all science as childish Narcissism. The reader is left to infer that only other modes of inquiry—poetry perhaps, or religion?—can provide solid, objective knowledge.

Elsewhere, regardless of conventionalist claims, conservative commentators exploited the very revision of scientific theory in polemics against the authority of science. In February 1920, an anonymous reviewer in *The Spectator* suggested that Hugh Elliot's 'confidence' in his materialist philosophy of science, and, by association, his dogmatic agnostic position, may have been shaken by Einstein's 'prophecies' concerning the orbit of Mercury.[86] The reviewer does not claim that Einstein's theory is anti-materialistic as such; rather, he implies that the undermining of one scientific theory radically diminishes the credibility of all. Though Einstein appeared to many to be a 'bolshevist' of science, here he is recruited as part of a conservative argument against materialism. Some weeks later, the editor suggested that Matthew Prior's *Ode on Exodus iii. 14* (1688) was peculiarly apposite: it is a poem that warns man against 'trying' (that is, testing) 'unfathom'd Wonders' with 'dangerous Curiosity'. The scientist who 'shows his Friend's mistake' will only confirm his own.[87] The sentiment is much the same as that voiced in the review of Hugh Elliot, though the use of a literary quotation additionally implies that literary knowledge is more secure than scientific. While some writers used Einstein's theory and the contemporaneous crisis in epistemology to argue that all viewpoints are relative, the *Spectator* writers produce a conservative version of this argument: they imply that all *scientific* viewpoints are relative, and additionally that the only stable framework for knowledge is conservative and Christian. However, *The Spectator*'s argument is a relatively rare one: more commonly, the new physics was attractive because it simultaneously carried the authority of science, but seemed to undermine some of that authority.

[86] [F. C. Moore], review of Hugh Elliot's *Modern Science and Materialism*, *The Spectator*, 124 (14 Feb. 1920), 214. Unsigned, authorship identified courtesy of *The Spectator*'s librarian.

[87] [John St. Loe Strachey], 'Einstein's Hypothesis and the Theory of Relativity', *The Spectator*, 124 (6 Mar. 1920), 302. Strachey associated this quotation with the Einsteinian revolution again in *The Spectator* (2 Feb. 1924).

The debates surrounding science in the war years and immediately after provide an important and largely overlooked context for T. S. Eliot's thinking about the nature of poetry, tradition, and poetic knowledge. The dominance of 'Tradition and the Individual Talent' in discussions of this subject has served to obscure some of the relations of Eliot's thinking with contemporaneous debate. Frequent comment on the scientific content of Eliot's 'catalyst' analogy has served to obscure the less obvious relations.[88] Moreover, the widespread anthologization of 'Tradition and the Individual Talent' has led to the neglect of the immediately contemporary lecture 'Modern Tendencies in Poetry', published as an essay in the Indian journal *Shama'a* in 1920, and never reprinted. The lecture, delivered on 28 October 1919, explicitly acknowledges *The Athenaeum* and draws upon an important debate about the relations of art and science which had occupied its pages since April 1919.[89] These debates in turn drew on the work of Henri Poincaré.

The most important text for the literary reviewers was Poincaré's *Science et méthode* (1908), which had been published in two English translations in 1913 and 1914.[90] Poincaré's work developed the constructivist aspects of Mach's epistemology, and explored concepts such as non-Euclidean space which were later (though independently) to inform Einstein's work. In the purely scientific sphere, Poincaré's philosophy of science provided an important framework for the justification and explanation of Einstein's work. But its impact in the broader cultural sphere was at least as important. The war-time discussions of imagination in science created a receptive audience for Poincaré's ideas, and he was enthusiastically adopted by critics and cultural commentators in the post-war years.

[88] Though Eliot's 'howler in elementary chemistry' was first alluded to in 1932 (Michael Roberts, review of Eliot's *Selected Essays*, *Adelphi*, 5/2 (Nov. 1932), 141–4), the criticism relates to Eliot's use of the word 'sulphurous'; no one has claimed that he misunderstood catalysis itself.

[89] I have previously considered the roles of Sullivan, Eliot and Murry in '*Pièces d'identité*: T. S. Eliot, J. W. N. Sullivan and Poetic Impersonality', *English Literature in Transition*, 39 (1996), 149–70; though the narrow time-frame of that article necessarily excludes the war-time context, the reader is referred to it for a more detailed biographical account of Sullivan's encounters with Eliot. Roger Fry's part in the debate, which was marked by a more psychological orientation, has been touched upon by Linda Hutcheon, *Formalism and the Freudian Aesthetic* (Cambridge: Cambridge University Press, 1984), 52–5.

[90] *Science and Method*, tr. Francis Maitland (London: Thomas Nelson, n.d. [*c.* 1914]), and *Science and Method*, tr. G. B. Halsted (New York: The Science Press, 1913). Subsequent references are to the Maitland translation.

Poincaré's essays 'The Selection of Facts' and 'Mathematical Discovery' were particularly influential. Poincaré begins 'The Selection of Facts' by confronting the common misconception of pure science as the random collection of facts. He paraphrases one version of this argument against science:

We cannot know all the facts, since they are practically infinite in number. We must make a selection; and that being so, can this selection be governed by the mere caprices of our curiosity? Is it not better to be guided by utility, by our practical, and more especially our moral, necessities? Have we not some better occupation than counting the number of lady-birds in existence on this planet?[91]

Poincaré argues that the applied science of the businessman or the industrialist would not be possible without the disinterested selection of facts. Such a selection is not capricious, because the scientist is interested only in those facts 'which have a chance of recurring' (17). This in itself is not enough: facts in complete conformity with the rules can teach us nothing new (20), so the scientist seeks 'cases where the rule stands the best chance of being found in fault' (21). In seeking these rules and exceptions, the scientist is motivated by the beauty of nature—not the beauty 'of qualities and appearances', but the beauty of nature's 'harmonious order' (22). Poincaré develops Mach's definition of science as the 'economy of thought', reinterpreting it in terms less utilitarian and more aestheticist, reminding the reader that the economical can also be the beautiful.

That Poincaré's adoption of 'harmony' and 'beauty' as key concepts made his theory a more attractive proposition than Mach's in the post-war years is confirmed by Herbert Read's response in 1921; in Read's case there is no explicit indication that nationality was in any way a factor.[92] Read was aware of the work of Mach and Pearson, and drew attention to the common thread in the philosophy of Whitehead and Eddington, but the descriptionists took second place to Poincaré. Read's summary of 'Mathematical Discovery', in the form of a 'loose syllogism', tends to assimilate it to 'The Selection of Facts':

Sensibility selects harmonious combinations from the aggregations of images within the mind;

[91] Poincaré, *Science and Method*, 15.
[92] Read, 'Readers and Writers', *The New Age*, 30 (8 Dec. 1921), 68. Read's account of unconscious creativity in his column for 1 Sept. 1921 also appears to draw on Poincaré.

Mathematical entities are always harmonious combinations;

Therefore, a mathematician endowed with sensibility (or aesthetic feeling) is most likely to discover harmonious combinations, and so be the best mathematician. In such a mathematician the aesthetic activity will play the part of a delicate sieve.

Although Read does not acknowledge *The Athenaeum*, he was both a reader and an occasional contributor, and it is likely that his awareness of Poincaré's work had been sharpened by Sullivan's articles of 1919.

Sullivan had opened the debate about scientific method with 'The Place of Science', in which he explored the peculiar status of science as a rational process which was nevertheless 'the child of irrational impulse'.[93] The irrational impulse to explain 'local curiosities' is 'transformed into the desire for *significant* knowledge—significant primarily for contemplation, and secondarily for practice'. In addition to serving 'curiosity, comprehension and practice', science created theories which were in themselves aesthetically satisfying: 'the measure in which science falls short as art is the measure in which it is incomplete as science'.

Sullivan's remarks faintly echo *Nature*'s editorial of January 1915, and 'curiosity' continues to bear its war-time value (as seen in Bateson's and Benson's essays), denoting a desire for knowledge distinct from the enemy's utilitarian outlook. But his references to 'curiosity' also hinted at a debt to Poincaré, one he acknowledged explicitly in his next article on the aesthetic aspects of science, 'The Justification of the Scientific Method'; the article quoted Poincaré on the importance of beauty in scientific motivation.[94] Like Poincaré, Sullivan confronted the popular misconception of science as 'a mere collection of random facts', in his case not ladybirds, but 'the number of nightingales heard in Hertfordshire during a certain month'. Like Poincaré, he argued that the aim of science was not to create catalogues, but to form theories, and, as the theories express the 'harmonies' which exist in nature, the theories themselves 'must have an aesthetic value'. In a later article on relativity, he would argue that, even if Einstein's theory were not accepted, it would remain a 'beautiful and ingenious mathematical speculation'.[95] The

[93] Sullivan, 'The Place of Science', *The Athenaeum* (11 Apr. 1919), 176.
[94] Sullivan, 'The Justification of the Scientific Method', *The Athenaeum* (2 May 1919), 274–5.
[95] Sullivan, 'The Equivalence Principle', *The Athenaeum* (6 June 1919), 433.

contributors to *Cambridge Essays on Education* had deplored
catalogues of facts, but for them, 'beauty' was the sole preserve of
'literature, ancient and modern'.[96]

However, 'The Justification of the Scientific Method' was not
merely a paraphrase of 'The Selection of Facts'. The prospect of
Newtonian theory being replaced by or incorporated into Einstein's
more comprehensive theory brought a new topicality to Poincaré's
ideas: if Newton's theory had always been factually incorrect, then
its truth must have inhered in some other quality; its aesthetic harmony seemed the likeliest basis for its truth. Moreover, if scientific
'results' as pre-eminent as Newton's could be proved wrong, scientists would have to look to scientific method as the basis of their
truth. Sullivan was aware of the paradox involved: if the method was
infallible, as so many apologists had claimed, then 'why are the
results reached by it provisional?' Scientific method appeared to be
'excellent as a means of obtaining plausible conclusions which are
always wrong, but hardly as a means of reaching the truth'.[97] The
paradox was more apparent than real, he explained, because 'there
is a part of every discarded hypothesis which is incorporated into
the new theory'. Although Newton's theory of gravitation was 'very
probably not exactly true', it was still very nearly true for a large
range of situations. Sullivan did not name Einstein's theory, though
he was clearly preparing the ground for his later expositions of relativity; for the purposes of his argument on method, he suggested
that the new theories were themselves probably only an approximation to the truth.

Drawing on war-time debates, Sullivan gave further expression to
his conception of science in two articles on scientific education.[98]
Some aspects of these articles are anticipated in other people's work,
but comparison also reveals Sullivan's individual features. As early
as 1914, Henry E. Armstrong, F. R. S., had argued for a change in
the method of science teaching. His model for scientific method was
'the method of the Chancery Court': 'the collection of all available
evidence and the subjection of all such evidence to the most search-
ing examination and cross-examination'. But scientific method

---

[96] Bateson, 'The Place of Science in Education', in Benson (ed.), *Cambridge Essays*, 137, 133.
[97] Sullivan, 'Justification', 275.
[98] Sullivan, 'On Learning Science', *The Athenaeum* (4 July 1919), 559 and 'Scientific Education', *The Athenaeum* (12 Sept. 1919), 885–6.

went beyond that of the courts, in that scientists were always willing to reconsider their judgements. They 'dare[d] to be positive' only in rare instances when the facts had confirmed the theory time after time. (Ironically, in retrospect, Armstrong cited the Newtonian theory of gravitation and the Daltonian theory of atoms as two generalizations 'which fit all the facts'). Armstrong's emphasis on the examination of evidence led to his dissatisfaction with current science teaching: 'too much that is now taught under the guise of science is pure dogma'.[99]

Sullivan was also dissatisfied with current educational methods: as he said in 'On Learning Science', the 'modern text-book' presented scientific theories with an 'air of infallibility', which students inevitably associated with the scientific man.[100] In 'Scientific Education' he took Professor A. Gray's British Association Address as his starting point, and, like Gray, once again questioned the relative importance of the classics and the sciences, and the role of the classics in government.[101] Sullivan could afford to be more direct than many had been in war-time: 'The cost to the country, in blood and money, of omitting science from the education of its political leaders, is now gradually becoming apparent.'[102] He accepted that many who learn science would not go on to work as scientists: the value in learning science lay in its ability to expand and discipline the imagination. Armstrong had blamed the shortcomings of scientific education on the literary culture, with its tradition of 'set lessons and literary study by blocks of learners', but Sullivan was more careful to distinguish the classics from literature. He adopted a trope familiar from the *Cambridge Essays*, comparing the present method of scientific education to the rote learning of Latin grammar, but he added that 'literary' education should be distinguished from the classics. While Armstrong's distaste for dogma was rooted in a preference for the experimental method, Sullivan's was inspired by an historical understanding of science. Learning science through the 'historic method', and particularly through the original memoirs of the great discoverers, preserved the intelligent student's 'delicate web of doubt, of half-seen alternative explanations', and

---

[99] Henry E. Armstrong, 'The Place of Wisdom (Science) in the State and in Education', *Nature*, 94 (22 Oct. 1914), 213–19 (p. 215).

[100] Sullivan, 'On Learning Science', 559.

[101] Professor A. Gray, Presidential Address to the Mathematical and Physical Section of the British Association, *Nature*, 104 (18 Sept. 1919), 52–9.

[102] Sullivan, 'Scientific Education', 885.

allowed the child to feel the 'hesitations and difficulties' of scientists as they first formulated their new theories.[103] Sullivan's historical understanding of science reduced the distance between science and literary culture. If his proposed method of teaching were adopted, '[m]any misunderstandings, including the present absurd "conflict" between science and literature, would vanish'.[104] While Sullivan was clearly aware of the war-time debates about the nature of scientific method and its relation to education, the displacement of Newton by a theory in which experimental data played a secondary role meant that the thinking of men like Armstrong had been superseded. Science advanced not only by incorporating sense data into a theory, but by incorporating earlier theories into an aesthetic whole.[105]

Eliot's October lecture follows Poincaré's and Sullivan's thinking quite closely. Eliot distinguished only three aspects to the scientist's work: the analytic; the observational (which he later terms 'the interest of curiosity'); and the constructive. He distinguished two aspects to the poet's gift, the analytical and the constructive.[106] His reason for excluding the observational becomes more clear when he considers the 'unconstructive' poetry of the Dadaist Tristan Tzara. Such poetry was, Eliot asserted, unpoetic, being 'no more art than a postage stamp album'; it was, by the same count, 'unscientific', 'because the interest in mere data is not a scientific interest at all'. That Eliot does not support this assertion may be because he was addressing an audience already familiar with the idea, if not from Poincaré directly, then from Sullivan's account of him.

The relevance of Sullivan's 'historic method' to Eliot's conception of tradition may already be apparent. Sullivan's articles landed on fertile ground. Eliot had before him the example of Ezra Pound, who had frequently adopted scientific metaphors, and, more importantly for Eliot, had compared the discipline of poetry to that of science. In his prescriptions for imagists in 1913, Pound had warned that the scientist does not expect to be acclaimed as a great scientist 'until he has *discovered* something', and that, before he can discover something, he 'begins by learning what has been discovered already'. The poet was in the process of becoming a

---

[103] Sullivan, 'On Learning Science', 559.   [104] Sullivan, 'Scientific Education', 886.
[105] The question of whether Einstein's theory replaces or incorporates Newton's has continued to be debated: see Kuhn, *The Structure of Scientific Revolutions*, 98–9.
[106] Eliot, 'Modern Tendencies in Poetry', *Shama'a*, 1/1 (April 1920), 9–18 (p. 11).

professionalized expert.[107] Eliot had repeated this idea in 1918, though his account subordinates the individual talent still further to its cultural context: 'A poet, like a scientist, is contributing toward the organic development of culture: it is just as absurd for him not to know the work of his predecessors or of men writing in other languages as it would be for a biologist to be ignorant of Mendel or De Vries.'[108] The difficulty for Eliot was to reconcile this model of poetic development with a 'classicist' scepticism about progress. If, as T. E. Hulme had said, 'Man is an extraordinarily fixed and limited creature whose nature is absolutely constant', then the belief in mankind's continuing improvement was unfounded.[109] Hulme's belief in 'tradition and organization' as the only solution broadly anticipates Eliot's adoption of tradition as a principle, but 'tradition' can denote both a process and a product, and Hulme's conception of tradition is far more static than Eliot's. Hulme imagines 'tradition' as an enclosed space within a permanent structure, while Eliot conceives it as a configuration of structures, statues in a gallery perhaps, in which the order of the 'existing monuments' can be readjusted to accommodate new works; the process of movement is an integral part of 'tradition'.[110]

Eliot confronted the problem of 'progress' in 'Modern Tendencies in Poetry'. After introducing the catalyst analogy, Eliot paused to examine the reliability of the poetry/science analogy: 'we know, or think we know, what is meant by progress in science; but is there the same kind of progress in poetry—is there any progress in poetry?'[111] The obvious objection rested on a distinction of value: the poetry of the past retained a 'permanent value', while 'past work in science appears of value only because of its being the basis of present conclusions and future discoveries'. Eliot expresses the belief that the objection might be attenuated from both sides, but addresses only the literary aspect; he argues that the value of past poetry is sustained only by the continuing production of poetry in the present.

---

[107] Ian F. A. Bell, *Critic as Scientist*; Pound, 'A Few Don'ts for Imagists' (1913), *Literary Essays of Ezra Pound*, ed. T. S. Eliot (London: Faber and Faber, 1954), 6; Louis Menand, *Discovering Modernism: T. S. Eliot and his Context* (New York: Oxford University Press, 1987), 113–32, esp. 121, quoting Rebecca West on the imagists.

[108] Eliot, 'Contemporanea', *The Egoist*, 5/6 (Jun.–Jul. 1918), 84. Eliot also compared the critic to the scientist in *The Egoist*, 5/9 (Oct. 1918), 113–14.

[109] Hulme, *Collected Writings*, ed. Karen Csengeri (Oxford: Clarendon, 1994), 61.

[110] Eliot, 'Tradition and the Individual Talent', *Selected Prose* ed. Frank Kermode (London: Faber, 1975), 38.

[111] Eliot, 'Modern Tendencies', 12.

The scientific aspect had already been examined by Sullivan in *The Athenaeum*. Though past science appears meaningless when viewed through the lens of the modern text-book, viewed through Sullivan's 'historic method', it becomes valuable again. Of course, this transformation of value depends on a transformation of science from a practical discipline to an object of contemplation, but the war years had increased the popular desire for exactly such a change. When present science is placed in the lens of Sullivan's historic method, it too is transformed: the provisionality of its hypotheses is emphasized; the appearance of progress is turned into the reality of neutral change. Although the process of tradition involves the incorporation of old works into new works—literally, in the case of Eliot's poetry—the process of incorporation is a mode of change rather than a mode of progress.[112]

The treatment of facts and the idea of tradition are not the only areas of similarity between Eliot's conception of poetry and Sullivan's conception of science. The problem of impersonality was also a central feature of *The Athenaeum*'s art/science debate, though one that had fewer precedents in the war-time debates. Sullivan's analysis of the topic again owed something to Poincaré, though his immediate occasion was the death of Lord Rayleigh on 30 June 1919. Sullivan's appreciation of Rayleigh's career applied what we would now term the 'author function' to Rayleigh's works, seeking unity in a consistent idea of authorial identity. Part of the identity that Sullivan found was due to nationality: like Maxwell and Kelvin, Rayleigh had the peculiarly British 'quality of scientific imagination' that needed to construct mechanical models. However, he also had individual qualities: he was a 'fine stylist' and a 'superb critic' of other scientists' work, 'fastidious' in his distaste for logical incoherence. He had an 'instinctive sense of form' which made his treatments of scientific problems 'aesthetically as well as logically satisfying'.[113]

Sullivan developed this idea in the following week. He began 'Science and Personality' by contrasting the 'obliteration of personality' which was supposedly the foundation of science with the 'expression of individuality' which many took to characterize art.

---

[112] Sullivan's scepticism about 'progress' is confirmed by his review of F. S. Marvin's *Recent Developments in European Thought*, a review which he (or Murry) significantly titled 'The Historical Method', *The Athenaeum* (16 Apr. 1920), 509.

[113] Sullivan, 'A Stylist in Science', *The Athenaeum* (11 Jul. 1919), 593.

He claimed, however, that analysis 'can discover the personal element in a great scientific work'. Though his terminology is inconsistent at first, he develops a more stable definition, according to which a work could have 'individuality' without the obtrusion of 'personality'. The 'delicacy and richness' of personality could not find expression in the 'limited medium' of science, but individuality could.[114] He gave no examples, but both Rayleigh and Einstein could have been adduced: in an earlier article, Sullivan had identified Einstein as the rare type of genius who could perceive things 'with "the eyes of a child"'.[115] Though Sullivan had less to say about art, he suggested both that the 'insistence on personalities' was the cause of the lack of great contemporary art, and that this insistence was now declining.

Eliot took up this theme in 'Modern Tendencies', apparently drawing on Sullivan's discussions of Rayleigh and Einstein. Eliot asserted that when one studied the work of a scientist, one would recognize that his achievement was due not to 'a desire to express his personality', but to 'a complete surrender of himself' to the work. However, 'if he is a great scientist there will be—I believe scientists will corroborate this statement, a cachet of the man all over it'.[116] The scientist's 'personality' has not been lost, but has gone into the work: 'the inferences seem to have drawn themselves, the demonstrations constructed themselves, the relations flown into each other's arms; but without him it would not have happened'. Eliot does not substantiate these claims, but the corroboration he alludes to was clearly available in Sullivan's *Athenaeum* articles.

Eliot was not the only writer to respond to the contemporary discussions of the relations of art and science. After the Royal Society meeting, the 'Georgian' J. C. Squire took up the theme of poetry and science in *The New Statesman*. Squire's ostensible occasion for this theme was a poem about Einstein—almost certainly Shanks's—and his own feeling of 'discomfort' in the face of relativity theory; but Squire had attended Eliot's lecture in the previous month, and would almost certainly have been familiar with *The Athenaeum*.[117]

[114] Sullivan, 'Science and Personality', *The Athenaeum* (18 Jul. 1919), 624–5.

[115] Sullivan, 'The Notion of Simultaneity', *The Athenaeum* (23 May 1919), 369.

[116] Eliot, 'Modern Tendencies', 10.

[117] J. C. Squire (as 'Solomon Eagle'), 'Books in General', 223; Squire's presence at the lecture was remarked by Murry in a letter to Mansfield, 29 Oct. 1919, *The Letters of John Middleton Murry to Katherine Mansfield*, ed. C. A. Hankin (London: Constable, 1983), 199.

He remarked that, increasingly, 'our scientists approach the condition of imaginative artists'. He presented a rather different picture of scientific activity from Eliot and Sullivan, emphasizing 'the endless routine of experiment, observation, and measurement' more than they did, and giving, by implication, more weight to the factuality of science. However, this picture of laboratory-bound drudgery acted as a foil to Squire's conception of scientific leaps of the imagination, 'the infrequent moment of the superb deduction, the huge hypothesis'. The great physicists and the great poets were all, Squire believed, 'men of imagination', though the one group had a 'feeling for mathematics' and the other 'feeling for words'. If Einstein's theory could '[work] so powerfully on sensitive minds' in spite of its obscure mathematical form, 'what would not be the result of a theory of equal grandeur embodied in great verse?'

Squire's rhetorical question sounds like a prescription for the worst form of poetic bombast, but his call for poetry to 'extend its province' has much in common with discussions of poetry in modernist circles. Sullivan had praised Einstein's general theory for being 'immensely comprehensive', and its comprehensiveness seemed to set a new standard for other forms of imaginative activity.[118] In his editorial for 19 December 1919, Sullivan surveyed the 'apparent chaos' of the contemporary cultural scene, a situation without any set of shared conventions.[119] He expressed the hope that an artistic 'Einstein' would come: he would 'unify the most disparate phenomena' and would perhaps 'disturb something as fundamental as our notions of space and time'. Until such a figure arrived, art would be weak: 'If art is to survive it must show itself worthy to rank with science; it must be as adequate, in its own way, as is science. To do that, it must become, to an unprecedented degree, profound and comprehensive, for it is living in a world which is unprecedentedly wide and deep.' With a dissenting glance at J. C. Squire, Sullivan added that he was not 'asking poets to write about the Milky Way', and that the necessary comprehensiveness did not consist in 'painting the signs of the Zodiac', 'reciting the facts of geology' or 'composing a symphonic poem on the death of the Sun'; rather, he required the poet to locate himself in relation to the full range of contemporary phenomena. In writing this, Sullivan may have been drawing on Eliot's earlier lecture and essays: Eliot

---

[118] Sullivan, 'The Equivalence Principle', *The Athenaeum* (6 Jun. 1919), 433.
[119] Sullivan, 'Dissolving Views', *The Athenaeum* (19 Dec. 1919), 1361–2.

had said, in 'Modern Tendencies', that the poet 'may be perceptive of any or all of the ingredients in the modern world', and elsewhere had noted Ezra Pound's poetic ambition to acquire 'the entire past'.[120] However, the traffic ran both ways: Sullivan's remarks may in turn have influenced Eliot's better-known and more forceful declaration that, like the Metaphysical poets, the modern poet 'must become more and more comprehensive'.[121] Not only was the ideal of comprehensiveness modelled in the shadow of science's cultural dominance, but such an ideal implies that poetry should include science. For Herbert Read, a few years later, the modern physicists provided the clearest example of an 'intelligent minority' distinct from 'the crowd', one whose work provided 'a whole system of thought and imagery ready for fertilization in the mind of the poet'.[122] Read cautioned that the scientific ideal could, like the religious ideal before it, be superseded, but recommended it nevertheless as a way of entering 'the full stream of all that is valuable in our age'. Such positive reactions to the new physics were possible not in spite of a literary hostility to mechanistic science, but because of that hostility.

[120] Eliot, 'Modern Tendencies', 14–15; 'The Method of Mr Pound', *The Athenaeum* (24 Oct. 1919), 1065.

[121] Eliot, 'The Metaphysical Poets' (1921), *Selected Prose*, 65.

[122] Read, 'The Nature of Metaphysical Poetry' (1923), *Collected Essays in Literary Criticism* 2nd edn. (London: Faber and Faber, 1951), 87–8.

5

Invisible Men and Fractured Atoms

CONCEPTIONS of matter developed rapidly in the period 1890 to 1930. In December 1895 Wilhelm Konrad von Röntgen discovered the rays named after him, later known as X-rays. In 1898, the Curies hypothesized the existence of a new chemical element 'radium', one of many radioactive substances which caused phosphorescence in neighbouring bodies; they isolated it in 1902. In 1899, Ernest Rutherford distinguished alpha and beta rays. In 1900, Max Planck advanced the theory that energy, rather than being infinitesimally variable in magnitude, exists in discrete 'quanta'. In 1903 Rutherford and Frederick Soddy theorized the instability of radio-active atoms, and in 1910, Rutherford went on to split the atom.[1] 1911 saw the publication of Rutherford's 'solar' model of the atom, in which electrons orbited around the nucleus. 1913 saw Niels Bohr's model of the atom, in which electrons behaved according to classical mechanics while revolving in their orbits, but were capable of leaping from one orbit to another.[2] By 1925, this model was deemed incoherent, and was replaced by various models in quick succession, developed by Werner Heisenberg, by Max Born and Pascual Jordan, by Paul Dirac, and by Erwin Schrödinger.[3] As the investigation of matter was more closely related to experimental work than Einstein's theorization of gravity, advances tended to be smaller and cumulative. In consequence the newspapers and intellectual journals could not present the new theories as a single 'revolution', nor focus on a single scientific 'genius', as they were able to with Einstein. There were numerous popular articles on the subject, and some radio broadcasts, but their authors were often slightly out of step with the most recent developments, as a result either of

---

[1] 'Radioactivity' (by Ernest Rutherford) and 'Radium' (unsigned), *Encyclopaedia Britannica*, 11th edn. (1910–11), xxii.793–802, xxii.807–8.
[2] Russell, *ABC of Atoms*, 44–5; Eddington, *Physical World*, 2–3.
[3] Eddington, *Physical World*, 206–25.

ignorance or caution.[4] As Eddington wrote in autumn 1926, the door of the quantum theory should carry a sign saying 'Structural alterations in progress—No admittance except on business'.[5]

As was noted in the introduction, many histories of modernism have emphasized the last, quantum mechanical phase of theorization; in doing so, they project the ideas of indeterminacy and complementarity back to a period when they did not necessarily carry the authority of physical science. If we wish to look at complementarity before the 1920s, we should look to William James, who may well have been one of Bohr's sources.[6] The popular science expositions of the 1920s continued to introduce ideas which derived from the turn of the century: matter being insubstantial was as important as particles being indeterminate. The crucial idea in the 'two tables' of Eddington's introduction to *The Nature of the Physical World*, and in the often-discussed 'threshold' scene, is that matter is porous: the idea derives from Rutherford's experiments in the first decade of the century.[7]

Atoms and matter are a rich source of metaphor. The atom provides metaphors for the self, and particularly, as W. E. Adams's *Memoirs of a Social Atom* (1903) ironically acknowledged, for the self in a urbanized mass society, in which any one individual seems interchangeable with any other.[8] The atom at this time had a fertile ambiguity about it, being both a thing that was indivisible, and a thing that experimental science had succeeded in subdividing. Matter likewise was both solid and permeable, no more so than in the emblem of Eddington's two tables. By virtue of this ontological instability, coupled with the atom's actual instability in Rutherford's laboratory, atom and matter seem to embody modern dilemmas. The scientific use of the term 'body' creates another route of transmission. Physicists frequently referred to molecular movements or vibrations as being a 'dance' or a 'jostling' of bodies.

In many respects the most significant examples are those where the metaphor remains concealed. The exuberant over-extension of metaphor, on the other hand, can be a strategy for acknowledging its artificiality, as in *The Grammar of Science*, where Karl Pearson

---

[4] Lodge discussed matter in his 'Ether and Reality' broadcasts, and there was a later series titled 'Atoms and Worlds' (6 Oct. to 10 Nov. 1926).

[5] Eddington, *Physical World*, 211.   [6] Holton, *Thematic Origins*, 137–42.

[7] Eddington, *Physical World*, xi–xii, 342.

[8] W. E. Adams, *Memoirs of a Social Atom* (London: Hutchinson, 1903). Adams does not elaborate this metaphor.

asks whether two particles might not, 'like two dancers, *hold hands*, and so the one "enforce" the other's motion?'[9] A more playful instance occurred in a discussion at the Royal Astronomical Society in 1918, in which Eddington asked why, when physical bodies tend to be spherical, our 'small irregular bodies are not': 'If we were built on a somewhat larger scale we should have to be spheres'.[10] The 'body' metaphor sustains the conceptualization of the self for reasons unconnected with science. The unity of the human body is a ubiquitous metaphor for the unity of the self.[11] The best-known theorization of the relation of body to self is Lacan's account of the mirror stage, in which the infant child, unable to co-ordinate the movements of its limbs, sees an idealized image of unity and control in its reflection. In the same way, the isolated bodies of physics—whether particles, atoms, molecules, planets or stars—provide idealized images of individualism. The most celebrated literary examples are Birkin's metaphors of stars and twin star equilibria, metaphors for the self which he contrasts with the Mino's state of being, 'a mere stray, a fluffy sporadic bit of chaos'.[12]

These metaphors for personal identity are transferable to the identity of a text, in other words, to literary form. Just as the unity of the body supports the impression of a unified self, so the physical unity of the book provides a metaphor for textual unity, in spite of the diversity of textual sources. Qualities that may be attributed to matter may also be applied to novels and poetry: solidity, porosity, inertness, volatility, substantiality and luminosity. Birkin's ideal condition of twin star equilibrium could almost describe the relation of *The Rainbow* to *Women in Love*, as two independent texts, distinct in form and tone, yet linked.

If atoms provide models for selves and for texts, then the interactions of atoms offer models for social interaction and for narrative form. Narrative can emphasize causal relations, or describe successive events and leave the reader to infer causal patterns. In 'Phases of Fiction', Virginia Woolf explores different forms of

---

[9] Pearson, *Grammar*, 325–6.

[10] Eddington, quoted in 'Meeting of the Royal Astronomical Society', *The Observatory*, 42 (Jun. 1918) 231–42 (pp. 237–8).

[11] The best-known theorization of the relation of body to self is Lacan's account of the mirror stage, in which the infant child, unable to co-ordinate the movements of its limbs, sees an idealized image of unity and control in its reflection.

[12] Lawrence, *Women in Love*, ed. John Worthen, Lindeth Vasey, and David Farmer (Cambridge: Cambridge University Press, 1987), 150, 152.

narrative relation, hinting at the atom metaphor without bringing it to the surface. Her description of Defoe's world as a mechanism, 'bright and round and hard', consisting of 'facts' and 'solid objects in a solid universe', suggests a Newtonian world of ball bearings related through cause and effect. Her accounts of other novelists are similarly dependent upon a very abstract model of the novel as system of movement. In the case of Dickens, his grotesques 'serve as stationary points in the flows and confusion of the narrative'. Woolf's metaphors are abstract and mixed: turning, out of chronological sequence, to Jane Austen, she initially draws on architecture. However, her description of Austen's characters as having 'edges' that are kept 'sharp' could refer to the boundary either of a building or of an atom. The metaphors return to physics when Woolf contrasts Austen with George Eliot: because Eliot's horizons are larger, her characters are smaller and their 'impact' on each other is less 'sharp'.[13] While the architectural metaphors share with the scientific ones a degree of abstraction, they are unable to describe dynamic narrative form, and Woolf turns again to physical metaphors of 'impact'. These metaphors do not depend on the discoveries of the mid 1920s. To establish a context for them, we need to turn back to the late-nineteenth century.

The discovery of Röntgen rays in 1895 was unusual in the field of research into matter for the level of publicity it aroused. Within a matter of years, the medium of X-ray photography had aroused fantasies of seeing one's own death, reading the thoughts of others, seeing through walls, and seeing through clothes: the X-ray occupied a peculiar position between scientific research and fairground sideshow.[14] From a popular perspective, radium was surrounded by a certain mystique, and had an ambivalent status. Its ability to damage organic matter was soon recognized (a phenomenon known as the 'Becquerel burn'), but it was also believed to have vital powers. In 1905, one Cambridge scientist believed he had discovered a new form of matter: in mixing radium compounds with gelatin media, he seemed to have created something neither organic nor inorganic,

[13] Woolf, 'Phases of Fiction' (1929), in *Collected Essays*, 4 vols. (London: Hogarth, 1966), ii. 56–102 (pp. 58, 72, 79).

[14] Yuri Tsivian, 'Media Fantasies and Penetrating Vision: Some Links Between X-Rays, the Microscope, and Film', in John E. Bowlt and Olga Matich (eds.), *Laboratory of Dreams: The Russian Avant-Garde and Cultural Experiment* (Stanford: Stanford University Press, 1996), 81–99.

but intermediate, which he christened 'radiobes'.[15] Such bridges between the organic and the inorganic implicitly promised to 'solve' the riddle of the creation of life by pointing to the material nature of the vital spark. No doubt the ability of radium to cause phosphorescence added to the impression of its hidden vitality.

Nascent modernists were well aware of this early phase of the new physics: Joseph Conrad met an early British pioneer of X-ray photography, and had his hand photographed; the young Virginia Stephen went, albeit by accident, to a lecture on the Röntgen rays in 1897.[16] Most importantly, though, in *The Invisible Man* (1897), H. G. Wells capitalized on the possibility of metaphorical exchange between the discourses of self, body, and matter. *The Invisible Man* facilitates the reading of later exchanges between literature and science, both in works that explicitly acknowledge Wells's novel, and in those where the metaphorical transfer may have occurred quite independently.

Wells's novel explores the ramifications of a simple metaphor: just as bodies of solid matter can produce invisible rays, so might human bodies produce invisible rays, and indeed, become invisible. When Griffin explains his process to Kemp, he establishes the metaphorical connection by saying that his process involves placing matter between two 'radiating centres of ethereal vibration', even though these are, he claims, not the Röntgen rays.[17] However, this is not the only metaphor involved in the text. Much of the power of Wells's novel for later writers is due to Griffin's literal invisibility being a metaphor for social invisibility. This is most readily apparent in the scenes in central London, where invisibility turns from being an advantage to being a positive danger: Griffin, the individual, is in constant danger of being crushed or destroyed by the crowd (94–5).

Lawrence implicitly reads *The Invisible Man* in this way in *The Rainbow*. When Ursula has been reunited with Skrebensky, she sees the town as 'a gleam of coloured oil on dark water', and the 'composure and civic purposefulness' of the townsfolk as a sham: they

[15] John Butler Burke, 'On the Spontaneous Action of Radio-active Bodies on Gelatin Media' [letter], *Nature*, 72 (25 May 1905), 78–9; 'On the Spontaneous Action of Radium on Gelatin Media' [letter] *Nature*, 72 (27 July 1905), 294; 'The Origin of Life', *Fortnightly Review*, o.s. 84 (Sept. 1905), 389–402.

[16] Conrad, letter to Edward Garnett, 29 Sept. 1898, *Letters*, ii. 94–5 and pl. 1; Woolf, diary entry for 9 Jan. 1897, *A Passionate Apprentice: The Early Journals 1897–1909*, ed. Mitchell A. Leaska (London: Hogarth, 1990), 10.

[17] Wells, *The Invisible Man* (1897), ed. Macdonald Daly (London: Dent, 1995), 86.

resemble the Invisible Man, 'a piece of darkness made visible only by his clothes'.[18] Lawrence interprets the idea of invisible light so as to align it with romantic ideas of the ineffable essence of the self. This allusion opens up the significance of many of Lawrence's other references to darkness, radium, radiation, and phosphorescence. It is the culmination of several pages in which Lawrence explores, more loosely, the idea of a dark, essential, pre-social self, which, variously, glimmers and vibrates. Its forms of radiation are distinct from those of the city, which, glittering and twinkling, is a world of distinctly visible but 'artificial' light.[19] To thicken and enrich his mythologization of this distinction, Lawrence tries to superimpose the unscientific idea that the dark light of X-rays vibrates while visible daylight does not. In these exploratory passages, Lawrence juxtaposes vocabularies and hints at scientific knowledge: for example, the darkness preferred by Ursula and Skrebensky is a primitivist darkness, 'heavy with fecundity in which every molecule of matter grew big with increase'.[20] Lawrence's use of 'molecule' is essentially hyperbolic, but it hints at the idea that matter, like the body and the self, contains hidden stores of energy.

Lawrence continued to develop these vocabularies in his later novels. The stages of the development are nowhere more clear than in *Women in Love*. The scene of the lovers Gerald and Gudrun walking together in the darkness recapitulates the external details of Ursula and Skrebensky in *The Rainbow*, and borrows much of its vocabulary from that scene. However, in the first, 1916 version, this was not so clear. Gudrun, admiring Gerald's beauty, thinks to herself: 'How much more of him was there to know. Ah much, much, many days harvesting for her large, yet perfectly subtle and intelligent hands, upon the field of his living, plastic beauty'.[21] However, in the more familiar 1920 and 1921 versions of the novel, his 'living, plastic beauty' becomes his 'living, radio-active body'.[22] In revising this passage, Lawrence apparently detected the scientific undertones of 'field', and allowed these to draw him towards the idea of radioactivity. In the revised version, 'field' is left suspended between two meanings, with 'harvesting' on one side and 'radio-active' on the other.

[18] Lawrence, *The Rainbow*, 415.   [19] Ibid., 418.   [20] Ibid., 413.
[21] Lawrence, *The First 'Women in Love'*, ed. John Worthen and Lindeth Vasey (Cambridge: Cambridge University Press, 1998), 306.
[22] Lawrence, *Women in Love*, 332.

However, Lawrence's revisions were not confined to this paragraph. Three paragraphs previously, in the 1916 text, Gudrun looks up at Gerald's 'shapely, male face', and 'a thrill of pleasure passed through her soul'.[23] She feels like Eve with the apple. In the later versions, however, though Gerald's face remains male and shapely, and Gudrun continues to resemble Eve, Lawrence eliminates Gudrun's subjective response and the reference to her soul. The revised version is more objective, and also prepares for the later reference to radio-activity: 'There seemed a faint, white light emitted from him, a white aura, as if he were visitor from the unseen.'[24] Like several of Lawrence's appropriations of scientific vocabulary, terms like 'aura' and 'the unseen' become dialogic, open both to spiritualist, Blavatskyan readings, and to scientific ones.[25] The revision does not substantially alter Gudrun's relation to Gerald, which remains one of subjected adoration, but Gerald becomes more uncanny, a figure from scientific romance, a visitor from another dimension.

A scientific vocabulary enabled Lawrence to delete a religious and romantic vocabulary, exemplified here by 'soul', and replace it with a vocabulary which was still, at the time, mysterious, and which broke with a conventional humanist philosophy. The 'soul' is more than human, but has a stable position within Christian humanist philosophy: radiation is inhuman, miraculous, and unstable in its signification. Lawrence employed his scientific vocabulary for the same purposes in revising a later passage in *Women in Love*. In both versions, Gerald and Gudrun are pressing Birkin for his opinions on the future of England, and in both versions Gudrun's sardonic persistence forces Birkin into silence. In 1916, Gudrun turns away from him to look at Gerald:

She looked at Gerald. He looked like a fruit made to eat. He was her apple of knowledge. She felt she could set her teeth in him and eat him to the core. She smiled to herself at her fancy. And what was the core then, the part she would throw away? Something worthless to her, perhaps.[26]

[23] Lawrence, *The First 'Women in Love'*, 305.   [24] Lawrence, *Women in Love*, 331.
[25] The most focused case is that of the 'Chladni patterns' in Lawrence's letter to David Garnett: see C. P. Ravilious, 'Lawrence's "Chladni Figures"', *Notes and Quotes*, n.s. 20 (1973), 332, and Thomas Gibbons, '"Allotropic States" and "Fiddlebow": D. H. Lawrence's Occult Sources', *Notes and Quotes*, n.s. 35 (1988), 338–40.
[26] Lawrence, *The First 'Women in Love'*, 364.

In the later texts, the Christian apple is replaced with modern science:

> She looked at Gerald. He was wonderful like a piece of radium to her. She felt she could consume herself and know *all*, by means of this fatal, living metal. She smiled to herself at her fancy. And what would she do with herself, when she had destroyed herself? For if spirit, if integral being is destructible, Matter is indestructible.[27]

The complexities of the revised version arise from the revision which has made Gudrun's act of consumption an act of self-consumption, and transformed Gerald from the object of consumption into a mysterious agent of it. Knowledge in the revised version is closer to a form of mystical knowledge, in which the knowing subject is annihilated in the known object. The oxymoronic 'fatal, living metal' provides Lawrence with an appropriate metaphor for such annihilation. In becoming the agent of this transformation, Gerald resembles a novel form of X-ray machine. Just as the X-ray machine 'eliminates' the flesh, so Gerald's radioactivity will eliminate the superficial 'self', leaving only the self's 'indestructible' skeleton.

Lawrence returns to the figure of the invisible man in *Aaron's Rod*, developing the association of invisibility and the essential self. While staying at the house of Sir William Franks, Aaron realizes that there has always been a gulf between his 'passional soul' and his 'open' conscious mind.[28] Aaron's mental self-image is compared to a passport description, 'ready-made and very banal': 'eyes blue, nose short, mouth normal, chin normal'. As he realizes this, Aaron's mask falls, and he feels 'transmuted' as the invisible man did. The narrator characterizes Aaron's inner self as being an 'essential plasm' and being like 'electric vibrations'. In doing so, the narrator realizes the essential paradox of his own position, conceding that he is articulating that which he claims is unutterable: the electric vibrations are invisible, 'no matter how many words they may purport'.

'Electric vibrations' is a vague phrase, but this model of the self has a structural similarity to that found in two other novels of the same year, Middleton Murry's *The Things We Are*, and Woolf's *Jacob's Room*. Murry's reference is localized and explicit. Its line of descent is clarified by Murry's actual biographical relation to Sullivan, by his textual relation to Sullivan's science columns, and by the fact that one of the novel's central characters, Bettington, is clearly modelled on Murry's friend: like Sullivan, Bettington is a

---

[27] Lawrence, *Women in Love*, 396. [28] Lawrence, *Aaron's Rod*, 163.

journalist, an enthusiastic talker, a devoted reader of Dostoevsky, and a former part-time student at London University. If Bettington's name derives from anywhere in particular, it might well be from 'Eddington'. At one point in the novel, Bettington travels by bicycle to see his friend Boston, and is described as feeling like 'an isolated atom'.[29] This part of the metaphor could have been employed at almost any time in the history of the concept of the atom, but the following phrase is more distinctly modern. Bettington is described as being drawn not to Boston personally, but 'to some centre of disturbance of which Boston was at most the symbol'. This most succinct gloss to this passage is Bertrand Russell's aphorism: 'matter' is 'a convenient formula for describing what happens where it isn't'.[30] In saying this, Russell was summarizing an idea developed in more detail by many earlier scientists and philosophers. 'Matter' and 'the atom' are dummy subjects, providing a notional grammatical subject for sentences like 'the atom is radiating', just as 'it' provides a dummy subject in the sentence 'it is raining'. The distant ancestor of this idea is Ernst Mach: for a Machian, 'the atom' provides an economic formula for grouping sense impressions, but has in itself no substantial reality; it is, at most, the symbol for certain perceptual disturbances. The more immediate ancestor is A. N. Whitehead, who in *Science and the Modern World* (1926) had criticized the idea that matter has 'simple location', identifying this as the 'fallacy of misplaced concreteness'. As he later wrote, 'For physics, the thing itself is what it does, and what it does is this divergent stream of influence.'[31] Russell had given an account of the electron in similar terms, notably using the word 'disturbance': 'it is possible that an electron is a certain kind of disturbance in the aether, most intense at one spot, and diminishing very rapidly in intensity as we move away from this spot'.[32] Bettington consciously chooses to give his 'disturbance' a simple location in the form of Boston, but acknowledges the artificiality of the process.

Woolf's novels of the 1920s do not refer explicitly either to Wells or to the discoveries of the 1890s, but *Jacob's Room* at least is suggestive in relation to both, not so much in any particular passage,

[29] Murry, *The Things We Are* (London: Constable, 1922), 257.
[30] Russell, *An Outline of Philosophy* (London: Allen and Unwin, 1927), 165.
[31] Whitehead, *Adventures of Ideas* (Cambridge: Cambridge University Press, 1933), 201–2.
[32] Russell, *ABC of Atoms*, 153–4.

but in its larger structure. If the novel is a parody of a *bildungsroman*, in which the hero fails to reach maturity,[33] it is also a parody of a biography, in which the biographer-narrator fails to capture his subject, fails to accommodate him within the conventional framework of biography, but cannot concede the impossibility of the task he has set himself. Jacob is very rarely glimpsed 'in himself', but is reconstructed through the scraps of evidence and information the narrator has managed to piece together: the short life of Mr Floyd, himself the editor of ecclesiastical biographies; the 'report' of Mrs Norman, who met Jacob on a train; or that of Mrs Papworth, Bonamy's cleaner.[34] The reports received are often generic, and their repetition, far from confirming earlier reports, draws attention to their emptiness: Jacob is 'distinguished-looking' and 'slightly awkward'. They resemble the passport-style descriptions of Jacob's contemporary, Aaron Sisley, and their very blankness structures a central absence which represents the non-articulable essence of the character. Woolf develops this duality in later work, aligning it with her sense that art must contain both granite and rainbow, the prosaic, ordinary experience, and the poetic or miraculous. In *A Room of One's Own* she argues that 'Woman' is both 'Mrs Martin, aged thirty-six, dressed in blue, wearing a black hat and brown shoes', but is also 'a vessel in which all sorts of spirits and forces are coursing and flashing perpetually'.[35] While the prosaic description approaches Aaron Sisley's idea of a passport description, the 'vessel' resembles many things, among them a cathode-ray tube. By the time of *A Room of One's Own*, she may have been consciously drawing on the 'two tables' of Eddington's *The Nature of the Physical World*. While the 'spirits and forces' suggest a more positive valuation of the interior of the self than we see in *Jacob's Room*, there is an underlying continuity between the earlier and the later work.

The resemblance of Jacob to Wells's invisible man has been obscured by Woolf's antipathy to Wells's later realist work, as seen in the series of essays that began with 'Modern Novels' (1919).[36] In a letter in 1922, Woolf paraphrased her own novel, saying that 'No one can see it [the human soul] whole . . . The best of us catch a

[33] Judy Little, '*Jacob's Room* as Comedy: Woolf's Parodic *bildungsroman*', in Jane Marcus (ed.), *New Feminist Essays on Virginia Woolf* (London: Macmillan, 1981), 105–24.

[34] Woolf, *Jacob's Room* (1922), ed. Sue Roe (London: Penguin, 1992), 16, 24, 87–8.

[35] Woolf, *A Room of One's Own* (1929; London: Penguin, 1945), 45–6.

[36] Woolf, *Essays*, iii. 30–7.

glimpse of a nose, a shoulder, something turning away, always in movement', and contrasted this form of representation with the method of Wells and Hugh Walpole, who made 'large oil paintings of fabulous fleshy monsters complete from top to toe'.[37] The irony is that one of Wells's most enduring, fabulous, and monstrous creations was quite the opposite of fleshy. In Wells's novel, the character himself must complete his own portrait, clothing the emptiness and improvising a face from goggles and a serviette, while in Woolf's, the biographer-narrator fleshes out the factual details. The final emblem of *Jacob's Room*, Jacob's empty shoes, is a particularly vivid point of similarity: Wells emphasizes the nakedness of his man's feet in many chapters, and in the epilogue, the sign for the pub 'The Invisible Man' is a board empty 'save for a hat and boots' (137).

It seems likely that the similarity between Woolf's conception of character and the new ideas about matter is due to a more widespread set of homologies, particular instances of which may be found in science, philosophy, linguistics, and other disciplines: 'relativity', in its broadest sense, the belief that in knowledge there are no positive terms, only relations. The same is true for Lawrence, and the scientific vocabulary in Lawrence's work seems, from this point of view, to be an attempt to grope towards an understanding of the new ontology. According to this 'relativity', the self exists not as an essence, nor as a cluster of a moral abstractions or biological characteristics (as, say, in Lombroso's biologistic criminology), but through its social relations. To some extent, *The Invisible Man*, *Women in Love*, and *Jacob's Room* continue to attempt to define the individual in opposition to 'society' and the crowd. They begin as if the individual essence could, without the contamination of society, be fully realized, but in trying to articulate that essence, they come to the brink of recognizing its non-existence. Accordingly, its absence is always represented as death, darkness, and silence, another example of modernist writing mourning the loss of order and positive knowledge. In this respect, there is a genuine difference in the emotional tone of modernist writing about the self and contemporaneous popular scientific writing about matter. In the scientific accounts, the absence of matter implies a liberation of energy,

[37] Woolf, letter to Gerald Brenan, Christmas Day 1922, *The Letters of Virginia Woolf*, ed. Nigel Nicolson and Joanne Trautmann (London: Hogarth, 1975–80), ii. 598. Cp. *Jacob's Room*, 23.

whether it is understood in nineteenth-century terms as a universal ether, or twentieth-century terms as vibrations and pulsations.

Woolf responds more directly to the new ideas of matter, and more positively, when thinking about matter as a barrier to the realization of the self. She responds more positively because the new ideas of matter suggest that such barriers are no longer as absolute as they had once appeared. Woolf began to explore this theme in *Mrs Dalloway*, in the relationship of Septimus and Clarissa. Her treatment of it owes something to the French unanimist school of writing, though a comparison with a work from this school also reveals significant differences, and allows us to see the extent to which Woolf's use of scientific concepts blended them with Bergsonian influences.[38]

Jules Romains' novel *Mort de quelqu'un* (1911) is the unanimist work closest to Woolf's circle: a translation by Woolf's friends Desmond MacCarthy and Sydney Waterlow was published in 1914, with an introductory letter by MacCarthy to Roger Fry.[39] *Mort de quelqu'un* is a simple narrative. It begins with the death in Paris of Jacques Godard, a solitary train driver, and goes on to describe, in parallel, the process by which news of his death is transmitted to his father in rural France, and the process by which Godard's 'soul' escapes his body and enters the bodies of acquaintances and strangers, uniting them into one soul. Souls are described with physicality equal to that of Godard's dissolving corpse: as his father travels in the stagecoach to Paris, the collective soul of the people in the carriage hangs 'in equilibrium just above their heads, under the grooved wooden roof' (56). Godard's soul, having left his body, oscillates, especially 'between the third and the fourth floors' (89). Though the pedantry of these specifications verges on the comic, it establishes the possibility of metaphorical movement between the idea of the soul, as something almost material, and matter, as something almost 'spiritual'. The 'soul' encounters the physical boundaries of bodies and walls, and these are described most clearly when Godard's father reaches Paris: 'Each row of windows saddened him. Every detail of the house marked the separation of human being into definite hard-and-fast compartments, as incapable of overlapping as

---

[38] For a general discussion, see Allen McLaurin, 'Virginia Woolf and Unanimism', *Journal of Modern Literature*, 9 (1981–2), 115–22.

[39] Jules Romains, *The Death of a Nobody*, trans. Desmond MacCarthy and Sydney Waterlow (London: Howard Latimer, 1914).

the severely just divisions of a graveyard' (94–5). While this description clearly owes much to Bergson's critique of mental compartmentalization, Romains's literal presentation of such compartments as rooms allows one to speculate what would be the case if the partitions between them were permeable or semi-transparent. If X-rays can see through solid flesh, then unanimism seems plausible.

In very general terms, *Mrs Dalloway* posits a similar relation between its 'nobody', Septimus Warren Smith, and Clarissa. They never meet, but the novel intimates a connection between them; a 'mechanical' point of connection is given (Dr Bradshaw), but the sense of similarity exceeds it. There are many local points of similarity between the two novels: *Death of a Nobody* repeatedly uses the image of a stone being dropped into a pool to describe the spreading influence of Godard, an image which anticipates the explicit and implicit imagery of events rippling outwards in *Mrs Dalloway*—the backfiring motor-car, for example, sent 'a slight ripple'. There are also significant differences: while the word 'soul' is ubiquitous in Romains's novel, Woolf hardly uses the word, preferring to refer to the 'self', or to use imagery to circumvent the problem of naming the inner essence of people. This opens the way, as it did for Lawrence, for an account of the self which uses scientific imagery, but in *Mrs Dalloway*, Woolf has not assembled all the pieces. Although Septimus uses X-ray imagery, when he tries to understand why he has seen a Skye terrier turning into a man ('Scientifically speaking, the flesh was melted off the world'), the imagery of melting, transparency, and porosity is not used in connection with social barriers.[40]

In *To the Lighthouse*, when Lily notices the Ramsays watching Prue and Jasper on the lawn, the scene becomes 'symbolical' (80). The transformation of the actual characters into symbols is described in terms of their acquiring an 'outline', but also in terms of their becoming 'sharp-edged and ethereal and divided by great distances'; for a moment, 'it seemed as if solidity had vanished altogether' (80). The vocabulary recalls that of 'Mr Bennett and Mrs Brown'. There, Woolf had diagnosed the idea of character as having lapsed into 'shapelessness', and had described the Georgian novelists as needing once again to 'sharpen [the] edges' of character.[41] The scene on the lawn is one of the novel's many epiphanies, or, in

---

[40] Woolf, *Mrs Dalloway*, 74.   [41] Woolf, *Essays*, iii. 387.

Woolf's terms, 'moments'. Later, in 'The Lighthouse', Lily contrasts the idea of the moment—'little daily miracles, illuminations, matches struck unexpectedly in the dark'—with the idea of a single great revelation (175–6). In the manuscript version of this passage, Woolf develops a more elaborate metaphor of illumination, drawing on new theories of matter. The passage is heavily revised, and contains many alternative phrases in apposition, such that their exact grammatical relations are not clear, but crucial phrases may be isolated. A moment 'could be held in the fingers'; it threw out its meaning 'like radium', and could be stored in a jar, 'throwing out light heat colour'; life consists of a 'succession' of moments like 'stepping stones'. Certain 'sights & memories' have 'the power of radium': this appears to be associated with a power of 'life' (though Woolf deleted the word), or with a 'creative' power, the power 'to accumulate & shed light'.[42] Though Woolf's stepping stones are not far removed from Wordsworth's 'spots of time', which have a 'fructifying' virtue, Woolf's conceptualization of the moment in metaphors of matter externalizes the psychological process. Although this passage did not appear in the final version, the ideas she explored there remained important to her: in one of her early plans for 'The Moths' (*The Waves*), she envisaged 'islands of light' in the 'stream' of life.[43]

The sudden transformation of the people on the lawn deepens our understanding of Lily's artistic processes: her vision consists, in part, of a process of X-raying. She quite explicitly sees Charles Tansley's character as if it were an 'X-ray photograph'; his 'desire to break into the conversation' is the bone that lies beneath the flesh of social convention (99). If the scene on the lawn becomes simultaneously 'sharp edged' and transparent, that is surely because the flesh has been melted off the world as in an X-ray photograph. Lily's artistic process consists, in part, of a process of X-raying, reducing realistic representations to forms which can be accommodated within her post-impressionist aesthetic. A mother and child are reduced into 'a triangular purple shape' without 'irreverence' (58–9). Although at the turn of the century X-ray photography was a sensational spectacle on a par with the cinematograph, the two were taken to lend support to opposing aesthetics: the one, an

---

[42] Woolf, *To the Lighthouse: The Original Holograph Draft*, transcribed and ed. Susan Dick (Toronto: University of Toronto Press, 1982), 294.

[43] Woolf, entry for 28 May 1929, *Diary*, iii. 229.

aesthetic of surface texture and detail, the other, an aesthetics requiring 'the elimination of materiality and opacity and the cult of invisibility, silence, and transparent things'.[44]

The idea of transparency also enters into Mrs Ramsay's vision. As she goes upstairs at the end of the dinner party, she tries to clear away the 'chatter and emotion' and reach something more permanent. This she achieves by thinking of the continuity of the generations, focused, of course, by the idea of marriage. This affects her sense of the house's physical fabric:

she felt . . . that community of feeling with other people which emotion gives as if the walls of partition had become so thin that practically . . . it was all one stream, and chairs, tables, maps, were hers, were theirs, it did not matter whose, and Paul and Minta would carry it on when she was dead.[45]

Woolf continues to draw upon the idea of permeable matter in her most unanimist novel, *The Waves*. Interestingly, though, the most explicit examples are associated not with a celebration of unanimism, but with an ontological insecurity, concerning both the being of the self and of objects in the world. In his summing up, Bernard confesses that he has begun 'to doubt the fixity of tables, the reality of here and now, to tap my knuckles smartly on the edges of apparently solid objects and say, "Are you hard?"' He has lost the 'thin hard shell' around the soul, the snail's shell which symbolizes the public self throughout the novel, and which may be seen as roughly equivalent to Aaron's 'passport' description.[46] A similar insecurity about solidity affects Rhoda, who feels that she may fall through the surface of the world at any moment. Eddington had by this time published his vivid account of the porous nature of matter, the threshold scene, in its best-known form:

I am standing on a threshold about to enter a room. It is a complicated business . . . I must make sure of landing on a plank travelling at twenty miles a second round the sun—a fraction of a second too early or too late, the plank would be miles away. The plank has no solidity of substance. To step on it is like stepping on a swarm of flies. Shall I not slip through?[47]

---

[44] Tsivian, 'Media Fantasies', 87.   [45] Woolf, *To the Lighthouse*, 123.

[46] Woolf, *Waves*, 221–2.

[47] Eddington, *Physical World*, 342. The similarity to *The Waves* is also discussed by Beer, *Open Fields*, 170–2, and *Virginia Woolf: The Common Ground* (Edinburgh: Edinburgh University Press, 1996), 121–2.

The resemblance to Woolf's novel is remarkable, but Eddington is by no means the sole progenitor. Bernard's table derives from a long line of philosophical tables, the most important of which is Bertrand Russell's. Russell had noted in 1912 that his table was, according to science, 'a vast collection of electric charges in violent motion', and like Bernard had rapped his table with his knuckles as one test (though an inadequate one) of its continuing reality.[48] In *The Waves*, the particular phrase dates from the last stage of revision: in the second draft, completed in February 1931, Bernard doubts fixity and reality, but does not submit the table to an experimental test.[49] However, the lateness of this interpolation need not imply that Woolf had discovered the idea only after February 1931. In November 1929, she had expressed doubts about the substantiality of her fictional creations, fearing that when she had discovered something interesting, she had 'no quite solid table on which to put it'.[50] For Woolf the late interpolation represents a return of those doubts and of the associated image, rather than a new discovery. The drafts of *The Waves* do not in themselves allow us to track Woolf's scientific learning: her knowledge of the non-solid table may date back to Russell's *Problems of Philosophy* or before.[51]

Though insubstantial matter gives rise to ontological insecurities, the novel hints that solidity can be equally oppressive. Louis expresses his security in his identity as a businessman in terms of solid matter, loving 'the table and its sharp edge' (128), his 'desk of solid mahogany' (168) just as he loves the punctuality of seeing 'Mr Prentice at four; Mr Eyres sharp at four-thirty' (128). It is clear, though, that the creation of such meticulous patterns of order is Louis's compensatory response to his insecurity, and in a novel that dissolves sharp edges and provides no exact dates or times, such patterns are implicitly subject to criticism. Being 'half in love' (127) with the routines of office life is close to being, in Keats's phrase, 'half in love with easeful death'. When the sharp edges belong to the self, they prevent the merging of the group into unanimism. 'There

[48] Russell, *The Problems of Philosophy*, 6, 13.

[49] Woolf, *The Waves: The Two Holograph Drafts*, ed. J. W. Graham (London: Hogarth, 1976), 726.

[50] Woolf, diary entry for 5 Nov. 1929, *Diary*, iii. 264.

[51] Ann Banfield's *The Phantom Table: Woolf, Fry, Russell and the Epistemology of Modernism* (Cambridge: Cambridge University Press, 2000), came to my attention too late to be taken into consideration.

is always somebody', complains Neville, 'when we come together, and the edges of meeting are still sharp, who refuses to be submerged' (163).

This ambivalence about the solidity of matter becomes one of the organizing principles of the self for each of the characters in *The Waves*: their selves oscillate between a porous, diffuse state and a hard, focused, particular one. This pattern has been associated with the wave / particle duality of the 'new' quantum theories of the mid 1920s.[52] While there are certainly some suggestive similarities, a retrospect of Woolf's earlier novels reveals that Woolf had developed many aspects of her own wave/particle model of the self in anticipation of the physicists.

The scientific basis of the dualism derived from Planck's quantum theory, which led scientists to ask how large a quantum of light must be. As Eddington states, it must be simultaneously large enough to fill the largest object glass of any existing telescope—at that time, a hundred inches across—and yet small enough to enter an atom.[53] It must be, then, simultaneously a wave and a particle. Subsequent theories attempted to resolve the dualism. In Schrödinger's theory, the universe is filled with a rippling sub-aetheric medium. The ripples are themselves undetectable, but when several ripples combine to form a particularly large disturbance—what Eddington refers to as a 'stormy area'—it can be recognized as matter, in particular, as an electron.[54] This theory has a general similarity to one that had long been advanced by the ether physicists. Joseph Larmor had suggested in 1900 that the 'points of strain in the aether' could move through it much as a knot could slip along a rope; Oliver Lodge expounded this idea in his 'Ether and Reality' broadcasts as if it were still current.[55] On such a theory, matter is a deformation of an otherwise imperceptible medium. Although this theory of matter did not in itself make reference to waves, one of the principal functions of the ether in nineteenth-century theory was to provide a medium for the undulations of light-waves.

Eddington anticipated that it was possible to misunderstand the Schrödinger theory by assimilating it to ether physics, and in his

---

[52] Judith Killen, 'Virginia Woolf in the Light of Modern Physics' Ph. D. thesis (University of Louisville, Kentucky, 1984), 99–102.

[53] Eddington, *Physical World*, 200–1. [54] Ibid., 211.

[55] Larmor, *Ether and Matter* (Cambridge: Cambridge University Press, 1900), quoted in Kenneth F. Schaffner, *Nineteenth-Century Aether Theories* (Oxford: Pergamon, 1972), 217–18; Lodge, *Ether and Reality*, 94.

account he emphasized that Schrödinger's waves were not waves of actual imperceptible stuff, but waves of probability existing in a virtual 'configuration space'.[56] Thus, an 'extended stormy area' in the Schrödinger theory does not represent diffused matter, but represents 'one particle which is equally likely to be anywhere'.[57]

Although the discussion has moved from atoms to electrons, the same possibilities for exchange between scientific and literary discourse exist: Jeans's comparison of electron-waves to suicide-waves brings out the connection of modern statistical physics to statistics as the nineteenth-century science of the state; the electron comes to represent the individual.[58] The 'electrons' of *The Waves* frequently express anxiety about 'particularity', mostly the particularity that language imposes on experience. For Bernard, the phrase 'love of Percival' is 'too small, too particular a name' to describe the 'width and spread' of their feelings (95), while for Neville, his own name represents the 'narrow limits' of his life, not the widespread 'net' of his self (164). As the characters gather in a restaurant to mark Percival's departure, the arrival of Jinny seems to create an acceptable kind of particularity: 'She stands in the door. Everything seems stayed. . . . She seems to centre everything; round her tables, lines of doors, windows, ceilings, ray themselves, like rays round the star in the middle of a smashed window-pane. She brings things to a point, to order' (90). When she moves again, the wave-like existence returns, and 'all the rays ripple and flow and waver over us' (90). It seems that Percival has a similar effect, bringing, says Neville, 'solidity' (91). This solidity is a quality of the united group, and is won at the expense of the solidity of any individual member: he makes them aware that attempts to say '"I am this, I am that"' are false (103). The exact effect of Percival is unclear: at one point Bernard says that his arrival makes the group believe in their own endurance (92), yet shortly afterwards he acknowledges that the thing they have made by coming together is 'not enduring' (95). However, such inconsistencies can readily be explained in psychological terms—the belief in endurance being a transient expression of youthful optimism, for example—and is not central to a consideration of Woolf's relation to scientific discourse. When Bernard recalls the Hampton Court reunion, and recalls the dissolution of the group, he compares it to a wave breaking (214). In Eddington's terms, a stormy area, the

---

[56] Eddington, *Physical World*, 219.   [57] Ibid., 214.
[58] Jeans, *Mysterious*, 122.

particle formed by the united group, subsides into imperceptible flatness. This account goes some way to explaining the relevance of the vision around which Woolf shaped the novel, the fin in a waste of waters. The fin represents actuality in the midst of probability, a discontinuous particularity which develops from and subsides back into the continuous medium.

Woolf might also seem inconsistent in the extensions she makes of the idea of the wave and the particle. Elsewhere in *The Waves*, the idea of widespread phenomena gathering to a point is used to describe time: 'This drop falling is time tapering to a point. Time, which is a sunny pasture covered with a dancing light, time, which is widespread as a field at midday, becomes pendant' (141). Like Lawrence, Woolf seems to have detected the potential for playing on 'field', or to have been led towards a scientific vocabulary by a pastoral one. Although she extends the wave/particle duality so that it refers to time, this does not in itself sever her discourse from Schrödinger or from the new physics.

However, any attempt to make too close an identification of Woolf's discourse with Schrödinger's is disrupted by the counterclaims of other scientific discourses. Firstly, magnetism. The six speakers of *The Waves* often characterize their 'open', nonparticular state as something that endows them with 'filaments' or 'fibres': one filament connects Bernard to Neville (66), another represents shared memories (93), while another represents hyperaesthetic nerves, bringing sounds from far away (101). That these 'filaments' could also be associated with spider's webs or telephone lines is less of a difficulty than their association with the idea of fields of force in magnetic theory. Lodge describes magnetism thus: 'We pull out infinitesimal lines of force and make them extend across perceptible space . . . If we liken the lines of force to elastic threads, they are elastic threads of infinitesimal length, capable of being stretched ad libitum, without limit; the lines never snap, nor do they ever shrink up into absolute nothingness.'[59] If Woolf learned science from broadcasts, she may as easily have heard Lodge's anachronisms as Eddington's up-to-date accounts.

Similarly, the idea that Jinny brings the diffuse group to a 'point' has an antecedent in *Mrs Dalloway*, in the scene of Clarissa at her dressing table. Clarissa, aware of the passage of time as a series of

---

[59] Lodge, *Ether and Reality*, 109.

drops, attempts to transfix the moment, 'collecting the whole of her at one point', creating a self which is 'pointed', 'dartlike' and 'definite'.[60] This passage is consistent with the model of the self seen in *Jacob's Room*—the construction of a social mask around a more diffuse interior—and with the models seen in *The Waves*. But Schrödinger's theory could not have been an influence on *Mrs Dalloway*. Not only does the composition of this passage predate the development of the new quantum theories, but it has an equally plausible antecedent in Bergson's theory of the self. In Sydney Waterlow's 1912 account, which Woolf might well have known, one's 'mental life' moves between states of contraction and expansion:

At one end of the scale is the state of things that occurs when I react to an imminent danger, as to a sudden blow threatening my eye. Here there is no memory, but a close approximation to pure perception; my mental life is narrowed down to a point and consists solely of a reflex action caused by my brain-process. But normally my mental life is immensely wider than the actions which correspond, point to point, with brain-process. At the other end of the scale is the diffused mental state which, when we merely remember or are sunk in reverie, includes no perception of a present object; and, by a process which he [Bergson] describes as one of dilatation and contraction, our minds range through all the stages between these two extremes.[61]

The probability of a particle can also range between these extremes. The counter claim of Bergsonian discourse does not altogether eliminate Schrödinger from the mixture of discourses to be found in *The Waves*, but it suggests that in discovering Schrödinger (assuming that she did), Woolf attempted to synthesize his ideas with those of more familiar thinkers, assimilating his ideas to theirs, but also reinterpreting theirs in the light of his. By a similar process, Woolf's vision of the fin in the waste of waters—meaningless in itself—was given some sort of intellectual context by Eddington's imagery of 'stormy regions' in the sub-aetheric sea. Each phase of this development requires the author to 'mythologize' the system of thought and imagery, in order to recognize its underlying metaphorical system, and to discard its factual content.[62] However, such a 'thinking

[60] Woolf, *Mrs Dalloway*, 40.

[61] Waterlow, 'The Philosophy of Henri Bergson', *Quarterly Review*, no. 430 (Jan. 1912), 152–76.

[62] My terminology here is indebted to Veronica Forrest-Thomson, 'Poetry as Knowledge: The Use of Science by Twentieth-Century Poets', Ph.D. thesis (University of Cambridge, 1971), 64–5, 120–5.

through' is not achieved by a detached autonomous subject, but by a subject which is also rethinking itself. In August 1922, Woolf reimagined her self in Bergsonian terms, the occasion being, appropriately enough, a visit from Sydney Waterlow: his presence forced her to become 'Virginia', 'very, very concentrated, all at one point' at a time when she would have preferred to have been 'merely a sensibility', 'scattered & various and gregarious'.[63]

In *The Years*, Woolf returns to the idea of the 'walls of partition' expressed in *To the Lighthouse*, the walls in this case being the walls of Victorian patriarchy. While the associations of the original title 'The Pargiters' with 'pargetting'—whitewashing and concealment—may seem far removed from the world of modern physics, they introduce the idea that the solidity of a partition is a deceptive appearance. The novel's narrative of liberation is chiefly symbolized by the raising of blinds and the opening of doors, but Woolf supports these symbols with more subtle references to the nature of matter. In 1908, Eleanor considers her lack of education:

But what vast gaps there were, what blank spaces, she thought leaning back on her chair, in her knowledge! How little she knew about anything. Take this cup for instance; she held it out in front of her. What was it made of? Atoms? And what were atoms, and how did they stick together? The smooth hard surface of the china with its red flowers seemed to her for a second a marvellous mystery.[64]

One of Woolf's techniques for compression in *The Years* is to juxtapose a character's internal question with an apparently unrelated external visual image, and to leave the reader to decide how the image prompts or answers the question. The present example is a variant: Eleanor's 'leaning back on her chair' is relevant, but the real answer to her question comes in the very characterization of her knowledge. Its being composed of 'vast gaps' and 'blank spaces' leads towards Rutherford's conception of the atom as mostly empty space. In the words of an earlier Hogarth Press novel, perhaps these atoms are only 'masquerading' as solidity.[65] If the chair is relevant, it is because of the philosophical tradition of referring to everyday domestic objects in discussions of matter and reality: as Russell points out in the introduction to *The ABC of Atoms*, tables and

[63] Woolf, diary entry for 22 Aug. 1922, *Diary*, ii. 193.
[64] Woolf, *The Years* (1937; Harmondsworth: Penguin, 1968), 126.
[65] Sylva Norman, *Nature Has No Tune* (London: Hogarth, 1929), 339.

chairs 'seem to present an unbroken surface', and we think 'that if there were too many holes the chairs would not be safe to sit on'.[66] While a collocation merely of 'chair' and 'atom' would not point with any great certainty to popular science, the phrase 'blank spaces' provides decisive additional support.

Eleanor's attribution of the china's hardness to its surface relates her questions about matter back to the question of pargetting, and to the family masquerade. Her question about how atoms 'stick together', with its implication that cohesion is somehow miraculous, might have been a surprising one in 1908: only more recently have we become accustomed to the idea that solid atoms contain vast quantities of energy. But if we read this as a displaced question about her family and its ability to 'stick together', it seems altogether more natural: as Martin later realizes, the Pargiters are 'boxed up together, telling lies' (239). Eleanor's question is ambiguous—'sticking together' could refer to the unity of the subatomic particles that form an atom, or of many atoms forming a tangible piece of matter—but within the Pargiter family, this ambiguity is of secondary importance. The first possibility is more suggestive, in that the break up of the atom would liberate the repressed energies of the Pargiter children. In this context, it is suggestive that in 1932 Woolf recalled a discussion of prison reform alongside one about the break up of the atom.[67] For as long as the Pargiter family atom sticks together, it imprisons the Pargiter children.

Thinking about atoms allows Eleanor to displace questions about her family into an emotionally neutral discourse, while allowing Woolf to inscribe historical ironies into Eleanor's questions. The reader who knows that atoms contain 'vast gaps' may well expect the Pargiter family to mutate or break up in some way. They may also be inclined to reassess metaphors of knowledge, and to question whether the solidity of 'solid' knowledge cannot itself become confining. As Jo Shapcott, or her 'Mad Cow', puts it: 'Most brains are too / compressed. You need this spongy / generosity to let the others in.'[68]

The later chapters of *The Years* confirm and develop this association of matter with barriers to the self. In 1917, Eleanor again projects the nature of society onto the nature of objects:

[66] Russell, *ABC of Atoms*, 7.

[67] Woolf, diary entry for 8 May 1932, *Diary*, iv. 96.

[68] Jo Shapcott, 'The Mad Cow Talks Back', in *Phrase Book* (Oxford: Oxford University Press, 1992), 41.

A little blur had come round the edges of things. It was the wine; it was the war. Things seemed to have lost their skins; to be freed from some surface hardness; even the chair with its gilt claws, at which she was looking, seemed porous; it seemed to radiate out some warmth. (310)

This description is developed in the 'Present Day' chapter, where 'An edge of light surrounded everything . . . Even the little red brick villas on the high roads had become porous' (329). While an object could have been said to 'radiate' warmth long before the discovery of radiation and X-rays, the term 'porous' suggests that a particular kind of radiation is intended.[69] That physical objects have 'lost their skins' suggests that Eleanor, like a saner version of Septimus, can now see them with X-ray vision. That Woolf emphasizes the oddity of 'even' the chair with gilt claws becoming porous suggests that it, like the later 'red brick villas' is a symbol of middle-class respectability; one might also recall that in *The Invisible Man*, the parts of a cat which could not be rendered invisible were its tapetum and its claws.[70]

The Years shows Woolf thinking through the implications of atomic theory and incorporating them within a larger mythology more consistently than in any of her other novels. However, had this consistency not been combined with artistic tact, and had the scientific ideas obtruded in the texture of the novel to the extent that they do in this reading, the very authority of science would raise difficulties. The danger is not the danger of 'mentalism', the belief that the external world, and hence the socio-political world, is merely a mental construct.[71] This danger is relevant to the descriptionist tradition from Mach to Eddington, and to *The Waves*, but *The Years*, while adopting the new physics' view of matter as porous, is ostensibly committed to it as something external to the self. Rather, the danger lies in aligning a particular state of society with a scientific idea that appears to be natural and inevitable. Such an alignment is politically conservative, even when the state of society might itself seem 'progressive'. The only explicit allusion to the nature of matter in Woolf's final novel treats more satirically the claims of science, and the claims which are based on scientific authority. As the audience of Miss La Trobe's play disperses, a voice remarks: 'It's odd that science, so they tell me, is making things (so

---

[69] Eddington, *Physical World*, 1.   [70] Wells, *The Invisible Man*, 87.
[71] Beer, *Virginia Woolf*, 122–3.

to speak) more spiritual . . . The very latest notion, so I'm told, is, nothing's solid . . . There, you can get a glimpse of the church through the trees . . .'[72] It would be possible, of course, to align the 'thinning' of discourse seen in these sentences, the lack of a solid argument, with the thinning of matter, but Woolf's satire seems directed elsewhere. Popular science writers have always been tempted to interpret scientific ideas in religious terms, and there have always been a number who have resisted this temptation. Even a noted atheist like Bertrand Russell raised the question of whether 'the Creator' would have made a rational or irrational universe, though he very pointedly declined to answer it. The conflict between the religious and the atheistic conceptions of popular science was sharpened by responses to Eddington—not only the 'Science and Mysticism' chapter of *The Nature of the Physical World*, but also his Swarthmore Lecture, *Science and the Unseen World*—and to Jeans's final chapter of *The Mysterious Universe*. While many continued to argue that science was becoming more spiritual, there was no shortage of critics insisting on a separation of the disciplines. As one Cambridge philosopher had said in 1929, 'You cannot turn matter into spirit by making it thin.'[73] The voice in *Between the Acts* implicitly compares the porosity of matter to the thinness of the trees: in each case, we get a glimpse of the church. There may be a concealed pun on the Greek *hyle* ('matter', 'wood'), but this does not redeem the underlying banality of the observation. The single word 'there' becomes brilliantly and satirically dialogic, blending the gestural ('look there'), the consolatory ('there, there') and the pseudo-logical ('At that point or stage in an argument'). Each meaning undermines the others. Drawing on extra-textual sources, we can also recognize that the 'thinness' of matter was in fact no longer 'the latest notion', but was rather more a distraction from the imminent war. In a novel that is sceptical about the claims of authority, Woolf indicates her scepticism about the scope of scientific authority.

[72] Woolf, *Between the Acts* (1941), ed. Gillian Beer (London: Penguin, 1992), 118.
[73] quoted by Needham, 'Biology and Modern Physics', *The New Adelphi*, 2 (Mar.–May 1929), 286–8 (p. 288).

6
Simultaneity:
A Return Ticket to Waterloo

New technologies not only affect the material circumstances of our lives, but they introduce new metaphors by which we live. Through these metaphors, new technologies can change our relationship to concepts as abstract as space and time, and phenomena as intangible as the velocity of light. At some point in the early twentieth century, the concept of simultaneity changed: to say that two events were simultaneous was no longer to say that they happened at the same time, with reference to an absolute framework of space and time, but to say that they were perceived simultaneously. Because all phenomena are perceived through a material medium, and because even the fastest possible medium, light, has a finite velocity, no event reaches our senses at the instant of its happening. That light has a finite velocity had been known since 1675, but Einstein's Special Theory of Relativity placed it at the centre of scientific theory, and the publicity surrounding the theory brought it to the attention of many for the first time. The simplest story one could tell here would be that Einstein's Special Theory influenced modernist conceptions of space and time. The problem with this story is that modernist writers were treating space and time in unusual ways many years before they had heard of Einstein, and in some cases, years before Einstein had published his theory. The purpose of this chapter then, is to explore a more complex story: one in which Einstein is important, but in which Einsteinian accounts of simultaneity are placed in comparison with technological innovations and the metaphors they made possible.

The metaphors occasioned by technology are very often deeply embedded, and only occasionally rise to the surface. Their 'depth' is no guarantee of profundity. When, in Lawrence's *The Lost Girl*, the heroine Alvina feels that time passed 'like an express train', the metaphor is not particularly striking, nor would it have seemed so in 1920.[1] However, it registers a set of deep assumptions about time—its externality and its pace—which are significant for life in the early twentieth century. When, in the same novel, Lawrence invokes telecommunication technology, the effect is altogether more interesting. Early in the story, Alvina begins a relationship with a medic called Alexander Graham, who soon completes his studies and returns to his homeland, Australia. Alvina feels ambivalent about him, at times feeling him to be her inferior, and at time feeling intense attraction to his 'potent and magical' qualities. At these times, 'she wished with all her force that she could travel like a cablegram to Australia'.[2] She cannot, of course, but the simile indicates how far technological innovations can reach: it is not simply a case of a historically unchanging human self being offered new ways of extending itself, but of the self being offered new metaphors for self-conceptualization. These are not absolutely new: in so far as Alvina imagines her self as a fast-moving, disembodied thing, she has not broken with the tradition of thinking of the self as roughly equivalent to the soul, within a dualistic view of the soul/body. Nevertheless, to conceptualize the self as information passing along a wire is to break significantly with Christian tradition, and to gesture towards a science-fiction world. The name of the man, Alexander Graham, hints at the telephone pioneer Alexander Graham Bell, implying in a more light-hearted way that, by 1920, distance and travel could no longer be understood without reference to the technology that had been established for about seventy years.

Telegraphy allowed the Victorians to think about space and time in new ways. For a writer at the start of the twenty-first century, the apparent newness of the 'world wide web' may obscure the extent to which the Victorians had created a global communications network; thinking of the telegraph as the 'Victorian Internet' partially redresses the balance, though at the risk of obscuring the different power interests which created the two media.[3] The Victorian

---

[1] Lawrence, *The Lost Girl* (1920), ed. John Worthen (Cambridge: Cambridge University Press, 1981), 32.

[2] Ibid., 24.

[3] My main sources are Jeffrey Kieve, *The Electric Telegraph: A Social and Economic History* (Newton Abbott: David and Charles, 1973), and Carolyn Marvin, *When Old Technologies Were New: Thinking About Electric Communications in the Late Nineteenth Century* (Oxford: Oxford University Press, 1988); Tom Standage's *The Victorian Internet* (London: Weidenfeld and Nicolson, 1998) derives most of its historical information from Kieve, and is significant only for its title. Stephen Kern also includes

telegraph network was first established in close association with the railways, and grew to serve financial and imperial interests. The first practical trials of telegraphs were made in 1837 by the London and Birmingham Railway, and in 1843 lines were laid from London Paddington station to Slough.[4] By August 1850 the first cross-channel cable from London to Paris had been installed; it was short-lived, but was replaced by a more durable cable in September 1851. By November 1851 the new cable was being used to link the London and Paris stock markets. By August 1858 the first transatlantic cable had been laid; it too was short-lived. By the time a successor was installed, in July 1866, cables had been laid in other directions, most notably from Britain to India. In 1872 a line was completed from Madras to Australia, thus creating the telegraphic route from Britain to the antipodes which Lawrence's Alvina required. A great deal more could be said about the immense technical difficulties which the telegraphic pioneers needed to overcome, particularly as regards deep undersea cables, but these are not relevant to the conceptual questions of space and time.

The global telegraph network made time travel possible, in two metaphorical senses. Firstly it allowed a person in one country to communicate with someone in a different time zone: indeed, the standardization of time zones in 1884 came about partly because of telecommunication.[5] Secondly, it allowed the metropolis to communicate with its imperial territories, and, as the native inhabitants of these territories were believed to be less fully evolved than their European masters, the filaments of the telegraph led backwards in evolutionary history. As Carolyn Marvin notes, European depictions of the telegraph tended to place Europe at the centre of attention. The instant global communication of news had apparently changed mankind, argued W. Hepworth Dixon, one-time editor of *The Athenaeum*. An event such as the defeat of Napoleon could take place 'in a dozen hours', and, thanks to the telegraph:

in another dozen men are talking in their breathless haste and fever of these great events, not only in Paris and Berlin, but in the mosques of Cairo and in the streets of Arkangel, in the bazars of Calcutta and on the quays of Rio, by the falls at Ottawa, in the market place of San Francisco and in the

telecommunications in his *The Culture of Time and Space 1880–1918*, but tends to under-emphasize differences between telegraphic and physical concepts of space and time.

[4] Kieve, *Electric Telegraph*, 25–37.   [5] Kern, *Culture of Time and Space*, 12.

shops at Sidney [sic] . . . That is drama. All the corners of the earth are joined, kindled, fused.[6]

Even when the process of diffusion was presented from the point of view of the spectator—for example, of the provincial peasant who received international telegraphic news through the medium of the newspaper—the effect was still to unite radically dissimilar lifestyles.[7] Ezra Pound, adopting the new rhetoric of global comparisons, emphasized temporal differences:

It is dawn at Jerusalem while midnight hovers above the Pillar of Hercules. All ages are contemporaneous. It is BC, let us say, in Morocco. The Middle Ages are in Russia. The future stirs already in the minds of the few. This is equally true of literature, where the real time is independent of the apparent . . .[8]

While the difference between Jerusalem and the Pillar of Hercules might at first seem to be the difference of time zones, the later examples make clear that Pound is imagining a difference of distinct evolutionary stages. While the idea of contemporaneity was also realized by such things as anthropological museums and imperial exhibitions, telecommunication connected not only cultures, but individuals.

The ability of the telephone to create incongruous juxtapositions can be registered directly, or, as in Woolf's *Night and Day*, by implication. The telephone in the Hilbery household is one of the modern voices which calls Katharine away from the 'nineteenth century', from her distinguished forebears in general, and her grandfather Richard Alardyce in particular. Its particular form of modernity does not annihilate the past, but recombines its fragments into new wholes. The alcove where the Hilbery telephone is housed 'was a pocket for superfluous possessions', the 'wreckage of three generations.'[9] These include the characteristic imperial traces—'[p]rints of great-uncles, famed for their prowess in the East' and 'Chinese teapots'—alongside the works of Cowper and Scott. 'The thread of sound, issuing from the telephone, was always

---

[6] Dixon's views were quoted or paraphrased in the *Electrical Review* in 1885, quoted in Marvin 199. I have been unable to locate the original.

[7] Nordau, *Degeneration* (London: William Heinemann, 1895), 39; I have discussed this example in more detail in 'Within the Ray of Light', forthcoming in Proceedings of the 1999 Leiden October Conference, to be edited by Valeria Tinkler-Villani (Rodopi).

[8] Pound, *The Spirit of Romance* (London: J. M. Dent: 1910), vi.

[9] Woolf, *Night and Day*, 262.

coloured by the surroundings which received it, so it seemed to Katharine. Whose voice was now going to combine with them, or to strike a discord?' Elsewhere in the novel Mary Datchet employs the familiar global imagery when thinking of her suffragist work, which is assisted significantly by the telephone: she lives at 'the very centre of it all', a centre 'which was constantly in the minds of people in remote Canadian forests and on the plains of India'.[10] Katharine's telephone compresses the global survey into an alcove. This new experience of space and time suggests new forms of writing, anticipatory both of Barthesian intertextuality, in which the text 'is a tissue of quotations drawn from the innumerable centres of culture', but, more importantly, of Woolf's later writings.[11] Crowding round 'the far end of the telephone' is a 'welter of voices', an 'enormous range of possibilities'.[12] Though this range of possible states must collapse into a single actuality when the call is answered, thinking of the telephone exchange is one way of imagining a literary form in which a welter of voices crowd together. As we saw in Chapter 3, the telephone exchange was a common metaphor for the relation of the brain to the nervous system, so such metaphorical pathways were available in scientific literature.

Pure science provided equally striking ways of thinking about space and time. Olaüs Roëmer had shown in 1675 that light has velocity, a fact which became more significant when descriptionists advanced the argument that science consists of the economic arrangement of sense impressions. If the fastest medium of communication, light, is itself finite in speed, our retinal image of the world will never coincide with the world itself. In 1872, the popular science writer Camille Flammarion devised a thought experiment which was to influence generations of other popular writers, not to mention scientists: if we were to look at the earth from a suitably distant planet, we would in theory be able to see the battle of Waterloo happening 'now', in our present moment.[13] An observer moving away from the earth faster than light would be moving deeper and deeper into the earth's past, and would see events reversed, with the battle of Austerlitz occurring before

---

[10] Woolf, *Night and Day*, 38.

[11] Roland Barthes, 'What is an Author?', in David Lodge (ed.), *Modern Criticism and Theory: A Reader* (Harlow: Longman, 1988), 170.

[12] Woolf, *Night and Day*, 263.

[13] Flammarion, *Lumen* (1872), trans. A. A. M. and R. M. (London: William Heinemann, 1897), 89–92.

Waterloo. Henri Poincaré drew on this idea in his discussion of chance and causality.[14] Flammarion was also to explain the nature of light in his *Popular Astronomy*, and though he did not introduce the vivid image of an epoch-making event like Waterloo, he was not reluctant to speak of this physical fact in metaphysical terms: light 'makes the past an eternal present'; it enables 'a transformation of the past into the present'.[15]

The fanciful quality of Flammarion's treatment of light should not be allowed to create an absolute division between popular science and the activity of real scientists. Not only did Poincaré find Flammarion's idea useful in thinking about causality, but it is not entirely dissimilar from the thought-experiment which Einstein set himself as a sixteen-year-old student: if he were to pursue a beam of light at the velocity of light, what would he see? He ought to see 'a spatially oscillating electromagnetic field at rest', but according to 'experience' and Maxwell's equations, there should be no such thing.[16] His theories of relativity were to provide a solution to this paradox.

The feeling that events are never quite the same as their images creates a disturbing sense of belatedness when extended to the self: even if we feel firmly installed within our own bodies, light is always taking images of our bodies away from us. Eddington describes in 1920 how, in a universe that is finite but unbounded, the light rays from a star could travel round the universe and converge again at the starting point: '[t]he ghost of a star appears at the spot where the star was a certain number of million years ago'.[17] If this theory were true—and Eddington expressed caution—the same could be said, in theory, for anything that emits or reflects light. If perceptions never quite coincide with the event, we live among ghostly images of each other. Both the image and the phrase are memorable. When Vita Sackville-West reviewed James Jeans's *The Mysterious Universe* in 1930, she claimed that the 'occasional glimmerings of comprehension' from a difficult book like Jeans's were 'more exciting . . . than the total understanding we get from an easier book':

[14] Poincaré, *Science and Method*, 71. This essay was first published as 'Le hasard', *Revue du Mois*, 3 (1907), 257–77; see also Poincaré's 'Camille Flammarion', *Revue des Revues*, 95 (1912), 217–19.

[15] Flammarion, *Popular Astronomy: A General Description of the Heavens*, trans. J. Ellard Gore (London: Chatto and Windus, 1894), 319, 616–17. First published in French in 1880.

[16] Holton, *Thematic Origins*, 358.

[17] Eddington, *Space, Time and Gravitation*, 161–2.

Thus, if for one second I catch the ghost of an idea of what Einstein may mean by the ghost of a star, returning after its inconceivable journey in light-waves round the universe to its original starting point, I cannot help feeling that I have gained something in the enlarging of my experience which I do not get in reading how Mrs Smith of Croydon or elsewhere squabbled with her husband.[18]

The reader of this review could be forgiven for thinking that Jeans describes such a phenomenon in his best seller, but he does not discuss the structure of the universe. In *Eos* he had talked of seeing 'light which had travelled round the universe', and in *The Universe Around Us* he had explained how light could travel round the universe and 'return to its starting point', but in neither text did he speak of such light as a 'ghost'.[19] Sackville-West had been interested in relativity since at least November 1928, when she reported to Woolf having dreamt that she 'understood space-time'.[20] The quotation from Henry Vaughan which she associated with spacetime— 'I saw eternity the other night / Like a great Ring of pure and endless light'—suggests that she was already familiar with the idea of a curved spacetime, and light travelling round it. Whether she knew Eddington's phrase from reading him directly, or through conversation, and exactly when she first encountered it, are less important for the present argument than the simple fact of transmission, and the significance that Sackville-West creates for the idea: a self imagined like starlight, disembodied and sublime, is more attractive than a self like Mrs Smith's, suburban and mundane.

The idea has exerted a considerable fascination on novelists and poets. Woolf draws upon it in *Night and Day*, in the scene where Katharine Hilbery stares at the night sky in December, looking at the stars much as a literary person would browse in a library, 'pulling out volume after volume'.[21] The comparison establishes the idea that the stars contain records of the past. Katharine, though little interested in the Church, feels that at Christmas time 'the Heavens', 'with immortal radiance' take part in the festival.

---

[18] Vita Sackville-West, 'Books in General', *The Listener*, 4 (19 Nov. 1930), 844.

[19] Jeans, *Eos, or the Wider Aspects of Cosmogony* (London: Kegan Paul, Trench, Trubner, 1928), 16; *The Universe Around Us*, 75.

[20] Sackville-West, letter to Woolf dated 29 Nov. 1929, *The Letters of Vita Sackville-West to Virginia Woolf*, ed. Louise De Salvo and Mitchell A. Leaska (London: Hutchinson, 1984), 312–13.

[21] Woolf, *Night and Day*, 161.

Somehow, it seemed to her that they were even now beholding the procession of kings and wise men upon some road on a distant part of the earth. And yet, after gazing another second, the stars did their usual work upon the mind, froze to cinders the whole of our short human history, and reduced the human body to an ape-like, furry form, crouching amid the brushwood of a barbarous clod of mud.[22]

'[B]eholding' is an interesting word: its inflated register, like that of 'immortal radiance', contributes to the gentle satire on Katharine, not simply by being inflated, but by being shared with some popular astronomy writers. Flammarion writes about the 'observer' of a star seeing its past in his present, but when he waxes metaphysical, his (or his translator's) word choice shifts upwards: 'As the aspect of worlds changes from year to year, from one season to another, and almost from one day to the next, we can represent this aspect as escaping into space and advancing in Infinitude to reveal itself to the eyes of distant beholders.'[23] Whether Woolf learnt of this idea from Flammarion is difficult to determine, though he is a more likely source than an early popularizer of Einstein. Woolf was correcting *Night and Day* in early March 1919, and had taken the manuscript to Gerald Duckworth in April, at which date only one popular account of Einsteinian relativity had appeared.[24]

Two brief allusions to star-gazing in Aldous Huxley's *Antic Hay* (1923) help to tease out the significance of Woolf's scene—the significance being something which may, in 1919, have gone beyond anything Woolf could have intended or known when writing *Night and Day*. Huxley's Mr Coleman refers explicitly to Einstein's reformulation of Newton's laws, and so the reader is prompted to think of relativity when Casimir Lypiatt lies on his bed and imagines himself floating in the 'dark emptiness between the stars'.[25] The finite velocity of light has the effect of self-estrangement: '[f]rom those distant abstract spaces he seemed to be looking impersonally down upon his own body stretched out by the brink of the hideous well; to be looking back over his own history.' Here, although Lypiatt's whole history is simultaneously present to him, the sense of simultaneity as incongruity, which informed Woolf's

---

[22] Ibid., 164.   [23] Flammarion, *Popular Astronomy*, 617.
[24] Woolf, diary entries for 7 March and 2 April 1919, *Diary*, i. 250, i. 261; the popular article was G. W. De Tunzelman's 'Physical Relativity Hypotheses Old and New', *Science Progress*, 13 (Jan. 1919), 475–82.
[25] Huxley, *Antic Hay*, 59, 226.

juxtaposition of Christian and evolutionary history, is not alluded to. In an earlier passage, the effect of incongruity is emphasized. Relaxing from the composition of an advertisement for his Patent Small-Clothes, Theodore Gumbril imagines the world around him: below him in the basement are the cook and the parlourmaid, reading their newspapers; on one side are 'a teeming family of Jews', on the other a 'young journalist and his wife'; beyond the walls are birds sleeping, slum-children playing, and freight ships crossing the Atlantic bringing more cigars. At the centre of this passage is Gumbril's description of the world above: 'the city of models . . . a bedroom, a servant's bedroom, an attic of tanks and ancient dirt, the roof and, after that, two or three hundred light-years away, a star of the fourth magnitude.'[26] The effect of incongruity is transferred from the temporal incongruities of space to the social and personal incongruities of city space. Gumbril's neighbours are as distant from him socially as the star of the fourth magnitude is physically, yet they are also inescapably here and now.

For most writers, the finite velocity of light was an idea first encountered in popularizations of Einstein's theories; and for the minority who knew of it before 1919 (as Woolf probably did), the popularizations would have served as a reminder, and would have given the idea a patina of modernity. However, though new, the idea was easily assimilated to traditional literary metaphors and images: the star as the unattainable; light as God's light. The idea that the past is preserved in travelling light rays gives a new twist to the classical and Renaissance tradition of the stellification of the dead, though, unlike their earlier counterparts, the modern dead never reach a final resting place.[27] This combination of existing traditions and innovative imagery creates a degree of interpretative undecidability. In 1919 and 1920, Wilfrid Wilson Gibson published two pairs of sonnets which took rays of light as their central image.[28] Gibson was certainly in a position to have read about relativity, if we assume that he read the periodicals in which his work appeared: the first pair of sonnets, 'Chambers', appeared in *The Athenaeum* not long after Sullivan had completed his series of expository articles there; the

[26] Huxley, *Antic Hay*, 122.

[27] Alastair Fowler, *Time's Purpled Masquers: Stars and the Afterlife in Renaissance English Literature* (Oxford: Clarendon, 1996), 59–86.

[28] Gibson, 'Chambers', *The Athenaeum* (11 July 1919), 583; 'Windows', *Fortnightly Review*, 113 (Apr. 1920), 570–1. I have discussed these poems in greater detail in 'Within the Ray of Light.'

second, 'Windows', appeared in the *Fortnightly* three months after Lodge's critical article.[29] In the 'Chambers' sonnets, the 'ray of light' is the principle which grants the speaker moments of revelation, opening the chambers of his mind, allowing him glimpses of 'Beauty and terror' at the same time. In keeping with the astronomical tradition, the ray of light brings together the incongruous, but in Gibson's case the incongruity is diminished by the antithetical nature of 'beauty and terror'; it is not the post-colonial clutter of Katharine Hilbery's alcove. In the 'Windows' sonnets, the ray of light has a similar function, though Gibson gives less emphasis to the ray as an internal, psychological principle. In the first of the sonnets the speaker, looking at a sunset through a window in Wales, remembers another window overseas, beneath which a girl was murdered. In the second of the sonnets he tries to reconcile the incongruity. 'If I could live within the ray of light', begins the octave—the ray of light being the principle that reconciles 'things diverse in seeming'—'Then' (begins the sestet) 'might my heart have ease and rest content / On the golden upland under the clear sky'. Though Gibson could not have known it, his thought experiment echoes Einstein's of 1895–6. Though the form of proximity is not identical (travelling alongside in Einstein's case, living within in Gibson's), this ray of light marks a significant departure from the literary tradition: in earlier poets, rays of light were objects of distant sublime contemplation. However, Gibson's dream of resting content on 'the golden upland' belongs to an older tradition of consolatory verse, and if the pastoral landscape is heaven as well as Wales, then the ray of light would appear to be a form of divine illumination. The undecidability of the imagery rests uncomfortably with the strictly logical and deeply conservative form of the sonnet. The pattern of a conditional in the octave ('If') answered by a consequence in the sestet ('then') implies that all questions should be logically resolvable. However, a poem that expresses a wish to reconcile 'things diverse in seeming' may also be aiming to synthesize scientific and religious imagery: Gibson may deserve the benefit of the doubt.

A more extreme, and slightly earlier, case of interpretative undecidability comes in the form of Freud's schizophrenic judge, Dr Daniel Paul Schreber (1842–1911). I am less interested here in the

---

[29] Lodge, 'The Ether Versus Relativity', *Fortnightly Review*, 113 (Jan. 1920), 54–9.

diagnosis which Freud reached from reading Schreber's memoirs, than in the 'thought-structures' that Schreber evolved. Schreber's belief in his vocation as the redeemer of the world, and his belief that God communicated with him, are based on familiar cultural materials. For Schreber, the human soul consists of nerves, 'structures of extraordinary fineness, comparable to the finest thread'.[30] While humans consist of bodies and nerves, God is nothing but nerve. God's nerves have a capacity to intervene in the world, and in this capacity they are known as 'rays'. God communicated with Schreber through these rays. Although the velocity of the rays is not significant for him, his conception of them explicitly condenses the ideas of nerve fibres and light rays, and, as they are vehicles of communication, implicitly includes the idea of telegraphic cables. Furthermore, Schreber's 'rays' borrow from the classical tradition of stellification. When a man dies, the spiritual part of him, his nerves, is purified and reunited with God. Purified souls lose some of their individual consciousness, and are 'fused together with other souls into higher entities.' Schreber explains that 'Important souls, such as those of men like Goethe, Bismarck, etc., may have to retain their sense of identity for hundreds of years to come,' before being 'resolved into higher soul-complexes'.[31] Schreber's souls are less concerned than Einstein to watch the light ray as it travels, but like Gibson, they live within it, closer than the conventional observer.

If the religious tradition created one important precedent for the imagery of starlight, then the immediate circumstances of the postwar period made Flammarion's example of the battle of Waterloo particularly resonant. Many popularizers adopted it. Edwin Slosson adopted it directly in 1920; Charles Nordmann substituted the battle of the Marne, and Maurice Maeterlinck used the marriage of Napoleon III.[32] In 1920 H. H. Turner, Professor of Astronomy at Oxford, touched more directly than anyone else on its contemporary relevance. Because of the finite speed of light, he wrote, 'our universe is not co-existent: the past close around us belongs to the peaceful present, but the nearest star is still in the midst of the late

[30] Freud, 'Psychoanalytic Notes on an Autobiographical Account of a Case of Paranoia' (1911), in *Pelican Freud Library* (Harmondsworth: Penguin, 1979), ix. 129–223 (p. 152).

[31] Freud, 'Psychoanalytic Notes', 154.

[32] Edwin Slosson, *Easy Lessons in Einstein*, 42–5; Charles Nordmann, *Einstein and the Universe*, trans. Joseph McCabe (London: T. Fisher Unwin, 1922), 76 (first published in French in 1921); Maeterlinck, *The Life of Space*, 153.

War'.[33] The effect of simultaneity makes the past seem incongruously present. Though this may imply, troublingly or even terrifyingly, that we can never escape the past, it also sublimates the terrors of war, placing them at a comfortable distance, light-years away. It is a less troubling reminder of the war than, for example, 'All the legless soldiers grinding barrel-organs, all the hawkers of toys stamping their leaky boots in the gutters of the Strand.'[34]

The ray of light can function as a token not only of memory, but also of an individual's relation to posterity. Its function in relation to memory may be illustrated simply by reference to Murry's *The Things We Are*, where the central character Boston experiences a memory in a 'long trembling shaft of light'.[35] Memory becomes something externalized, objective, a feature of the physical world rather than the mind. Its use to anticipate posterity is less common, but occupies an important place in Woolf's *To the Lighthouse*. The first part of the novel, 'The Window', revolves around questions of personal and professional legacies: Mrs Ramsay's asking 'what have I done with my life', and her awareness that 'children never forget'; Mr Ramsay's pondering the importance of his contribution to philosophy. Lily Briscoe, looking at the distant view of the sand dunes, feels it outlasts the gazer 'by a million years', and seems 'to be communing already with a sky which beholds an earth entirely at rest'; as in *Night and Day*, 'beholding' is the phrase of choice, though the word seems less laden with satirical intent.[36] For the sky to behold the earth 'at rest' implies a Flammarion-like being who can travel away from the earth at the speed of light. This is not the only possibility—the phrase might imply that, on account of entropy, the universal machine has ground to a halt—but light rays are the most likely solution. Not least because of the lighthouse, the novel is haunted by rays of light. Mrs Ramsay imagines her own life at rest, as something laid out before her for inspection, 'a little strip of time . . . her fifty years'.[37] Mr Ramsay invokes the same stellar perspective as Lily: he considers his achievement as if he were looking from a mountain top down at the 'long wastes of the ages', from which vantage point he can see 'the perishing of stars'. He asks what would survive of him: 'His own little light would shine, not very

[33] Turner, 'Introduction' to Erwin Freundlich, *The Foundations of Einstein's Theory of Gravitation* (Cambridge: Cambridge University Press, 1920), p. xi.

[34] Huxley, *Antic Hay*, 62.   [35] Murry, *The Things We Are*, 58–9.

[36] Woolf, *To the Lighthouse*, 25.   [37] Ibid., 66.

brightly, for a year or two, and would then be merged in some bigger light, and that in a bigger still. (He looked into the darkness, into the intricacy of the twigs.)'[38] Mr Ramsay desires a modern form of stellification, to become a star in the philosophical firmament; the idea that his light will become absorbed within that of a greater soul is curiously like Dr Schreber's. The modern star, though, is not fixed: not only because of the expanding universe (which does not immediately concern us), but because its light too is constantly travelling. If the twigs evoke an essentially optimistic metaphor, in which every branch and root contributes its small part to an enduring intellectual organism, it is a metaphor implicitly posed against one of the individual contribution as an entirely isolated ray of light, travelling through a lonely cosmos.

Questions about posterity naturally raise the question of whether we can know the future. To imagine one's history as a ray travelling to a destination presents the possibility that one might overtake the ray and contemplate the destination. Though physically such a process is impossible, according to Einstein, the ubiquitous metaphor of travel makes it all too easy to imagine. The question Woolf asks while writing *To the Lighthouse*—'But what is to become of these diaries'—exactly echoes (or anticipates) Mrs Ramsay's question 'But what have I done with my life?'[39] It seems that Woolf's question about her own posterity was prompted by a dinner the previous evening, at which her companions discussed 'how if Einstein is true, we shall be able to foretell our own lives'. Though Woolf considered the argument to be 'passing my limits', the diary preserves a fragment of a culture in which scientific ideas and unscientific speculations were frequently discussed.[40]

These instances of imagery would not be so significant were it not that they are so appropriate to the form of *To the Lighthouse*. The ray of light in Murry's novel is significant as an archaeological fragment, contributing to a larger literary and intellectual history, but it bears the same tenuous relation to Murry's conventional novel as Gibson's imagery did to his conventional poems. *To the Lighthouse* is constructed around visual images, some remembered, some perceived, all

---

[38] Woolf, *To the Lighthouse*, 41.
[39] Woolf, diary entry for 20 Mar. 1926, *Diary*, iii. 67.
[40] Ibid., iii. 68. Present were Clive Bell, Roger Fry, and Lord Ivor Churchill: see letter to Vita Sackville-West, 29 Mar. 1926, *The Letters of Virginia Woolf*, ed. Nigel Nicolson, asst. by Joanne Trautmann Banks, 6 vols. (London: Hogarth, 1975–80), iii. 250.

with a sharpness of outline as clear as the pictures that James cuts out of the Army and Navy catalogue. Mr Bankes associates Ramsay's decision to marry with the image of a hen protecting its young, and associates Mrs Ramsay with a hotel being built at the back of his house; Lily associates Mr Ramsay's work with the image of a 'scrubbed kitchen table', cut out of context and placed, like an object in a surrealist collage, in the branches of a tree; Mrs Ramsay answers the question of what she has done with her life by looking at the plates arranged on the table. Lily sums up 'marriage' in the epiphanic image of 'a man and a woman looking at a girl throwing a ball'.[41] This instance is particularly important, not only because the narrator (or Lily) explains the process by which images acquire temporary symbolic significance, but also because of the trajectory of the girl's ball:

there was a sense of things having been blown apart, of space, of irresponsibility as the ball soared high, and they followed it and lost it and saw the one star and the draped branches . . . Then, darting backwards over the vast space (for it seemed as if solidity had vanished altogether), Prue ran full tilt into them and caught the ball brilliantly high up in her left hand, and her mother said, 'Haven't they come back yet?' whereupon the spell was broken.

The novel cuts out sharply remembered moments from the flux of time, and sends them out into space. Eventually they return. If the question of 'The Window' is 'what will become of me?', the question of 'The Lighthouse' is the one with which Lily opens it: 'What does it mean then, what can it all mean?'[42] The images return, like the ghosts of stars. In 'Time Passes', Mrs McNab's memories of Mr and Mrs Ramsay are 'faint and flickering, like a yellow beam or the circle at the end of a telescope'.[43] In 'The Window', Lily memorizes her decision to move the tree in her painting by placing the salt cellar on the pattern of a flower in the table cloth; in 'The Lighthouse', the image returns to her.[44] While this form does not break radically with the idea of memory as personal, psychological process, and while the sharp-edged images could be interpreted in Bergsonian terms, the association of memory with rays of light tends to transform it into something impersonal and external.

In *The Waves*, Woolf incorporates starlight imagery still more explicitly. Though its relevance to the novel's form is less direct than

[41] Woolf, *To the Lighthouse*, 79–80. [42] Ibid., 159.
[43] Ibid., 149, see also 152. [44] Ibid., 92, 191.

in the case of *To the Lighthouse*, it rewards examination. In his summing up, Bernard describes how he is surprised both at everyday things—people going about their daily routines of earning a living—and by 'the light of the stars falling, as it falls now, on my hand after travelling for millions upon millions of years'.[45] Though, locally, this image is difficult to interpret, on the larger scale it allows us to gloss remarks made earlier in the novel, during the Hampton Court episode. In a rare moment of direct communication, Susan invites her friends to appreciate a moment of silence and stillness. Jinny and Rhoda echo her thoughts, but Louis draws attention to the continuation of flux, asking them to listen instead 'to the world moving through abysses of infinite space. It roars; the lighted strip of history is past and our Kings and Queens; we are gone; our civilisation; the Nile; and all life.'[46] Louis's idea of history as a strip of light and Bernard's reference to a 'strip of time' gloss Mrs Ramsay's vision of her life as 'a little strip of time', a phrase which might otherwise be more readily associated with knitting than with astronomy. Louis's idea of history is also very close to Flammarion's. Notably, when Flammarion wrote of a succession of moments 'escaping' into space, he imagined them as 'a series of waves bearing from afar the past of worlds'.[47] This image seems particularly close to Louis's sense of his life as a palimpsest of past lives, though it is only one facet of the meaning of 'waves' in the novel in total.

Bernard too reflects on history during the Hampton Court scene, imagining our 'English past' as 'one inch of light', lost in the 'whirling abysses of infinite space'.[48] The idea of simultaneity disrupts sequentiality, revealing it to be a fragile psychological construct, 'a trick of the mind' which puts 'Kings on their thrones, one following another'. It is not merely official history which is threatened by 'this flood' of time: 'Our lives too stream away, down the unlighted avenues, past the strip of time, unidentified.' Indeed, simultaneity combines the public and the personal: the cause of King William III's death (his horse tripping on a molehill) was the same as the cause of Percival's.[49] The battle of Waterloo is not mentioned, but for Neville, 'all depends upon the battle of Blenheim'. Teasingly, too, at the end of the episode, Bernard is clutching a

[45] Woolf, *The Waves*, 206.
[46] Ibid., 173.
[47] Flammarion, *Popular Astronomy*, 617.
[48] Woolf, *The Waves*, 174.
[49] Ibid., 114, 174, 236–37 n.60.

return ticket to Waterloo: the detail is realistically accurate, in that Waterloo would be the usual London station for Hampton Court; but it is also symbolic of the new conception of time and history created by the new physics.[50]

The presence of this astronomical imagery in *The Waves* is undeniable, but its significance is open to question. It lends a form of scientific support to the simultaneity experienced by all three male characters, most notably to Louis and his metempsychotic memories of previous lives. This connection is significant in larger cultural terms, as it suggests that such an association of ideas may have worked for other writers who did not refer explicitly to science in their completed works. Through it we can gloss the simultaneity of works like *The Waste Land* just as we can gloss the phrase 'a little strip of time' in *To the Lighthouse*.

However, *The Waves* does not share exactly the form of simultaneity of those other works. It does not involve the complex mingling of past and present that we find in *Mrs Dalloway*, nor the co-presence of myth and modernity that characterizes *Ulysses* or *The Waste Land*. Although Woolf expresses scepticism about the reality of linear narrative, using Bernard as a mouthpiece, the novel itself is essentially chronological. Bernard mocks the 'happy concatenation of one event following another in our lives', comparing it to the 'knocking of railway trucks in a siding', and associating it both with the lives of 'small shopkeepers' and with the more authoritarian 'boasting boys'.[51] Yet as narrative, *The Waves* moves very smoothly from childhood to death. This is not to deny that the novel's technical innovations create a sense of timelessness. The characters respond to the same perceptual objects, but only rarely do they respond directly to the previous speaker; there is a lack of conventional lexical cohesion between speeches. The narrator possesses only one verb ('said') and six proper names. Taken together, these innovations give the reader the impression that several speeches are occurring simultaneously, though the reader also realizes that time moves forward within episodes and between them. The simultaneity of *The Waves* is heterotopic: like a telephone call, it brings two or more diverse places together in one. The simultaneity of *Mrs Dalloway* and other works of high modernism is heterochronic: it brings together two or more diverse times as if they were

---

[50] Ibid., 175, 180.   [51] Ibid., 179–80.

simultaneous. Heterotopia can create apparent heterochronia, for the reasons considered earlier in relation to telecommunications, but, in spite of Louis's uncertainties about his identity, this effect is minimal in *The Waves*: if evolution is understood as a series of steps, rather than a continuous curve, then all six characters belong to the same evolutionary level. The images of history as a strip of light are relevant only indirectly to the novel's form. If, through their use of this imagery Woolf's characters are commenting on her literary form, they are commenting belatedly on the novels of the 1920s, and not on the novel which they find themselves inhabiting.

What they might have to say about *Mrs Dalloway* would be interesting to know. Though Einstein is explicitly mentioned, the novel does not incorporate the stellar imagery already seen, and so the assistance of external texts is required. That is not to say that the allusion to Einstein is irrelevant. Occurring in connection with the aeroplane that soars over London, it is consistent with the allusions to light seen in *Night and Day* and in *Antic Hay*. In those novels, thinking about starlight created a sense of disembodiment. For the incidental character Mr Bentley, 'vigorously rolling his strip of turf at Greenwich', the aeroplane is a symbol of man's determination 'to get outside his body, beyond his house, by means of thought, Einstein, speculation, mathematics, the Mendelian theory'.[52] Though Mr Bentley might associate Einstein with disembodiment purely because of his reputation as a pure thinker, Woolf, by placing Mr Bentley at Greenwich, and the aeroplane above it, alludes to Einstein's role in changing ideas of space and time. It is a more intelligent, relevant allusion than that in Rose Macaulay's novel *Potterism*, where 'Einstein' betokens that the intellectual standards of the daily newspapers have risen, or Woolf's own in 'A Simple Melody', where he is merely the sort of topic an intense young man would discuss.[53] Though Mr Bentley has seemed to at least one critic to be a symbol of the scientific man, one who would bring Nature into submission, it seems more likely that Woolf intended a contrast between the earth-bound Bentley and the soaring Einstein.[54] As we have seen, a

---

[52] Woolf, *Mrs Dalloway*, 30.

[53] Macaulay, *Potterism: A Tragi-Farcical Tract* (London: Collins, 1920), 231–2; Woolf, *The Complete Shorter Fiction*, 202. I am grateful to Sylvia Vance for drawing my attention to *Potterism*.

[54] For the former opinion, see Allen McLaurin, *Virginia Woolf: The Echoes Enslaved* (Cambridge: Cambridge University Press, 1973), 154, and for the latter, Gillian Beer, *Virginia Woolf*, 162.

sharp evaluative distinction was commonly made in the post-war period between applied and pure science. The representatives of the former in *Mrs Dalloway* are Holmes and Bradshaw, and Mr Bentley's treatment of his turf anticipates their treatment of Septimus Warren Smith.

This favourable and carefully considered allusion authorizes a consideration of simultaneity in *Mrs Dalloway*. It was a formal quality that generates comparisons: one of the novel's earliest readers, Gwen Raverat, compared it to a ballet; more recently, the arrival of Peter Walsh, Sally Seton and other characters at Clarissa's party has been compared to the return of ghosts on All Souls' Day.[55] One may also compare the convergence of the various characters to the convergence of rays of light from diverse sources, each beginning at a different point in space and time, but arriving at the same here-now, London in the middle of June. The advantage of this latter comparison is its comprehensiveness. Not only do people return to London, but memories and visions: Clarissa's memories of Bourton; the singing woman, who seems to have endured since the time when London was a swamp; the image of London as the Romans first saw it, an image which is a double survival, mediated as it is through Conrad's *Heart of Darkness*.[56] The image of simultaneity found in Flammarion's image of the battle of Waterloo, taking place 'now', is particularly appropriate to Septimus's condition: the ghosts of the war keep returning to haunt him. The mixture of peace and war that H. H. Turner identified is adopted by Woolf, with a difference: the images of war have not travelled out to the nearest star, but have curved back on themselves and returned to post-war London. To frame Septimus's hallucinations thus is not to say that they are intended by Woolf to be anything other than psychological phenomena, but it allows us to understand the form of the novel in terms that distance it from Woolf's own episodes of insanity.

Though I wish to emphasize simultaneity as literary form, the idea that starlight travels at finite velocity may also have influenced certain writers' concepts of their literary vocation. Woolf's description of reading James's *What Maisie Knew* is a route into this topic:

---

[55] Gwen Raverat, letter to Virginia Woolf dated 22 Apr. 1925, Monks House Papers, University of Sussex; J. Hillis Miller, '*Mrs Dalloway*: Repetition as the Raising of the Dead', *Fiction and Repetition* (Oxford: Basil Blackwell, 1982), 190.

[56] Woolf, *Mrs Dalloway*, 88–9, 26; Conrad, *Youth, Heart of Darkness, The End of the Tether*, 49.

Maisie . . . can only affect us very indirectly, each feeling of hers being deflected and reaching us after glancing off the mind of some other person. Therefore she rouses in us no simple and direct emotion. We always have time to watch it coming and to calculate its pathway, now to the right, now to the left . . . we hang suspended over this aloof little world and watch with intellectual curiosity for the event.[57]

The vocabulary recalls descriptions of both special and general relativity: Maisie is a ray of light travelling through space, 'deflected' by the gravitational field of the sun; this deflection is the object of a calculation. The distance of Maisie from the reader could equally well be the distance of the author from the text. Light has several qualities which make it an appropriate metaphor for the text. It is an emanation, an expression, yet it has 'escaped' its author, and acquired a kind of aesthetic autonomy. Though it travels very quickly, it does not reach the observer immediately; because of the vast distances referred to in popular astronomy books, one is left with the impression that it moves rather slowly. The text, in other words, does not make an immediate impact.

By this date, D. H. Lawrence had already taken up the astronomical metaphor quite explicitly. For him, stars shared the isolation of human beings.

One is one, but one is not all alone. There are other stars buzzing in the centre of their own isolation. And there is no straight path between them. There is no straight path between you and me, dear reader, so don't blame me if my words fly like dust into your eyes and grit between your teeth, instead of like music into your ears. I am I, but you are you, and we are in sad need of a theory of human relativity . . .[58]

If the reader applies such a theory, says Lawrence, he or she will realize that his words arrive 'strangely changed and travel-worn' having come 'down the long curve of your own circumambient atmosphere'.[59] This model of literary production and reception implies not only a need for readerly flexibility and activity, to compensate for the incommensurable nature of author and reader, but also a licence for the author to be difficult, to write not for immediate consumption, but for a distant posterity.

[57] Woolf, 'Phases of Fiction', *Collected Essays*, ii. 81–2.
[58] Lawrence, *Fantasia of the Unconscious; Psychoanalysis and the Unconscious* (London: Heinemann, 1961), 19.
[59] Lawrence, *Fantasia*, 20.

The analogy I have described between Einsteinian simultaneity and the form of *Mrs Dalloway* could be readily extended to describe *The Waste Land* and other works of high modernism. Indeed, Sullivan's short review of Eliot's poem, which described it as a series of 'flashes', seeks to understand its fragmentariness as an optical phenomenon.[60] These flashes, we may say, extending Sullivan's metaphor, come from radically different sources, some many light years away from Eliot's London, others in close proximity; some from anthropology (and therefore from 'prehistoric' culture), some from the Renaissance, others from Eliot's immediate contemporaries.

However, any attempt to extend the metaphor must confront the ambivalence of British modernist writers, in their critical texts, to the idea of simultaneity. This ambivalence takes the form of outright hostility in several places, most notably in Wyndham Lewis's *Time and Western Man*. The roots of the ambivalence lie in British modernism's complex relation to its continental counterparts, particularly Italian futurism. Simultaneity was a central formal property of Italian Futurist painting and experimental writing. The leader of the futurists, Filippo Marinetti, had declared in 'Geometric and Mechanical Splendor', that one of the 'essential elements' of Futurism's 'new beauty' would be 'the simultaneity that derives from tourism, business and journalism'.[61] His praise elsewhere of 'the beauty of speed' implies that futurist simultaneity derived not simply from the experience of 'tourism', but from the experience of travelling at high speed.[62] The belief that Pound expressed in 1910, that all ages are contemporaneous, might have made him receptive to the futurist vision, but the Futurist attitude to history—'Why should we look back . . . We will destroy the museums'—differs greatly from Pound's Provençal antiquarianism, and from his later attitude. By September 1914 Pound, as a spokesperson for the Vorticist movement, was arguing that the Futurists offered nothing but 'accelerated impressionism', and implied that its fault lay in 'simultaneity'.[63] The Vorticist manifesto of July 1914 had similarly claimed that Futurism was merely the latest form of Impressionism.

[60] Sullivan, unsigned notice of *The Criterion*, *TLS* (26 Oct. 1922), 690.
[61] F. T. Marinetti, *Selected Writings*, ed. R. W. Flint (London: Secker and Warburg, 1972), 97.
[62] Marinetti, *Selected Writings*, 41.
[63] Pound, 'Vorticism', *Fortnightly Review*, 102 (Sept. 1914), 47–61.

It had termed Marinetti's movement 'Automobilism', and had ridiculed its valorization of magnitude and velocity: 'Elephants are *Very Big*. Motor cars go quickly.'[64]

The reasons for this hostility are open to interpretation. It was not simply due to a nationalist impulse to create a British avant-garde, though this was certainly a motivating factor in the creation of Vorticism.[65] It was not simply because Futurist simultaneity was rooted in technology: although this may have been a contributing factor during the war, Lewis makes little mention of it in his later criticism, which is directed at philosophy and pure science. It has frequently been argued that the Vorticist preference for hard outlines and sculptural solidity, as against the softness of outline created by Impressionism and Futurist simultaneity, reflects a psychological insecurity about masculinity.[66] While this interpretation is certainly plausible, it is peripheral to the philosophical issues: one could just as easily explain Marinetti's enthusiasm for fast cars as an expression of his insecure masculinity. What is clear is that modernist writers distinguished several different species of simultaneity, but distinguished them fitfully. If they appear ambivalent, it may be because they were attracted to one species, and sceptical about another, but lacked any developed vocabulary in which to articulate these preferences and distinctions.

Many commentators noted similarities between Henri Bergson's philosophy and the philosophy implied by Einstein's special theory, and some—for example, Wildon Carr—interpreted Einstein in Bergsonian terms.[67] The origin of the comparisons was Bergson's distinction between two forms of time, *temps* and *durée*.[68] The

---

[64] [Lewis], 'Long Live the Vortex', *Blast*, 1 (Jul. 1914), 7–8.

[65] Paul Peppis, *Literature, Politics and the English Avant-Garde* (Cambridge: Cambridge University Press, 2000).

[66] Hal Foster, 'Prosthetic Gods', *Modernism / Modernity*, 4/2 (1997), 5–38; Jessica Burstein, 'Waspish Segments: Lewis, Prosthesis, Fascism,' *Modernism / Modernity*, 4/2 (1997), 139–64.

[67] H. Wildon Carr, 'The Principle of Relativity and its Importance for Philosophy,' *Proceedings of the Aristotelian Society*, 14 (1913–14) 407–24 (a paper read on 13 Jun. 1914); *The General Principle of Relativity in its Philosophical and Historical Aspect* (London: Macmillan, 1920); 'Bergson's Theory of Knowledge and Einstein's Theory of Relativity,' *The Philosopher*, 2/1 (Jan.–Mar. 1924), 8–12. Bergson himself tackled the question in *Durée et simultanéité* (Paris: F. Alcan, 1922).

[68] Bergson advanced the distinction in *Essai sur les données immédiates de la conscience* (1888); near-contemporary British accounts may be found in Waterlow and Solomon, and a more recent introduction in Leszek Kolakowski, *Bergson* (Oxford: Oxford University Press, 1985), 13–14.

former, 'clock time', spatializes our time sense: literally, on a clock face, where each second, minute, and hour is given a portion of space; metaphorically, in the way we think about time. Bergson had arrived at the distinction as a result of trying to explain Zeno's paradox, and in more general terms, trying to understand nature as process rather than a succession of static snapshots. Zeno's paradox is this: Achilles is running a race with a tortoise, and the tortoise has a head start. Common sense tells us that Achilles will overtake the tortoise, but a spatializing analysis suggests otherwise. By the time that Achilles reaches the tortoise's starting point, the tortoise will have moved on to another, further point. By the time Achilles reaches that point, the tortoise will have moved on again. And so on, *ad infinitum*. The problem with this mode of analysis is that it segments time into distinct moments. It sees Achilles and the tortoise as being 'at' a given point in time, rather than continuously moving through it. Bergson solved the problem by positing the existence of *durée* as the form taken by time before it is spatialized. Every moment of *durée* overlaps every other; indeed, for this reason it is misleading to talk of a 'moment' of *durée*. Viewed as *durée*, every moment of time is simultaneous with every other.

The character of Bergsonian simultaneity, and hence its difference from the Einsteinian species, may best be illustrated by a brief quotation from *The Trespasser*. Helena and Siegmund's assignation on the Isle of Wight takes places in a dream-like atmosphere. Whereas, Helena comments, the days 'used to walk in procession like seven marionettes, each in order and costume, going endlessly round', now for them, the days and nights are 'smeared' into one. Siegmund agrees, asking rhetorically why he should be 'parcelled up' into segments of time; '*I* am not made up of sections of time.'[69] This is clearly Bergsonian in its derivation, and the characteristic vocabulary is of smearing and blurring. Time loses its sculptural solidity. In Einsteinian simultaneity, the simultaneous existence of distinct moments does not imply any blurring of them. Indeed, the movement of light creates a very un-Bergsonian spatialization of time. The characteristic vocabulary is of juxtaposition. The dramatic example of peace juxtaposed with war emphasizes discontinuity.

Wyndham Lewis's assault on the 'time philosophy' in *Time and Western Man* does not make this distinction. J. W. N. Sullivan,

---

[69] Lawrence, *The Trespasser*, 98.

responding to an earlier essay by Lewis on the subject, had urged him to distinguish Einstein's work from the 'time philosophy', on the basis of the 'scientific' status of the theory of relativity.[70] Though in his *Athenaeum* essays Sullivan had himself associated Einstein with the contemporary *zeitgeist*, he had not done so on the basis of the 'time philosophy', and he expressed scepticism about Lewis's method. In Lewis's account, he wrote, the 'time philosophy' was so all-pervasive that it had the character of a 'curious madness', or at best an 'excessive flowering of a certain type of mind under exceptionally favourable conditions'.[71] Sullivan agreed that history and art were 'pliable things', and conceded that 'to some extent', so too was science. But, he asserted, 'it would be, I think, wholly untrue to say that the theory of relativity has borrowed anything from Bergson and Co.' The 'pedigree' of Einstein's theory was not the time philosophy, but the non-Euclidean geometries, Maxwell's equations, and the Michelson–Morley experiment: these were matters of logic and experiment. For Sullivan, only a scientific critique could 'demolish' Einstein's strictly scientific achievement.

With the benefit of hindsight, various criticisms may be levelled at Sullivan's argument. Sullivan emphasizes the Michelson–Morley experiment and the experimental verification of Maxwell's equations, and thus gives his account of Einstein an 'experimenticist' bias. Unaware of Einstein's 1895–96 thought-experiment, he says nothing of the imaginative element in the origins of Einstein's theory. Finally, he does not ask about the circumstances that framed Einstein's theory: although in itself the theory may rest on logic and experiment, such an account does not explain why the problems that Einstein solved became problems at that particular moment in history. In retrospect, Lewis was right to argue that, in so far as Einstein was working with 'imaginative material', it was 'inconceivable' that he 'should not be to some extent metaphysical'.[72] However, he did not sufficiently distinguish Einstein's 'metaphysic' from Bergson's.

Lewis acknowledged Sullivan's criticisms of 'The Revolutionary Simpleton' in the text of *Time and Western Man*, but did not take

---

[70] Lewis, 'The Revolutionary Simpleton,' *The Enemy* 1 (Jan. 1927), 27–192; Sullivan, letter to Lewis dated 23 Feb. 1927, Lewis papers, Carl A. Kroch Library, Cornell University.

[71] Sullivan, letter to Lewis, 23 Feb. 1927.

[72] Lewis, *Time and Western Man* (1927), ed. Paul Edwards (Santa Rosa: Black Sparrow, 1993), 139.

their substance seriously.[73] In spite of Sullivan's assertion concerning Bergson, Lewis claimed that it was 'unlikely' that Einstein 'had not at least read the work of Bergson, and formed some opinion upon it, favourable or otherwise'.[74] Neither Sullivan nor Lewis presents a sufficient level of evidence to make it possible to adjudicate between their claims.

In his account of Einsteinian simultaneity Lewis followed Sullivan's advice in so far as he summarized the physical basis of the special theory, but his account distorts the physical facts to minimize the difficulties they present to his argument. The root of Lewis's objection was the Machian aspect of Einstein's philosophy, and its emphasis on sense data as the fundamental elements of science; he termed this 'the Theory of Sensa'. To Lewis, to adopt such a philosophy was to abandon the adult capacity for abstract thought and judgement, and to lapse into the childishness he termed the 'child cult'. He satirizes the Theory of Sensa's obsession with the present moment:

The intensity, nakedness, *reality* of the immediate sensation, even though it gives you no ideal *whole*, though it is dogmatically a creature of the moment, even though it gives you the 'objects' of life only as strictly experienced *in Time*; evanescent, flashing and momentary . . . is nevertheless, is it not? *the real thing.*[75]

The presentation of sensations 'flashing' leads into Lewis's more detailed account of the scientific aspect of the Theory of Sensa; that it accidentally echoes Sullivan's comments on *The Waste Land* was probably not something of which Lewis was aware. Lewis goes on to say that the Theory of Sensa

admits that all its assumptions are based on optical illusions, the phenomena of distorting media, and the 'physically' abnormal or seldom experienced; just as psychoanalysis is founded upon the curiosities of the clinic. Physically these philosophic theories are the exact counterpart of the psychology of the freudian. But imported into the centre of them are also a set of astronomical curiosities. For instance, one of the key-illustrations to show the credibility of 'sensa'—the new specifically optical 'object'—is the fact that, owing to the immense distances separating us from many of the stars, the star's light that reaches us today may be the light of a world now dead. Hence the point of light that we see is a sort of apparition.[76]

---

[73] Ibid., 135, 138–39, 162, 205, and Paul Edwards's note, 578.
[74] Lewis, *Time and Western Man*, 139.   [75] Ibid., 389.   [76] Ibid., 389.

For Lewis, the limiting effect of the velocity of light is identical to the kind of optical illusion that occurs due to the different refractive indexes of air and water: a straight stick seen partly submerged in water will appear to be bent.[77] He gives the misleading impression that the finiteness of light's velocity is a physical abnormality or exception, rather than an absolute limit to all sense impressions. By choosing the example of a star which is immensely distant and which is 'now' dead, he gives the impression that light from nearby objects reaches us immediately. Lewis needs to maintain this erroneous distinction in order to maintain his faith in 'the eye'.[78] For Lewis to admit that the eye is subject to the limitations of its environment would be to admit to the fallibility of the 'I', the will.

The distinction between Einsteinian simultaneity and that which is due to telecommunications is of a different order. While we can distinguish Einsteinian and Bergsonian simultaneities on the basis of metaphors of continuity and discontinuity, the simultaneity of telecommunications produces incongruous juxtapositions which are similar to those produced (in thought experiments) by light travelling. In physics, and particularly astronomy, light is commonly discussed as a medium of communication, a carrier of messages. These metaphors found their way into expository works: H. H. Turner, for example, compared the time difference between the 'actual' occurrence of an event and the arrival of the light signal to the time difference between news transmitted over the electric telegraph and through the post office.[79] The telephone introduces an additional point of similarity, in that, like the ghostly star, the telephone call creates an uncanny combination of absence and presence.

The similarities may be explored by returning to *The Waves*. Though Louis's multiple identities are associated, in the Hampton Court episode, with Einsteinian simultaneity, they are associated at least as strongly with telecommunications. As a successful businessman, Louis unites 'the furled and close-packed leaves' of his 'many-folded life' not only through the act of signing a single name, but with 'letters and cables and brief but courteous commands on the telephone to Paris, Berlin, New York'.[80] Interpreted realistically, those on the end of the line are his business associates or representatives; but *The Waves* encourages other forms of

---

[77] Lewis, *Time and Western Man*, 391.   [78] Ibid., 134.
[79] Turner, 'Introduction' to Freundlich, *Foundations*, p. xi.
[80] Woolf, *Waves*, 127.

reading, and it is not difficult to interpret Louis's phone calls as conversations with his multiple selves. He has achieved what Lawrence's Alvina desired, and has become a cablegram.

The image of Louis fusing his lives together may seem to contradict the idea that the global telecommunications network created modernist simultaneity: for Louis, the telephone facilitates the imposition of clock time, 'Mr Prentice at four; Mr Eyres sharp at four-thirty.'[81] Rather, though, Louis's fusion clarifies the problem: the idea of the network creates the idea of simultaneity, as did Katharine Hilbery's 'welter of voices'; individual telephone calls suppress it. This is particularly the case when the person making the call exercises authority: although a telephone call may create a heterochronic state, the subordinate party's reckoning of time is of little importance; the metropolitan centre imposes its own time on the provinces, territories, and dependencies. Louis's case is particularly interesting because we are allowed to see the insecurity of his authoritarian time, and to recognize that it is won at a cost. Louis's obsessive repetition of 'Mr Prentice at four; Mr Eyres at four-thirty' betrays an awareness that clock time is an extraordinarily fragile structure; doubly so in the hands of a man who embodies a whole succession of historical figures.[82] The cost of clock time to Louis is the sacrifice or suppression of his complexity.

Only by reintroducing the question of power can we differentiate the simultaneity created by the finite velocity of light from that created by telecommunications. Put crudely, it is a distinction between nature and culture. This is crude, in that the 'natural' phenomenon of simultaneity is itself activated by cultural forces. Nevertheless, it carries the authority of 'nature' and telecommunications do not. 'Natural' simultaneity is a universal phenomenon, whereas, in the late nineteenth and early twentieth centuries, telecommunications were far from universal. The rapid expansion of the telegraph system into a global network came about because that network served imperial interests. The use of the London to Paris cable to connect the stock exchanges in 1851 illustrates the alignment of telecommunications with business interests. So too does a map of the London District company's telegraph network in around 1861, which shows a concentration of lines on the financial district of the City of London.[83] As David Harvey argues, '[s]uperior command

---

[81] Ibid., 128.   [82] Ibid., 129, 130.   [83] Kieve, *Electric Telegraph*, 60–1.

over space has always been a vital aspect of class (and intra-class) struggle'.[84]

The growth of telephony followed similar elitist patterns. These were somewhat complicated in Britain by the fact that the government had acquired the telegraph network in the 1870s, and had subsequently attempted to restrict the growth of the new telephone technology. However, the crude figures both for the United Kingdom and the United States indicate that owning a telephone remained exceptional. Bell made his first experiments in telephony in 1875, and took out patents in March 1876. There were impressive rates of growth in the early years, but they soon reached a plateau. By 1900, there were 1,356,000 phones in the United States, an ownership level of 1.76 per cent; by 1905 the figure had reached 5 per cent. In the United Kingdom, in 1885 there were only 3800 subscribers in London, and 10,000 in the whole country. By 1890, the national figure had reached 55,000. By 1910 the level of ownership, although the second highest in Europe, was still little over one per cent of the population.[85]

What these figures do not indicate is the number of telephones made available to the public. Had public telephones been widespread and affordable, then the technology could not so readily be presented as divisive. Public telephones were proposed as early as 1884 in Edinburgh, and installed in 1888 in Glasgow. However, it is significant that the Edinburgh proposal encountered strong opposition from existing subscribers, on the basis that the usefulness of telephones was directly proportional to their exclusivity: businessmen were concerned that 'triflers and intruders' would too easily be able to waste their time.[86] The very features of the telephone that made it so advantageous to the middle and upper classes were also the features that made it potentially threatening. A telephone call pierced the secure walls of the bourgeois home and business with an immediacy surpassing that of the letter. The stability of the network relied on tacit agreements about access and behaviour, such as would be observed in a gentleman's club. In 1895 the Postmaster-General declared to Parliament that 'the telephone could not, and never would be an advantage which could be enjoyed by the large

[84] David Harvey, *The Condition of Postmodernity* (Oxford: Blackwell, 1990), 232.

[85] Marvin, *When Old Technologies*, 64; 'Telephone,' *Encyclopaedia Britannica*, 11th edn. (1910–11), xxvi. 556.

[86] Quoted in Marvin, *When Old Technologies*, 103.

mass of the people'.[87] The telephone provided prompt communication, and this, he argued, was incompatible with a large number of users. This incompatibility was not simply due to a technical constraint. Although such constraints played a part in creating the exclusivity of the network, this exclusivity was sustained by a particular social politics. If subscription had to be limited, it was inevitable it would be limited to the ruling classes and authorities.

The subject position created by telecommunications was available only to a minority. Though some felt it indirectly, for example, as readers of newspapers that gathered news from across the world, their relation to the new simultaneity was essentially passive. It is tempting to treat it and the new physics as two mutually reinforcing influences on modernist literary form, combined by simple addition; but to treat their relation in this way would be to ignore the status of the new physics as a representation of 'nature'. The relation is more complex. Though telecommunications were the tools of a social elite, the literary writers and cultural commentators of that elite viewed them at times with suspicion, at times with hostility. For Max Nordau, they were one of many forces of cultural acceleration which would lead either to nervous exhaustion and degeneration, or to the evolution of a new form of human being possessed of nerves 'of gigantic vigour'.[88] While the modernist antipathy to 'bourgeois modernity' is not as fundamental as some critics have implied, and was certainly mixed with responses of excitement and wonder, there may have been greater sympathy to a simultaneity born of astronomical phenomena than one derived from the clamour of city life. However, representing the new simultaneity as a natural phenomenon is essentially an ideological move. Though no one was travelling close to the speed of light in 1919, a small economic elite was able to move information closer to that speed than anyone else. The new experience of space and time was not a politically neutral fact; nor were the subjectivities and literary forms it enabled.

[87] Quoted in ibid., 101.   [88] Nordau, *Degeneration*, 39, 541.

7

Non-Euclidean Humanity

OF all the sciences, mathematics might seem the one furthest removed from the conventional concerns of literature, allowing the fewest possibilities for metaphorical exchange. Indeed, if we take 'science' to refer to empirical and experimental science, then mathematics should not even be categorized as a science. Yet for many reasons, not least its very resistance to the methodology of this study, mathematics demands attention. Geometry in particular demands attention because of its centrality in Einstein's theory of gravity, his General Principle of Relativity. In granting importance to geometry in this study, however, one need not endorse the reductivist model of the sciences in which all the authority of all 'soft' sciences ultimately rests on that of harder sciences: biology on chemistry, physics on mathematics. While this story may have convinced some scientists at some periods in history, studies in the sociology and the history of science suggest that in many cases the authority of science rests on a far more complex network of factors, both within scientific institutions and in their relations to the larger culture.

Einstein's theory explained gravity not as an attractive 'force', but as an effect of the curvature of spacetime around particularly dense bodies. It described the curvature of spacetime using the form of non-Euclidean geometry developed by Riemann. Having dispensed with 'force' it did not require an imperceptible ether to act as a medium for the transmission of force. It did not disprove the existence of the ether, but simply dispensed with it as an unnecessary, uneconomical hypothesis. In very broad terms, Einstein's explanation follows the early twentieth-century trend of replacing mechanistic explanations with formalist ones. In this case, the resistance to non-Euclidean geometry and to formalist theory reveals a great deal about the ideological dimension of thematic commitments: the writings of Oliver Lodge, to which I shall return shortly, are a particularly rich field.

Non-Euclidean geometries had developed from attempts to discard the least satisfactory of the postulates in Euclid's geometry, that concerning parallel lines. Both Euclid's parallel postulate and the definition of parallelism rely upon references to infinity. Parallel straight lines are those which, 'being in the same plane and being produced indefinitely in both directions, do not meet one another in either direction'.[1] The difficulty with this definition is that it suggests one may physically demonstrate it, yet it demands the physically impossible task of drawing lines to infinity. Thus it exposes the conflicting ontological claims made for geometry in the nineteenth century. On the one hand the nativists claimed that the basis for a 'true knowledge of the natural world' was innate, while empiricists claimed that it derived from the evidence of the senses.[2] These were not merely academic arguments, but ideological ones. The nativist position is an essentially conservative one: it was the task of the educated elite to pass down the 'immutable truths' from generation to generation.[3] The empiricist argument about geometry, like many empiricist arguments in the nineteenth century, was tinged with radicalism: anyone could discover these truths using the evidence of their senses. Moreover, these ideological arguments influenced education at every level. Nineteenth-century school editions of *Euclid's Elements* reinforced the use of 'Euclid' as a byword for infallibility and for self-evident truth, presenting his geometrical axioms as the very foundation of civilization. One edition quoted many classical authorities on the importance of geometry in education, and quoted the contemporary William Whewell as saying that 'the truths of Elementary Geometry' had, 'in all ages, given a meaning and a reality to the best attempts to explain man's power of arriving at truth'; another school edition claimed that the *Elements* had been translated into the languages 'of all nations that have made any considerable progress in civilization'.[4] At university level, the nativist arguments about geometry influenced the education of the national elite, as the mathematics tripos was a compulsory part of a Cambridge education from 1848 onwards. The justification for the inclusion of Euclidean geometry, even for those wishing to study the

---

[1] Euclid, quoted in Joan Richards, *Mathematical Visions: The Pursuit of Geometry in Victorian England* (San Diego: Academic Press, 1988), 62.

[2] Richards, *Mathematical Visions*, 2–3.   [3] Ibid., 29.

[4] Robert Potts (ed.), *Euclid's Elements* 3rd edn. (Cambridge: Cambridge University Press, 1850), p. vi; James Thomson (ed.), *Euclid's Elements* 15th edn. (London: Longman, 1860), p. viii.

classics, was that it developed and cultivated the reasoning faculty, especially in the process of reasoning 'from fundamental principles to their consequences'.[5] Euclid underpinned logic, civilization, and the very idea that science could reach a single, absolute truth.

The non-Euclidean geometers imagined worlds in which Euclid's postulates did not apply: for example, on the surface of a sphere, where two lines might appear to be parallel, but on which they actually meet at the poles. Some important early researches had been published by Nicholai Lobachevskii in 1840, but non-Euclidean geometries became the object of debate in Britain only in 1870, when Hermann von Helmholtz published a brief article in *The Academy* describing Bernhard Riemann's ideas. For the nativist defenders of Euclid, the necessary truth of his propositions was based on the impossibility of conceiving an alternative geometry.[6] However, the nativist response to the empiricist challenge was to concede that non-Euclidean geometry would be applicable in a non-Euclidean world, but to assert that its applicability would not affect the truth of the Euclidean system. An early and influential form of this argument was presented by the economist W. Stanley Jevons in 1871, in direct response to Helmholtz's *Academy* article.[7]

The distinction between practical utility and absolute truth remained an important one in the later debates about Einstein's adoption of non Euclidean geometry. In an exposition of Einstein that appeared in the *Times Educational Supplement* in December 1919, F. M. Denton concluded that as Euclid had been contradicted by relativity, his readers should reject Einstein, 'for that which literally contradicts the principles of Euclid's geometry can only be non-sense'.[8] E. St John Brooks responded by saying that Euclidean geometry was a special case of the non-Euclidean—we could now describe it as a *subset* of the non-Euclidean—and so was not directly contradicted by the new development. To this Denton replied that he was prepared to concede the 'value' of the non-Euclidean geometry, but not its truth. St John Brooks made a similar concession and similar distinction, but attached opposite values to each of its terms: he conceded that *applied* sciences could retain Euclidean geometry, but that *pure* sciences such as physics would need to adopt the non-Euclidean.

[5] Whewell, quoted in Richards, *Mathematical Visions*, 21.   [6] Ibid., 91.
[7] W. S. Jevons, 'Helmholtz on the Axioms of Geometry', *Nature*, 4 (19 Oct. 1871), 481–2; Richards, *Mathematical Visions*, 86–7.
[8] F. M. Denton, 'The Modern Theory of Relativity', *TES* (4 Dec. 1919), 605–6.

Described thus, the argument between St John Brooks and Denton may seem to derive from purely intellectual positions. However, the confidence with which Denton asserted the absolute truth of Euclid and rejected Einstein is surprising, and suggests a personal commitment that goes beyond logical arguments. This commitment derives from a variant of the nativist view, most apparent when Denton argues that people innately possess 'a sense for force' and 'no sense for space distortion'.[9] Though Denton subscribes to the nativist view, he relocates innate knowledge in the body rather than the mind.

The underlying anti-intellectualism of this position becomes clearer in some of Oliver Lodge's writings against relativity in the years 1919 to 1921. Lodge frequently complained that the mathematics of general relativity were unduly complicated. He affected to praise their ingenuity, but, as we have seen, found many of the new mathematical methods genuinely difficult.[10] The expository failings of 'The New Theory of Gravity', the first of his popular pieces on relativity, are particularly interesting, though they become apparent only when the piece is quoted at length. Lodge introduces the theory portentously: 'A most complicated theory it is, elaborated by singular genius with the aid of innumerable symbols and difficult reasoning'.[11] While other expositors might have attempted to explain why the reasoning was difficult, or even to work through it in outline, Lodge is more concerned to deter the reader from proceeding further. He goes on to explain that theory 'lays its hands not only on ether and matter, on light and gravitation, but attacks the fundamental conceptions of Space and Time also' (1195). What might in other accounts have been praised as comprehensiveness here becomes transformed into a kind of greed or territorial acquisitiveness. Lodge then outlines the main features of the new theory:

It evolves a generalised theory of gravity to which the Newtonian theory is a close approximation. It attributes inertia to energy (not for the first time). It gives a theory of Space of which Euclidean space may be regarded as a special case. It involves a theory of Time which may be described as requiring four co-ordinates instead of three to fix a position, and so virtually making Time an aspect of a fourth dimension of Space. The timing of events on this theory becomes extremely complicated; it is barely possible to say even when two events are simultaneous, or to offer a criterion as to what is meant by simultaneity. Gravitation becomes a property of Space—

---

[9] Denton, 'Einstein's Theory' (letter), *TES* (18 Dec. 1919), 639.
[10] See Chapter 1. [11] Lodge, 'The New Theory of Gravity', 1195.

of four-dimensional Time-Space—it therefore affects everything that occurs in space. There are ten possible coefficients instead of the common quantity g, the intensity of gravity. A ray of light is not straight; the path of 'least action' is affected by a gravitational field, which acts like a change in optical density and so causes a sort of refraction . . . The theory of relativity . . . involves complications which at first look as if they would drive the older physicists to despair, and it is useless to attempt to instruct general readers in its intricacies.

(1195–6)

There are many localized peculiarities of phrasing here: many readers would have been distracted by asking who else had previously attributed inertia to energy; they would have wondered why it was '*barely* possible' to determine simultaneity, in a context where possibility and impossibility ought to be clear cut and mutually exclusive; they would have wondered whether the observed deflection of light beams was not in fact the optical effect of refraction, something claimed by several of those sceptical about the supposed 'proof'.[12]

However, the failings of Lodge's exposition lie not only in these localized peculiarities, but in the failure of the passage to trace any logical relations between these individual developments. While many expositors developed lines of argument which differed from Einstein's—beginning, for example, from experimental results rather than formal asymmetries—they generally attempted to present the general principle, and hence the adoption of non-Euclidean geometry, as the inevitable outcome of a chain of reasoning. In Lodge's presentation, there is no coherence. This may simply reflect Lodge's own difficulty in comprehending the theory, but it may, more cynically, be an attempt to bewilder 'general readers' to the point where they agree with the concluding sentence of the paragraph, and abandon further attempts to understand the theory. The disconnected statements of this paragraph contrast sharply with the fluent assured rhetoric adopted by Lodge when he returns to the ether theory:

We have already had to generalise our conceptions of mass and shape, on the strength of the electrical theory of matter, and we have done so

---

[12] e.g. E. Nevill, FRS, 'The Revolution in Science' [letter dated 14 Nov.], *The Times* (17 Nov. 1919), 8; Thomas Case, 'Theories of Space' [letter], *The Times* (22 Nov. 1919), 8; Arthur Fitch, 'A Revolution in Science' [letter], *The Nation* (London) 26 (29 Nov. 1919), 303–4.

joyfully. That was done before Einstein rose above the horizon. But let us not make the mistake of discarding, lightheartedly, that great reality, the Ether of Space; let us not think of light, in a vague fashion, as travelling with fixed speed through nothing, and being bent out of its path by unsubstantial geometry; let us not complicate Space unduly, nor jump to overhasty ideas about Time. Revolutionary changes such as these ought to be the result of long pondering and much experience, they should not be the outcome of a revolutionary period or be born among the harassments of war.

(1196–7)

The idea that the formalist mode of explanation was 'unsubstantial', leads to the most ideologically laden part of Lodge's objections to relativity, which received fuller expression in two later articles, one in *Nature* and the other in the *Fortnightly Review*. These objections were due to Lodge's commitment to the concept of force. In both articles he asserted a position very similar to Denton's: 'Force is essentially a human conception derived from our muscular sense, and, psychologically, is as basic as motion, and more directly apprehended than matter.'[13] It seems as if Lodge had embarked on his own version of the descriptionist programme of isolating the fundamental, non-metaphysical elements of physics. But whereas for Ernst Mach, the fundamental units were sense-data, for Lodge they were muscular sensations. While these could be taken essentially as a special category of tactile sensations, Lodge's emphasis is very different from those of Mach or Eddington. Stanley Goldberg has commented that Lodge had a 'metaphysical inability to conceive of two bodies affecting each other without a mechanical connection', and has suggested that he belongs to the tradition of mechanical model making exemplified by Kelvin.[14] In addition to this, it should be noted that Lodge's argument in his defence of 'force' derives from Whewell, who had justified the primacy of 'force' etymologically, noting that the 'original meaning' of the Greek word was 'muscle' or 'tendon'.[15] In Whewell's and Lodge's emphasis on the muscular body, we see something not quite covered by Goldberg's description of a 'metaphysical' thematic commitment: there is an ideological

---

[13] Lodge, 'Einstein's Real Achievement', 366. The sentence echoes 'Remarks on Gravitational Relativity (IV)', *Nature*, 107 (25 Aug. 1921), 817.

[14] Stanley Goldberg, *Understanding Relativity* (Oxford: Clarendon, 1984), 225.

[15] William Whewell, *The Philosophy of the Inductive Sciences*, 2nd edn., 2 vols. (London: John W. Parker, 1847), i. 185–6.

component. Rippling just below the surface of Lodge's discourse is the idea that the mathematical methods of the new physics are not only complicated, but unmanly. The 'full-bodied, concrete, absolute' reality has been replaced by 'superficial appearances, impracticable measurements, geometrical devices, and weirdly ingenious modes of expression'.[16] The 'muscular sense' of gravitational force has been replaced by a 'neat' and 'compact' mathematical nomenclature. True, this nomenclature can become a 'powerful weapon', but Lodge may have believed that fighting with powerful weapons was not the same as fighting with one's muscles. If, for the sake of emphasis, we inflate this position into a grotesque parody of itself, Lodge seems to imply that the hypergeometers are closeted aesthetes who have never in their lives done a day of honest physical toil; they are degenerate and anaemic cranks brought up with the comforts of a machine age, divorced from the realities of nature; finally, they are unpatriotic and morally evasive. Lodge was never this direct or extreme, and it may be that he was never fully conscious of his assumptions, but the relevant vocabulary is scattered throughout his popular and scientific articles of the period.

The suggestion that supporters of Einstein were unpatriotic is the crucial part of the jigsaw. We have already seen how Lodge associated the revolution in physics with a period of revolution and war, associating Einstein both with bolshevism, and with Bernhardi's 'Weltmacht oder Niedergang' attitude. The main point was to emphasize Einstein's foreignness. Many scientists regretted that Einstein had 'dethroned' Newton. Expositors who wished to overcome nationalistic antipathy to Einstein were able to point to a British forerunner in W. K. Clifford, who had suggested in 1875 that gravitation could be explained in terms of non Euclidean geometry.[17] Lodge preferred a strategy of denial, and adopted a metaphor of kingship, which allowed him to reassure his readers that 'for all practical purposes, Galilean and Newtonian dynamics still reign, perhaps no longer supreme, but as a limited monarchy'.[18] In 'Einstein's Real Achievement', he moderated his xenophobia, stating merely that 'in its laudable anxiety to be fair to foreigners, this country is apt to overlook the work of its own pioneers' (354). Notably Clifford was

---

[16] Lodge, 'The Geometrisation of Physics', 800.

[17] For example, see J. W. N. Sullivan, 'Relativity', *Athenaeum* (3 Sept. 1920), 311; a review of Einstein's *Relativity: A Popular Exposition*.

[18] Lodge, 'New Theory', 1201.

not numbered among Lodge's pantheon of pioneers: to place him there would have been to undermine Newton's pre-eminence. Approached from the context of his patriotic attachment to Newton, Lodge's thematic commitment to the idea of force takes on a more particular meaning: force, as something that can be felt on the muscles, seems to belong in a late nineteenth-century discourse of athleticism, muscularity, and manliness.[19]

Lodge writes nostalgically about the 'old simplicities' that have been 'replaced by complex mathematical machinery', and anticipates 'that before long there will be a revolt in favour of more physical conceptions and greater simplicity of expression. For there is probably no need to strain after such ingenuity, and express everything in this complicated fashion' (371). These phrases could be transposed directly into a conservative review of modernist poetry.[20] Lodge develops a strand of Carlylean conservatism too, rejecting 'machinery' in favour of physical toil. In the concluding page of 'Einstein's Real Achievement', Lodge declares that hypergeometry is inadequate to the 'fulness of existence'; physics 'is richer than geometry'; 'We live in a full-blooded universe, containing intelligence and emotion and will' (372). Lodge projects his idea of the complete imperialist Englishman onto his picture of the universe. Conversely, he projects his sense of the relativists' moral evasiveness onto the Einsteinian universe: he regretted the 'tendency to abolish the idea of "force", and to replace gravitation by a modified geometry; as if the earth sailed along, not so much obedient to all the forces acting on it, as free of any compulsion whatever' (365). In the Einsteinian account of gravitation the earth, in orbiting the sun, is following the line of least resistance. It would travel in a straight line, but spacetime is curved around the sun. This principle of least action is fundamental to Newtonian physics—the first law of motion states that a body stays at rest or continues in motion unless acted upon by a force—but Lodge gives the impression that Einstein is the sole author of this irresponsible universe in which bodies act disobediently, sailing carelessly along the line of least resistance, without making a manful struggle against the 'force' of gravity.

[19] See Bruce Haley, *The Healthy Body and Victorian Culture* (Cambridge, Mass.: Harvard University Press, 1978), 107–19, and J. A. Mangan, *The Games Ethic and Imperialism* (1986; London: Frank Cass, 1998), 48–9.

[20] Though, with only a small adjustment, their reactionary position could also be that of modernist writers themselves, regretfully adopting ingenious modes of expression, but nostalgically looking back to a period of order.

Not only does matter struggle with gravitational force, but in Lodge's world the good physicist struggles with reality. In Lodge's view, 'Einstein and his disciples' held that our physical theories are 'founded upon convenience'.[21] It is instructive to compare this phrase with Karl Pearson's summary of descriptionism as 'the economy of thought': the one phrase suggests a rational, prudent, and respectable allocation of resources within a household or a business, while the other suggests mental laziness and moral unreliability. It was not 'convenience' towards which scientists should 'devote time and energy', continued Lodge, but 'absolute truth'. For Lodge, there was a moral danger in the pragmatist position: it affected 'conduct'; we behave differently in the face of the pragmatic truth and the absolute truth.

Lodge had certain intensely personal reasons for rejecting Einsteinian geometry and remaining committed to the ether. Much of his scientific reputation was founded on his work in perfecting radio transmitters, and as ether was believed to be the medium through which radio waves were propagated, he could not very well abandon it. More idiosyncratically, Lodge was committed to Psychical Research, and when he writes in 'The New Theory of Gravity' that 'every kind of force' is transmitted by one and the same medium (1195), he leaves room for the term 'force' to refer to more than conventionally physical forces. Concluding 'Einstein's Real Achievement', he explained how science had gradually extended the functions of the ether, making it responsible at first for the transmission of light, then electricity, and then magnetism. 'Some day', he writes, 'we shall take a further step, and include among its functions the service of other forms of existence . . .' (372): this latter statement insinuates very strongly that the ether must be preserved for the sake of the spirits. Lodge's son Raymond had been killed in the First World War and was numbered among them. In the closing sentences of *Ether and Reality* he was more direct: ether 'is the primary instrument of Mind, the vehicle of Soul, the habitation of Spirit. Truly it may be called the living garment of God' (179).

Though Lodge had these uniquely personal reasons for his commitment to the ether, his arguments generally centre on the question of force. Force and the ideas that surround it define a subject-position that was held by a significant number of physicists, and, in

---

[21] Lodge, 'The Ether Versus Relativity', 54–9.

its non-scientific manifestations, by other citizens. Lodge was a realist rather than a descriptionist in science: he concludes one article
with an oratorical reminder to the scientist that 'his function is to
discover rather than create', and speaks slightingly of a philosophy
in which space and time are 'forms of thought constructed by the
observer'.[22] He wished to return physics to the body, seeing its
innate intuition of 'force' as the ultimate foundation for the truth of
physics. In this return to the body he differs subtly from the nativist
apologists for Euclid, whose orientation was mental. However, his
return to the body must not be confused with that of the descriptionists, who were regularly the objects of his criticism. He cautions
in 'Einstein's Real Achievement' that we must not 'too modestly
assume that our powers of conception are limited and tied down to
the apprehensions directly derivable from our senses' (367). For the
descriptionists, our physical conceptions derive from the evidence of
the senses alone, but their model of the perceiving body is invariably
of a passive, predominantly visual body. Lodge's ideal body is mus-
cularly engaged with the world and its forces.

The contrast between the realists and the descriptionists might
seem to be reducible to a difference in generations, and it largely
was, but in Wyndham Lewis's *Time and Western Man*, we find a
modernist writer defending a position very like Lodge's. Lewis
redefines his philosophy: it is not to be defined as a 'philosophy of
the eye' if by that we understand 'the eye' to be isolated from all
other senses. He positions himself in opposition to Bertrand Russell,
who had claimed that sight is a 'less misleading' sense than touch 'as
a source of fundamental notions about matter'.[23] He argues that, in
our 'everyday perceptive experiences', we associate tactile and visual
sensations, and use each to correct the other. However, in the following paragraph, Lewis goes on to grant superiority to the sense of
touch. This development is not carefully argued for:

It may be useful, in this place, as well, to add that the idea of *force* derives
from the sense of touch, it is generally supposed. This idea astronomical
mathematics, being visual, was naturally led to abandon. Again, the eye is,
in the sense in which we are considering it, the *private* organ: the hand the
public one. The eye estranges and particularizes more than the sense of
touch. Its images are of a confusing vivacity, and its renderings are readily
more subjective. The notion of one Space, they say, is due to the sense of

---

22 Lodge, 'The Geometrisation of Physics', 800; 'Einstein's Real Achievement', 362.
23 Lewis, *Time and Western Man*, 393.

'touch': and space is the 'timeless' idea. Space is the 'public' idea. And in order to be 'timeless', and to be 'public', it must be one.

The remark about force is offered and abandoned, without being developed in any explicitly logical way. There is, however, an underlying logic to the remark, which becomes apparent if we note the gendering of 'public' and 'private' as masculine and feminine spheres. Lewis, recognizing that his argument is potentially weakened by the association of the word 'touch' with night, sensuality, and privacy, redefines it in terms of public and masculine activities.

While the ether was necessarily too fine-grained to be available to human perception, its intangibility was of a very different kind to the intangibility of a geometric distortion of spacetime. The model-making of nineteenth-century ether physicists had established a tradition in which the ether was like matter, only smaller. While the idea of non-Euclidean spacetime provided a far more elegant explanation of gravitation than the ether theories, introducing these geometries to readers who had evolved in three-dimensions presented a particular expository challenge. Many of the other analogies used to describe non-Euclidean spacetime began with a familiar two-dimensional surface and invited the reader to imagine its 'distorted' form. In a particularly rich metaphor, Slosson (and later Nordmann) compared non-Euclidean geometry to a distorting fairground mirror.[24] The implied complementary comparison, of Euclidean geometry to a non-distorting flat mirror, is particularly interesting in view of the idea of realism, scientific and literary, as the mirror of nature. However, following this line of thought also weakens the effectiveness of the analogy, as, by imagining non-Euclidean geometry as a grotesque distortion, it reinforces the claims of Euclidean geometry to represent reality. One could just as easily claim that Euclidean geometry is itself a distortion of a naturally curved space.

Another common analogy, the 'flatland' analogy, required a more radical rethinking of the body. The analogy, which had first appeared in Britain in von Helmholtz's *Academy* article, but was better known from the 'geometrical romance' *Flatland*, required the reader to imagine what a two-dimensional being would perceive as

---

[24] Slosson, *Easy Lessons in Einstein*, 21; Nordmann, *Einstein and the Universe*, 50.

it moved around a two-dimensional surface.[25] In particular, it asked what it would perceive if a three-dimensional object were to fall through its space, and what it would perceive if it encountered a distortion of the surface in a third dimension. In the first case, if a solid sphere fell through the flatland, the flatlander would perceive a disk which grows and then diminishes in size. In the second case, the distortion would be perceived as an attractive force.[26] The analogy provided an introduction to the idea of gravitation as distortion of spacetime. Rethinking the body can lead by a simple chain of association to rethinking the self: if the apparently omniscient flatlanders cannot perceive a third dimension, the three-dimensional reader cannot help but wonder about a fourth one. The curved flat surface inhabited by the flatlanders can readily be misunderstood to be a 'sphere' (a three-dimensional object); this misunderstanding can lead to the paradoxical and disturbing idea that 'spheres' and other apparently solid bodies might have no interior. Again, as the body and the self are both conceptualized with container metaphors, and described in the same words—'heart', for example—it is no great leap to start contemplating a self which is entirely a curved surface without an interior.[27] We have already seen, in the work of the descriptionists, a tendency to think of the world as consisting purely of perceptual surfaces, without any depths. The geometrical analogy provides another way to the same idea of self.

Some appropriations of non-Euclidean geometry did not systematically think through it, but adopted it light-heartedly. Aldous Huxley's prose-poem 'Beauty' spoke of Helen of Troy's curves outwitting Euclid; a Cambridge undergraduate magazine, writing about the famously plump G. K. Chesterton, spoke of the 'Einsteinian curves of his commanding character'; and a reviewer in *The Spectator* wrote that modern poetry induces 'curvature of the brain'. This last example, hinting also at 'curvature of the spine', interprets non-Euclidean geometry and modern poetry as causes of

---

[25] Hermann von Helmholtz, 'The Axioms of Geometry', *The Academy*, 1 (1870), 128–31; Helmholtz, 'The Origin and Meaning of Geometrical Axioms', *Mind*, 1 (1876), 301–21; Edwin A. Abbott, *Flatland: A Romance of Many Dimensions* (London: Seeley and Co., 1884).

[26] 'W. G.', 'Euclid, Newton, and Einstein' [letter], *Nature*, 104 (12 Feb. 1920), 627–30. The analogy of a flatfish was often used: Pearson, *Grammar*, 321; Eddington, *Space, Time and Gravitation*, 95–6; Patrick Browne, 'The Fourth Dimension', *The Dublin Review*, 168 (Jan.–Mar. 1921), 93–106 (105).

[27] Lakoff and Johnson, *Metaphors We Live By*, 29–34.

physical deformity, and relies on the reader's prejudice in favour of the classically rectilinear Euclid; J. C. Squire's comment that non-Euclidean geometry 'tends to run in families, like chess and dipsomania', similarly implies, jestingly, that non-Euclidean space is deformed or degenerate.[28] These examples do little more than take 'non-Euclidean' to be synonymous with 'curved'. However such non-comprehending appropriations hint at the metaphorical possibilities contained within the apparently neutral language of geometry. The idea of a 'curved' universe can be interpreted either as a threatening distortion of nature, or as the 'natural' antithesis of mechanical straight lines.

The idea of non-Euclidean space as more 'natural' may explain its non-scientific appeal. Eddington provides a particularly resonant phrase, describing the Einsteinian theory of the curvature of spacetime as 'a world surveyed from within with standards conformable to it'.[29] Whereas the pure mathematician had imagined a world 'surveyed from outside with standards foreign to it', the physicist dispenses with the idea of 'pure' geometry, and returns the discipline to its etymological roots as the science of earth measurement.[30] The impression is that pure mathematicians and physicists who modelled their science on 'pure' mathematics were guilty of 'distorting the simplicity of things', working, like a cartographical Procrustes, to fit the curved universe onto a flat map. Eddington also provides the more fanciful image of the law of gravitation as a 'fastidious tailor' who will not tolerate 'wrinkles' in spacetime.[31] In consequence the seams of the garment—the world lines of matter through spacetime—must curve a little towards one another.

It is interesting to compare these remarks with Virginia Woolf's description of Lawrence Sterne's prose in A Sentimental Journey as flowing naturally into the 'folds and creases of the mind'.[32] In this case the similarity of Woolf and Eddington does not support the hypothesis of direct influence, because there is an obvious antecedent for both their remarks in Pater's essay 'Style' (1888). Pater quotes a French commentator on Flaubert, who distinguishes between the idea of style as a preformed mould and Flaubert's idea

---

[28] Aldous Huxley, 'Beauty', Coterie, no.1 (May 1919), 21–8 (p. 22); R. B. B., 'G. K. Chesterton', The New Cambridge, 14 (27 Jan 1923), 35; C. R. Haines, 'Obscure Poetry' (letter), The Spectator (13 Jan. 1923), 57; J. C. Squire, 'Books in General', The New Statesman, 14 (22 Nov. 1919), 223.

[29] Eddington, Physical World, 145.   [30] Ibid., 162.   [31] Ibid., 128.

[32] Woolf, 'A Sentimental Journey' (1928), Collected Essays, i. 96.

of style as something which evolves to suit the 'matter': 'the *matter*, the basis, in a work of art, imposed, necessarily, the unique, the just expression, the measure, the rhythm—the *form* in all its character-istics'.[33] Expressed thus there is still a distinction between matter and form, but in his commentary Pater pursues the idea further, repeating the claim he had made in 'The School of Giorgione' (1877) that in the most perfect art, the art of music, 'it is impossible to dis-tinguish the form from the substance or matter'. This antecedent significantly complicates the relations of literature and science in this territory. If we allow literature the strongest possible degree of influence, then the 'elegance' and 'economy' of Einstein's theory emerge as a form of aestheticism, notably in their identification of matter with 'folds' or 'puckers' in spacetime. If we allow literature a weaker influence, and physics a degree of autonomy, then the significance of Paterian aestheticism lies in its providing Eddington with a means of articulating Einstein's theory in such a way as to render it familiar, and providing literary writers with a matrix in which to accommodate relativity.

The alignment of non-Euclidean geometry with aestheticism does not redeem Huxley's reductive reference to Helen's 'curves', but Huxley is interesting to pursue, not least because 'Beauty' was pub-lished in the same month as Sullivan's articles on relativity. Huxley almost certainly knew these articles, and would at least have been acquainted with their contents through conversation. His first two novels continue to engage tentatively with Einstein and the language of geometry. *Crome Yellow*, published in November 1921, hints in its first chapter that it depicts a post-Einsteinian world, and in chap-ter 10 the physicist is alluded to by name. Characteristically, though, the allusion trivializes him, being due to Priscilla Wimbush, who worries whether relativity will affect her astrological charts.[34] The irony and the slightness of the allusion suggest that Huxley may have no coherent purpose in his scientific allusions, other than to assert his topicality and his modernity.[35]

The novel begins with Denis Stone in a train on a slow branch line, lamenting the loss of time his journey involves. When he reaches his station, his impatience and sense of urgency come into

[33] Pater, *Appreciations* (1889; London: Macmillan, 1924), 34–5.

[34] Huxley, *Crome Yellow*, 47.

[35] A position argued generally by June Deery, 'Cultural Trespass?', *University of Dayton Review*, 21/3 (1992), 73–84.

conflict with the stationmaster's more relaxed approach to life. By 1921, trains were 'inseparably coupled' with the popularization of Einstein, so much so that Sullivan, spotting another train approaching in H. W. Carr's exposition, commented 'We knew that something complicated was coming, because we are always meeting these trains in expositions of relativity.'[36] In this light, Denis's conflict with the stationmaster could be read as an Einsteinian allegory of the world viewed by two observers with different velocities. However, Huxley does not allow his readers to pursue this possibility: *Crome Yellow* abandons the special principle of relativity, and moves on to the general principle. Denis cycles the last few miles to Crome, and tries to find the right word to describe 'the beauty of those deeply embayed combes, scooped in the flanks of the ridge beneath him' (2). The scene alludes to curved spacetime, though 'curves' is the word that Denis finds least satisfactory, and also the word which blocks or represses all other possibilities. Eventually, by thinking of the French *galbes*, he moves to a sexualized vision of the landscape, in which 'the little valleys had the lines of a cup moulded round a woman's breast' (3). That association of 'curves' with non-Euclidean geometry is strengthened by Huxley's 'Beauty', and its reference to Helen of Troy. But while the earlier text concealed its embarrassment about sexuality, schoolboyishly, in the language of geometry, the novel moves in the opposite direction: not knowing how to develop the language of geometry in any coherent way, it returns to the language of sexuality, and specifically to a painterly version of it. Science is apparently more embarrassing for Huxley than sex: embarrassing, perhaps, because at this stage, he cannot find a literary form sufficient to accommodate his knowledge of the new physics, yet is aware of the large claims made for it, not least by Sullivan.

However, in chapter 4, Huxley returns to geometry. Denis has a faltering conversation with Jenny Mullion, who, being deaf, responds to his question 'Did you sleep well?' by replying 'Yes, isn't it lovely', and then talking about the weather.

Parallel straight lines, Denis reflected, meet only at infinity. He might talk for ever of care-charmer sleep and she of meteorology till the end of time.

---

[36] David Bradshaw, 'The Best of Companions', *Review of English Studies*, 47 (1996), 196; Sullivan, 'An Abstruse Theory', *Athenaeum* (5 Nov. 1920), 621–2.

Did one ever establish contact with anyone? We are all parallel straight lines. Jenny was only a little more parallel than most.

(15)

What place does Euclid have in the discourse of a satirical novel? In one respect, Denis is thinking like an exemplary interpreter of science and literature, recognizing that the apparently neutral language of geometrical postulates contains metaphors of human isolation and narratives of human contact. This passage is valuable, not only because it authorizes readers themselves to interpret the novel in this way, but also because it encapsulates the solipsism that is fundamental to Huxley's early novels, peopled as they are by eccentrics and caricatures. Jenny's deafness is merely incidental.

The term 'eccentric' is itself a geometrical one, and its potential richness is illuminated by a text by another writer who moved in Huxley's cultural orbits. Robert Gathorne-Hardy first visited Garsington while a third-year undergraduate at Oxford, in late 1921 or early 1922; Huxley was by then a long-established part of Ottoline Morrell's cultural circle. Gathorne-Hardy appropriated general relativity, and the idea that matter created a warp in space-time, to describe the Morrells, saying that they too 'produced such a warp in the spiritual world about them which caused everybody to behave eccentrically'.[37] It is possible that Gathorne-Hardy's perception of Garsington as being peopled by eccentrics was quite accurate, but it may also have been influenced by Huxley's thinly veiled presentation of it as Crome in *Crome Yellow*: in one passage Mr Scogan excuses the existence of the aristocracy on the grounds that it alone is capable of tolerating and even encouraging the 'eccentricities of the artist and the newfangled thinker' (53).

In this light, Gathorne-Hardy appears to have been attempting to outdo Huxley, and the modernity of his reference draws attention to the antiquity of Denis Stone's reflections. In a period when the failings of Euclid's parallel postulate had been brought to the attention of all intellectually inclined readers, it seems strange that Denis's world view should, at this point, be so assuredly Euclidean. If

[37] Gathorne-Hardy, 'Introduction' to Ottoline Morrell, *The Early Memoirs* (London: Faber, 1963), 29–30. Gathorne-Hardy matriculated at Oxford in Michaelmas Term 1919: *Oxford University Calendar for 1920* (Oxford: Oxford University Press, 1919), 488. Leonard Woolf's description of Garsington as a 'galaxy of male stars' provides an interesting supplement to Gathorne-Hardy's quip: *Beginning Again: An Autobiography of the Years 1911–1918* (London: Hogarth, 1964), 203.

Huxley was conscious of this, he may be implying that Denis is as much behind the times as Crome. Moreover, not only is Denis depending on Euclid, but he is subtly modifying him. The usual form of the parallel postulate states that parallel lines produced indefinitely do *not* meet at infinity. Denis says they meet *only* at infinity. Denis's re-writing of Euclid introduces the possibility that the isolation of characters can be overcome, and that communication can become possible. At this early point in the novel, it creates expectations of Denis being involved in a marriage plot, most obviously with Jenny. The novel goes on to complicate this expectation: in one sense, Denis's parallel lines do meet, in that he finally achieves empathy with Mary, but their empathy is only that of mutual commiseration over disappointed relationships.

Huxley's next novel, *Antic Hay,* develops and twists the theme of parallel straight lines. When the artist Casimir Lypiatt goes down on his knees and expresses his passionate love for Mrs Viveash, she pats his head comfortingly, 'as one might pat the head of a large dog', and thinks to herself:

If only one could manage things on the principle of the railways! Parallel tracks—that was the thing. For a few miles you'd be running at the same speed. There'd be delightful conversation at the windows . . . And when you'd said all there was to say, you'd put on a little more steam, wave your hand, blow a kiss and away you'd go, forging ahead along the smooth polished rails. But instead of that, there were these dreadful accidents; the points were wrongly set, the trains came crashing together.[38]

In the case of Lypiatt and Mrs Viveash, the space which on a narrow view appears to conform to the parallel postulate turns out, on a larger view, to be non-Euclidean.

Taken together with Gathorne-Hardy's anecdote, Huxley's first two novels suggest that there was something like a necessary connection between caricature and geometry. Such a connection could not be universally or timelessly true, but in the early 1920s it was widespread. In this light, a passing remark by T. S. Eliot from 1919 acquires greater significance, both for his work and for modernist writing generally. In his essay 'Ben Jonson', Eliot attempts to re-evaluate Jonson and implicitly, to appropriate him as a model for modern writing. He attempts to critique the convention according to which Shakespeare's plays were seen as having more emotional

---

[38] Huxley, *Antic Hay,* 74–5.

'depth' than Jonson's. He argues that there is a distinction between a 'superficial art' and an 'art of the surface', contrasting Beaumont and Fletcher, who wrote apparently emotional verse which was in fact 'superficial with a vacuum behind it', with Jonson, in whose work 'the superficies . . . is solid'.[39] In attempting to clarify the distinction, Eliot was able to move very easily from a discussion of surface and depth into the language of geometry:

Jonson's characters conform to the logic of the emotions of their world. It is a world like Lobatchevsky's; the worlds created by artists like Jonson are like the systems of non-Euclidean geometry. They are not fancy, because they have a logic of their own; and this logic illuminates the actual world, because it gives us a new point of view from which to inspect it.

The passage has been little commented upon, but it has been suggested that this allusion is part of an impudent charade in Eliot's early criticism, a 'masquerade of scholarship' modelled on Remy de Gourmont: 'We suspect that Eliot knows no more about Lobatchevsky than we do, but we know that the old fogeys he is attacking will *think* he does.'[40] If this were the case, then the only conclusion to be drawn would be that 'non-Euclidean geometry' was merely a metonym for 'modern science', a means of recruiting the cultural authority of science against a generation of critics who might feel inclined to disagree with Eliot's assessment of Jonson. Certainly Eliot could not have been unaware of the topicality of his reference. His article was published just one week after the Royal Society had heard the result of Eddington's test of Einstein's General Principle. He may later have regretted the topicality of the reference, for, while it remained in the 1920 and 1928 editions of *The Sacred Wood*, he removed it when revising 'Ben Jonson' for inclusion in the 1932 edition of *Selected Essays*, and never restored it. However, if the 1932 revision hints that Eliot was embarrassed at the comparison, this was more probably due to the developing association of non-Euclidean geometry with popular science writing and with esoteric interest in the 'fourth dimension', and not to a dissatisfaction with the comparison *per se*, nor to a sense of regret over a youthful

---

[39] Eliot, 'Ben Jonson', *TLS* (13 Nov. 1919), 637–8. Another version, 'The Comedy of Humours', appeared in *The Athenaeum* (14 Nov. 1919), 1180–1.

[40] F. W. Bateson, 'The Poetry of Learning', in Graham Martin (ed.), *Eliot in Perspective: A Symposium* (London: Macmillan, 1970), 31–44 (p. 35); see also Richard Sheppard, 'The Problematics of European Modernism,' in Steve Giles (ed.), *Theorizing Modernism: Essays in Critical Theory* (London: Routledge, 1993), 1–51 (pp. 40–1).

'masquerade of learning'.[41] To assume that Eliot knew as little about geometry as most late twentieth-century academic literary critics is to impose an alien set of cultural values on him. Eliot could have heard of non-Euclidean geometries long before Einstein's general principle drew attention to them: they are mentioned in at least one of the articles cited in his doctoral thesis, and were discussed frequently in *Mind* at a time when Eliot was referring to it in the course of his philosophical research.[42] The very topicality of geometry in November 1919 gave Eliot additional opportunities to learn.

Of course, even if we concede that Eliot knew what he was talking about, his reference to Lobatchevsky could still be termed impudent on the grounds that it gives the geometrically unlearned reader no explanation of the basis of the simile. Taking 'Ben Jonson' in isolation, these criticisms are fair, but by drawing comparisons between this essay and other work by Eliot and his contemporaries, it is possible to see how his idea of 'non-Euclidean humanity' is not an isolated topical reference, but is part of a larger system.

Eliot had been developing what we might call an 'aesthetics of the surface' for some time. In January 1918 he had praised Henry James in terms which, perhaps unexpectedly, anticipate those of 'Ben Jonson'. James's characters were 'Done in a clean, flat drawing, each is extracted out of a reality of its own, substantial enough; everything given is true for that individual; but what is given is chosen with great art for its place in a general scheme.'[43] In 'Ben Jonson', the flatness of the drawing is a precondition of the cohesion of the characters. While in Shakespeare, the characters 'act upon' one another, in Jonson's work they 'fit in' with one another: 'The artistic result of *Volpone* is not due to any effect that Volpone, Mosca, Corvino, Corbaccio, Voltore have upon each other, but simply to their combination into a whole.'[44] Later in 1918, Eliot identified Jonsonian qualities in Wyndham Lewis's *Tarr*. Lewis had an 'inhuman' intellectuality, but to Eliot this was praiseworthy: his humour was 'near to Dickens, but on the right side, for it is not too

---

[41] It is also possible, as Sheppard suggests, that by 1932 Eliot had 'achieved his own sense of centred, "Euclidean" certainty' ('The Problematics of European Modernism', 41).

[42] Bertrand Russell, 'Recent Work on the Philosophy of Leibniz', *Mind*, 12 (1903), 177–201, cited by Eliot in *Knowledge and Experience in the Philosophy of F. H. Bradley* (London: Faber, 1964). See also L. J. Russell, 'Space and Mathematical Reasoning', *Mind*, 17 (1908), 321–49; C. D. Broad, 'What Do We Mean by the Question: Is Our Space Euclidean?', *Mind*, 24 (1915), 464–80.

[43] Eliot, 'Henry James', *Selected Prose*, 151.   [44] Eliot, 'Ben Jonson', 638.

remote from Ben Jonson'.[45] (The wrong side of Dickens was presumably the sentimental side: though one might make a case for sentiment as kitsch, as a superficial form of emotion, such an argument belongs to a later era). In the Lewis essay, Eliot is caught between two possibilities, a 'human' or 'humane' outlook which is too indebted to romanticism and Victorian sentimentalism to be useful, and a modernist outlook which, at this time, he can describe only as 'inhuman'. Non-Euclidean geometry allows Eliot to break apart this pair of concepts and introduce a third, the concept of a humanity which is neither deeply human nor inhumanly superficial, but 'non-Euclidean humanity'.

Eliot's analysis of Jonson and caricature owes something not only to his reading of Lewis, but to Lewis's text itself, particularly Tarr's disquisition on art. Tarr directs his criticism primarily at the equation of art with vitality, but vitality, in this case, implies depth and interiority:

'Deadness, then', Tarr went on, 'in the limited sense in which we use that word, is the first condition of art. The second is the absence of *soul*, in the sentimental human sense. The lines and masses of the statue are its soul. No restless, quick flame-like ego is imagined for the inside of it. It has no inside. This is another condition of art; *to have no inside*, nothing you cannot see.'[46]

This line of thought can be traced back to Nietzsche, and frequently has been; specifically, to the distinction he makes in *The Birth of Tragedy* between 'the Apolline art of the sculptor and the non-visual, Dionysiac art of music'.[47] However, there are important intermediaries whose terminology is more suggestive for the purposes of the present comparison. The most significant is T. E. Hulme's essay 'Modern Art and its Philosophy' (1914), itself an appropriation of Worringer's work.[48] Hulme distinguished between two kinds of art, the geometrical and the vital. Vital art has lines which are soft and fluid; it aims to represent life, and to produce a relation of empathy between the art work and the viewer. It is essentially naturalistic or

---

[45] Eliot, 'Tarr', *The Egoist*, 5/8 (Sept. 1918), 105.
[46] Lewis, *Tarr: The 1918 Version*, ed. Paul O'Keeffe (Santa Rosa: Black Sparrow, 1990), 299–300.
[47] Friedrich Nietzsche, *The Birth of Tragedy* (1871), trans. Shaun Whiteside, ed. Michael Tanner (London: Penguin, 1993), 14.
[48] Hulme, 'Modern Art and its Philosophy', in *Collected Writings*, 268–85; Wilhelm Worringer, *Abstraktion und Einfühlung* (1908).

realistic. It is associated with the rise of humanism. Geometrical art abstracts from nature: the human body is represented as 'stiff lines and cubical shapes of various kinds' (272). Hulme gives Byzantine and Egyptian art as examples, but also modern art, which he associates with the contemporary decline of humanism.

It is central to Hulme's argument that these two forms of art correspond to two different kinds of relation to nature and to space. The vital, naturalistic art 'is the result of a happy pantheistic relation between man and the outside world' (273). The geometrical art is the result of a feeling of separation from nature, a state of mind which can derive from many dissimilar causes. Hulme's prime example is 'more primitive people': the 'lack of order' and 'seeming arbitrariness' of their world inspires them with a certain fear, which Hulme compares to agoraphobia. As a compensation for this 'space-shyness', they desire to create abstract geometrical shapes, which, 'being durable and permanent shall be a refuge from the flux and impermanence of outside nature' (274). Hulme gives the example of Greek archaic sculpture, in which 'the arms are bound close to the body' (275).

Worringer's distinction acquires an additional depth of meaning in Hulme's aesthetic system because it corresponds very closely to the distinction Hulme had earlier advanced in his essay 'Romanticism and Classicism'.[49] Hulme had distinguished the two temperaments in terms of space and spatial limitation. Hulme's 'classicist' sees man as 'an extraordinarily fixed and limited animal' (61). The 'romantic', who is equivalent to the creator of 'vital' and 'empathetic' art, sees man as potentially unlimited, and 'because he thinks man infinite, must always be talking about the infinite' (62). Taken together, Hulme's remarks suggest another way of interpreting the relation of Euclidean to non-Euclidean geometry. Although 'classical' would, in its usual acceptation, be best applied to Euclidean geometry (Greek, rational, established), if we use the term 'classical' in Hulme's sense, as denoting a certain relationship to the infinite, then non-Euclidean geometry, in so far as it rejects the parallel postulate, is the 'classical' geometry. Euclidean geometry ascribes the quality of infinity to space, just as romanticism ascribes it to man. W. K. Clifford's description of the coming of non-Euclidean geometry could fit comfortably into Hulme's essays: 'the

---

[49] Hulme, 'Romanticism and Classicism', in *Collected Writings*, 59–73. Csengeri suggests that the essay is the same as the lecture Hulme delivered on 15 July 1912.

knowledge of Immensity and Eternity is replaced by knowledge of Here and Now'.[50] Hulme's 'classical' qualities apply particularly well to a non-Euclidean space which is, like Riemann's, finite but unbounded: it is a space which is itself 'space-shy', fearful of the infinite.

In this context it is interesting to consider Clifford's lecture in further detail. Clifford concludes by comparing the properties of 'homaloidal' space (space without any curve or distortion), with those of the various alternatives. He notes that in some non-Euclidean spaces, after travelling a prodigious distance, you would return to the spot from which you started. Clifford declares that such a geometry is 'far more complete and interesting' than any Euclidean geometry. This remark might seem to express merely a mathematician's delight at the possibilities of pure thought, but Clifford implies a greater significance by adopting the vocabulary of consolatory literature: 'In fact, I do not mind confessing that I personally have often found relief from the dreary infinities of homaloidal space in the consoling hope that, after all, this other [non-Euclidean geometry] may be the true state of things.'[51] The abruptness with which Clifford adopts this tone, and the implications of what he says, suggest that he is parodying such consolatory literature. Clifford alludes to and subverts the habitual identification of God with the infinite, and seems in effect to say 'God: how dreary'. But even if his tongue was in his cheek, his mock confession suggests how a curved, non-Euclidean space could prove intellectually, imaginatively, and even emotionally satisfying. It provides a protection against infinite space. For Clifford, infinite space was merely dreary, but Eliot describes the 'depth', the 'third dimension' of Shakespeare, Donne, Webster, and Tourner as containing 'a network of tentacular roots reaching down to the deepest terrors and desires': the infinities of Euclidean space can be terrifying as well as monotonous.[52]

Eliot's essay on Jonson was also an exploration of his own aesthetics. He wrote it at a crucial point in his career, shortly after he had delivered 'Modern Tendencies in Poetry', and shortly before he

---

[50] W. K. Clifford, 'The Philosophy of the Pure Sciences. II.—The Postulates of the Science of Space', *Contemporary Review*, 25 (1875), 360–76 (p. 363). The second of three lectures first delivered at the Royal Institution, 1, 8, 15 Mar. 1873.

[51] Clifford, 'The Philosophy of the Pure Sciences, II', 376.

[52] Eliot, 'Ben Jonson', 638.

began work on *The Waste Land*.[53] His contemporaries recognized immediately that in his analysis of caricature, Eliot was, as Katherine Mansfield put it, 'finding himself'.[54] Mansfield's remark is interestingly ambiguous, in that 'himself' could refer to Eliot's already-established inscrutable public persona, or to his works; the ambiguity suggests one route at least by which writers may move between the self and literary form.

Relating the form of *The Waste Land* to general relativity is a speculative activity, and the only form of confirmation available for such speculations comes in the form of critical commentaries which themselves used the language or the imagery of the general principle and associated ideas. As a minimum, one can return to Eliot's observation that Jonson's characters do not 'act upon' one another, but 'fit it' together. The language of action and reaction suggests a Newtonian mechanics, in which space is a distinct backdrop to the movement of matter. Likewise, the language of accommodation can be associated with an Einsteinian model of space and matter: the 'fitting in' together of Jonson's characters can be taken to resemble the curvature of spacetime around matter. However, 'fitting in' is a characteristic of all coherent systems, of which Einsteinian gravitation is just one example: these phrases justify only the loosest of analogies.

To develop the idea of 'accommodation' more systematically, one needs to relate the form of *The Waste Land* to concepts of distortion, crumpling, puckering, and warping. This analogy can readily be developed, because it builds on long-established metaphors concerning language itself. In characterizing the distinction between literal and metaphorical statements, we draw upon metaphor, and one category of these metaphors is geometrical. The literal utterance is characterized as an unadorned flat surface, while the metaphorical utterance is characterized as a decorated or curved surface. A 'plain' speaker is also a 'plane' speaker: not only are the two words related etymologically (which would in itself prove nothing), but their meanings have not diverged significantly. Although hardness and rigidity are more familiar metaphors for literalism than flatness, all three metaphors are mutually sustaining: for a surface to remain flat

---

[53] See Eliot, letters to his mother dated 10 Nov. 1919 and 18 Nov. 1919, *Letters* i. 345–6, i. 350–1.

[54] Mansfield, letter to Middleton Murry [dated 19 Nov. 1919], *The Collected Letters of Katherine Mansfield*, ed. Vincent O'Sullivan and Margaret Scott, 4 vols. to date (Oxford: Oxford University Press, 1984–95), iii. 104. Mansfield was referring to 'The Comedy of Humours'.

when subjected to external pressure, it must also be rigid. The metaphor of flatness has been in use since at least the seventeenth century. The first stanza of George Herbert's 'Jordan', which Michael Roberts noted in this connection, is particularly apt:

> When first my lines of heav'nly joys made mention,
> Such was their lustre, they did so excell,
> That I sought out quaint words, and trim invention;
> My thoughts began to burnish, sprout, and swell,
> Curling with metaphors a plain intention,
> Decking the sense, as if it were to sell.[55]

While one cannot reduce Herbert's figures to geometry—'sprout' and 'swell' also implicitly associate metaphor with fertility, while the last line quite explicitly associates it with the market place—it is clear that the underlying metaphor was well established by this time.

The kind of semantic curvature that occurs in Eliot's poem is most concisely illustrated by one of the densest allusive passages, the superimposition of Marvell on Day:

> But at my back from time to time I hear
> The sound of horns and motors, which shall bring
> Sweeney to Mrs Porter in the spring.[56]

Much as Lawrence, in revising *Women in Love*, placed the word 'field' in a tension between its agricultural and its scientific meanings, so, if the reader recognizes the allusions, Eliot allows one phrase to distort another. This dialogism operates not only between phrases, but even within a single word: thus 'horn' refers dialogically both to hunting horns and car horns, and, by extension, to a feudal world and the modern urban world. While the semantic distortions this creates are the most noticeable feature of the poem, it has also been convincingly argued that Eliot's palimpsestic method creates prosodic distortions. For example, reading the line 'Sweet Thames, run softly till I end my song' in the context of Spenser's *Prothalamion*, one would be likely to identify five stressed syllables, but in the context of 'The Fire Sermon' it is more likely to receive only four, the stress on 'till' being dropped; it is 'a familiar line distorted by its modern surroundings'.[57] The pressures are created

[55] Herbert, quoted in Roberts, *The Modern Mind* (London: Faber, 1937), 96. Roberts also notes the metaphor of curled hair in Herbert's 'Dulness'.
[56] Eliot, *The Collected Poems and Plays of T. S. Eliot* (London: Faber, 1969), 67.
[57] Derek Attridge, *The Rhythms of English Poetry* (London: Longman, 1982), 323.

not only by the action of one phrase on another, but, if the reader responds to Eliot's 'mythical method', the action of the mythic subtext. Thus in one of the 'purest', least allusive sections of the poem, the second paragraph of 'What the Thunder Said', the pure dramatic meaning of a voice looking for 'water' and finding only 'rock' is situated in a distorted semantic space, where 'water' refers particularly to fertility myths.

This elaboration of the flat/curved contrast is not simply my own. Contemporary reviewers struggled to accommodate the strangeness of *The Waste Land* within familiar images and concepts, but were forced to abandon some of the conventional vocabulary of poetry reviewing and adopt more impressionistic metaphors. In this they superficially resemble scientists working in unfamiliar areas, and expositors attempting to convey difficult new ideas. More importantly, many of their metaphors identify *The Waste Land* with the concepts of flatness and distortion. Images of mosaics and kaleidoscopes were common. Beyond this similarity, there was a degree of divergence, particularly over the question of whether there was any underlying force acting to unify the fragments. This divergence may be emblematized in two of the earliest reviews. Edmund Wilson emphasized the unity created by myth; Conrad Aiken, who had read parts of the poem long before Eliot conceived of *The Waste Land*, and who was thus more acutely aware of Eliot's compositional process, emphasized heterogeneity.[58] Wilson contrasted the flatness of Ezra Pound's eight published *Cantos*, a 'bewildering mosaic', with Eliot's work, arguing that unlike Pound's work in progress, Eliot's poem had a 'central emotion' which provided 'a key'. Conrad Aiken emphasized flatness, borrowing an image from Louis Untermeyer's review, and describing *The Waste Land* as a kaleidoscope. Aiken also described it as being as flat as Prufrock's projection of 'the nerves' in 'patterns on a screen'. This second image is interesting for its larger implication, that the parts of the body most associated with depth (intellectual depth, in this case), could be projected in two flat dimensions.[59] Aiken went on to explain why the poem seemed flat: 'Mr Eliot has not wholly annealed the allusive

[58] Ronald Bush, 'T. S. Eliot and Modernism at the Present Time', in Bush (ed.), *T. S. Eliot: The Modernist in History* (Cambridge: Cambridge University Press, 1991), 191–204.

[59] Wilson in Michael Grant (ed.), *T. S. Eliot: Critical Heritage* (London: Routledge and Kegan Paul, 1982), 138–44; Untermeyer in ibid., 151–3, esp. 151; Aiken in ibid., 156–61, esp.160.

matter, has left it unabsorbed, lodged in gleaming fragments amid material alien to it.'[60] While such a failure could be represented in terms of a deep structural weakness, Aiken chooses to emphasize the gleaming surface. It might be argued that the ubiquity of this image does not so much indicate a critical consensus about the poem's form as a collective inability among critics to articulate their feelings, which resulted in mutual plagiarism: not only did Untermeyer and Aiken imagine *The Waste Land* as a kaleidoscope, but so too did Harriet Monroe.[61] Nevertheless, even if Monroe and Aiken did not originate the kaleidoscope image independently of earlier critics, that they chose it in preference to other images points to a kind of consensus.

Monroe's review is interesting additionally for her description of *The Waste Land* as a 'wild dance in an ash-heap before a clouded and distorted mirror'.[62] While this is essentially a way of describing the poem as superlatively obscure, and perhaps of indicating its primitivism ('wild dance'), Monroe's image of the 'distorted mirror' suggests a debt to the popularizations of relativity. In very general terms, like Joyce's image of Irish art as the 'cracked lookingglass of a servant', the distorted mirror symbolizes Eliot's ambivalent relationship to mimesis, but, given the use of the fairground mirror as an image for 'curved' space time, it suggests that Eliot's poem too takes familiar objects and warps them. Untermeyer also seems to have borrowed from the relativity expositions. His description of the poem as 'familiar quotations . . . imbedded in [a] formless plasma' recalls the description of the Einsteinian universe as consisting of world lines embedded in a jelly which is then distorted.[63] However, there are significant limits to this comparison: while Untermeyer's fragments are embedded, the medium is formless; the mathematical formulation of non-Euclidean space, though it may seem 'formless' to someone reared on Euclid, provides a very precise specification of form. Given the disparaging tone of Untermeyer's review, 'formless plasma' may be intended to remind the reader of 'ectoplasm', and thus to construct Eliot as a fraudulent spiritualist, raising the voices of the dead.

Ideas of distortion remained central to the critical discourse on *The Waste Land* for many years. One important cause was the

---

[60] Aiken, in *Critical Heritage*, 158.

[61] Monroe, in *Critical Heritage*, 167–70, esp. 167.   [62] Ibid., 167.

[63] Sullivan, 'The Equivalence Principle', 433; Eddington, *Space, Time and Gravitation*, 87–8; Nordmann, *Einstein and the Universe*, 136.

incorporation of this vocabulary in the critical discourse of the New Criticism. Because the New Critics developed their concepts from a reading of Eliot's critical essays, and took his poetry as an important reference point, their discourse is perhaps too neatly adapted to his poem to produce any significant insights: there is a lack of critical friction. Additionally, the New Criticism developed its vocabulary in a period when relativity theory was a paradigmatic science. When in 1965 one critic attempted to relate *The Waste Land* to relativity, he suggested that it was 'a mathematical and symbolic scheme of forces, pressures, tensions, oscillations'.[64] Putting aside the question of how *The Waste Land* can be a 'mathematical' scheme, one notes that the vocabulary of 'forces, pressures, [and] tensions' does little more than reproduce the dominant critical discourse of the period.

Nevertheless, this discourse tells us something about Eliot's work, precisely because it derives from Eliot's own critical essays, and from early criticism of *The Waste Land*. That New Criticism should adopt a scientific vocabulary is initially surprising: most critical accounts of the school emphasize its reaction against science, its belief in the difference between denotative scientific and connotative literary language. For example, one of the most influential New Critical books, Cleanth Brooks's *The Well-Wrought Urn*, begins by making the distinction: 'paradox is the language appropriate and inevitable to poetry. It is the scientist whose truth requires a language purged of every trace of paradox; apparently the truth which the poet utters can be approached only in terms of paradox.'[65] However, the surprise is unwarranted: in distinguishing the languages of poetry and of science, Brooks does not directly make any claims about the language of criticism. Critical discourse was placed in a more complex situation, which Brooks does not directly articulate: at an institutional level, literary study had to respond to the prestige of the sciences, and one response was to employ a more technical vocabulary; yet to employ such a vocabulary was to risk the charge of insensitivity to the connotative qualities of literary language, as defined by New Criticism. Brooks's adoption and discussion of Shakespeare's phrase 'assays of bias' is particularly revealing with respect to this dilemma. He introduces it with an attempt to

---

[64] Steven Foster, 'Relativity and *The Waste Land*: A Postulate', *Texas Studies in Literature and Language*, 7 (1965), 77–95 (p. 86).

[65] Cleanth Brooks, *The Well-Wrought Urn* (1947; revised edition, London: Dennis Dobson, 1968), 1.

describe literary language in geometrical terms: 'The poet must work by analogies, but the metaphors do not lie in the same plane or fit neatly edge to edge. There is a continual tilting of the planes; necessary overlappings, discrepancies, contradictions.'[66] This metaphor, however, suggested that literary language is continually making compromises and losing precision. Shakespeare's phrase 'with assays of bias / By indirections find directions out' suggests a higher degree of precision:

Shakespeare had in mind the game of lawnbowls in which the bowl is distorted, a distortion which allows the skilful player to bowl a curve. To elaborate the figure, science makes use of the perfect sphere and its attack can be direct. The method of art can, I believe, never be direct—is always indirect.[67]

Ostensibly, Brooks derives his critical discourse from the most literary of sources, yet the language of 'perfect spheres' and 'distortion' belongs also to the geometrical description of gravitation: the line followed by the bowl is the geodesic line of the physicists. The discourse can be applied to the eclipse observation of 1919: passing through the spacetime curved by the sun, starlight 'alludes' to its presence, but does not touch it directly. Had Brooks taken crown bowling as his example, the similarity to the physicists' discussions of flatlanders encountering a mound would have been closer still.[68] One cannot be sure if Brooks was fully conscious of the geometrical and physical basis for his metaphor for non-scientific language, though his adoption of a language of 'planes' suggests that he was. If so, then Brooks's censor displaces what would have been the shameful and unspeakable coupling of science and literature into the socially acceptable form of a quotation from Shakespeare. *The Waste Land* is mentioned only once in *The Well-Wrought Urn*, but Brooks's critical outlook is everywhere indebted to it and to Eliot's essays. That he too should resort to a language of 'planes' and 'distortion' suggests that, however impudent Eliot's allusion to Lobatchevsky might have been, it was also significant, and that it made sense as part of a coherent system of signs.

The adoption of geometrical metaphors in critical discourse was facilitated by dormant metaphors, slumbering deep within the

---

[66] Brooks, *Well-Wrought*, 6.   [67] Ibid., 6–7.

[68] F. A. Lindemann had compared warped spacetime to a distorted golf green, 'Introduction' to Moritz Schlick, *Space and Time in Contemporary Physics* (Oxford: Oxford University Press, 1920), pp. iv–v.

language. The depth of these metaphors has important consequences for a criticism which would concern itself with the association of geometry and language. My characterization of *The Waste Land*'s method as involving a distortion of semantic space between phrases implies that it is possible to write a plain language without such distortion. Similarly, Brooks's metaphor of imperfect spheres implies and depends upon the idea of perfect spheres. This class of paradox conforms to the logic of the supplement, as described by Derrida and adopted by Attridge: literary language defines itself as something which is both part of literal language, but also supplementary to it.[69]

Like Euclidean geometers, we assume that linguistic space has the property of 'elementary flatness'. Clifford defines this property quite concisely: 'Any curved surface which is such that the more you magnify it the flatter it gets, is said to possess the property of elementary flatness.'[70] However, as Clifford also notes, we can readily imagine surfaces in which successive magnifications reveal 'new wrinkles and inequalities': a coastline or a piece of string are the simplest examples.[71] What would happen if one granted logical priority to semantic curvature, treating straightness not as the standard, but as the exceptional case? As Eddington says, 'a level lawn stands more in need of explanation than an undulating field'.[72] If one starts with an inescapably wrinkled semantic world, one can account for the 'flatness' of literal utterance in much the same way that Rorty accounts for the 'hardness' of scientific facts, as the result of a social convention which agrees on certain interpretative rules: we agree to interpret certain utterances at a level of magnification which reveals their flatness, rather than one which reveals the larger curve, or reveals the more minute wrinkles. This argument, however, still grants too much value to the idea of flatness. Flatness might be better interpreted not as an absence of metaphor, but as an absence of information: flat statements are not factual ones, but predictable ones which, on account of their predictability, carry no information. Jakobson's phatic communion—for example, 'How are you?' 'I'm fine, how are you?'—is the best-known case. Any utterance which

[69] Attridge, *Peculiar Language: Literature as Difference from the Renaissance to James Joyce* (Ithaca: Cornell University Press, 1988), 22–8, and index entries under 'supplement'.

[70] Clifford, 'The Philosophy of the Pure Sciences, II', 368.

[71] James Gleick, *Chaos: Making a New Science* (London: Cardinal, 1988), 94–103.

[72] Eddington, *Physical World*, 138.

carries information can be characterized as creating a small warp in semantic space. My example of phatic communion would itself carry information if it were to occur in an unexpected context. Similarly, the phrase 'Good night sweet ladies' might itself be nothing more than phatic communion, but in the context of Ophelia's madness in *Hamlet*, it becomes less predictable, and so more curved. Eliot, by juxtaposing Ophelia's phrase with the equally banal 'Goonight Bill' and 'Goonight Lou', creates curvature out of phrases which are, when viewed closely and in isolation, flat. On this account, *The Waste Land*'s geometry is not absolutely different from that of other speech, prose, or poetry. All language is warped. The prominence of the warps in *The Waste Land* is due to the apparent unpredictability of its juxtapositions for a first-time reader. Eliot, in making an apparently absolute distinction between the Euclidean drama of Shakespeare and the non-Euclidean drama of Jonson, misleadingly represented the relation of the two geometries: as many expositors were at pains to point out, Euclidean geometries could be contained within non-Euclidean geometries, as special cases.[73] While one can elaborate Eliot's reference to a non-Euclidean drama as a model for a poetry of tensions and pressures, and while such an elaboration finds some confirmation in the remarks of contemporary critics concerning 'distortion', those remarks build upon a metaphorical system which prioritizes flat literalism. Within such a system, *The Waste Land* can only ever be seen as an aberration. If one modifies this metaphorical system on the lines suggested above, then, although one may obtain a better account of the production of meaning, one also deprives Eliot's geometrical metaphor of its ability to differentiate Jonson's (and hence his own) work absolutely. Furthermore, one deprives the contemporary critics of their confirmatory value: they ought not to have been surprised to find 'distortion' in a literary work, as any work of any value will disrupt our expectations and 'distort' the literary tradition.

It is not necessary for a discussion of the form of a work to be confirmed or supported by the content: the content may contradict the form, or exist in a relationship looser even than contradiction. However, in the case of *The Waste Land*, there are certain details of relevance to the questions of flatness and depth. The title itself

[73] More importantly, the 'semi-Euclidean', hyperbolic spacetime of four dimensions can be seen as a special case of non-Euclidean four-dimensional spacetime: Eddington, *Space, Time and Gravitation*, 47, 77–83.

suggests flatness, something confirmed by references to the 'endless plains', 'the arid plain' and 'the flat horizon' (lines 369, 424, 370). Eliot's metaphors of flatness and dryness relate primarily to infertility, but it is relevant to remember that they are also, dormantly, metaphors of literalness. Curiously, he had described the 'flat' and hollow work of Beaumont and Fletcher in very similar terms: although their work appears to have 'depth', in fact the 'blossoms' of their imagination 'draw no sustenance from the soil, but are cut and slightly withered flowers stuck into sand'.[74] More curiously still, in the essay which immediately preceded *The Waste Land* in *The Criterion*, T. Sturge Moore had characterized 'beauties of detail' which lack 'organic relation' to an aesthetic whole as 'cut or wired flowers, doomed to sterility.'[75] According to such a characterization, the three-dimensional world of Shakespeare might seem preferable, on account of its 'tentacular roots' which reach down to the deepest 'terrors and desires'. But in *The Waste Land*, as in 'Ben Jonson', this is not so. The cruelty of April is that it stirs the 'dull roots', and awakens 'memory and desire'. The speaker of the opening lines would prefer to preserve the flat covering of 'forgetful snow' as a way of suppressing post-war trauma, and in particular the knowledge that there are corpses buried in the gardens of Europe. In this light, the ideal of 'non-Euclidean humanity' provides not simply the resolution of an aesthetic problem, but the resolution of an emotional and psychological one: how to deal with 'deep' traumatic memories without simply hollowing out the depths. The problem is collective as well as personal, and requires that groups reach some form of accommodation, 'fitting in' with each other without referring directly to their shared traumatic memories. If we allow the content of the poem to govern the interpretation of its form, the aesthetic ideals of Jonsonian caricature and non-Euclidean humanity emerge not as permanent solutions, but as temporary expedients, necessary until a return to 'depth', 'terror' and 'desire' is possible. Such a reading is compatible with the characterization of modernism as expressing a nostalgia for lost order. Curiously, it places Eliot closer to the conservative physicists who, in their more accommodating moments, tolerated the use of mathematical symbolism as a temporary measure, but hoped for a return

---

[74] Eliot, 'Ben Jonson', 638.
[75] Moore, 'The Story of Tristram and Isolt in Modern Poetry', *The Criterion*, 1 (Oct. 1922), 34–49. The juxtaposition is noted by Bishop, 'Re:Covering Modernism', 314.

to 'more physical conceptions'.[76] It implies that while the modern poet must 'be *difficult*', 'allusive' and 'indirect' in response to a complex civilization, such measures are temporary.

[76] Lodge, 'Einstein's Real Achievement', 371.

Conclusion

IN 1991, N. Katherine Hayles critiqued the 'characteristic pattern' followed in most studies in literature and science:

First some scientific theory or result is explained; then parallels are drawn (or constructed) between it and literary texts; then the author says in effect Q.E.D., and the paper is finished. In my view, every time this formula is used it should be challenged: What do the parallels signify? How do you explain their existence? What mechanisms do you postulate to account for them? What keeps the selection of some theoretical features and some literary texts from being capricious? What are the presuppositions of the explanations you construct, and how do they connect with what you are trying to explain? None of these questions is easy to answer.[1]

These continue to be valuable questions, not least because there are strong institutional reasons for the continued dominance of the 'formula' described by Hayles. The audience for most 'literature and science' criticism consists of academic literary critics: such critics are usually familiar with the author or literary culture being discussed, but unfamiliar with scientific theory. There are good reasons for beginning a paper with an explanation of its scientific content, and no virtue in deliberate obscurity; exploration does not preclude explanation. Although a wholly formulaic method will often produce wholly predictable results, a method which abandons all familiar formulae will convey nothing to anyone. By the same token, if every critic in the discipline addressed Hayles's questions to the exclusion of all other methodological reflection, Hayles's questions would also lose their value.

The real problem faced by critics' explanations of scientific theory is that, ideally, they fulfil a very different purpose from popular science expositions. Most explanations of scientific ideas are organized in terms of container metaphors, unfolding layers of wrapping to reach the simple timeless idea at the centre. Explanations for the

[1] N. Katherine Hayles (ed.), *Chaos and Order* (Chicago: University of Chicago Press, 1991), 19.

purpose of the historical study of literature and science need to pay as much attention to the container as to the contents; they are descriptions as much as explanations. This is greatly facilitated by employing the actual popular science texts of the period, rather than more recent accounts. Historical texts may bring their own difficulties, in that their explanations may become incomprehensible in the course of time: their authors' assumptions about what the reader finds familiar and unfamiliar become gradually less reliable. If this is not a problem with relativity expositions, that is because we have reached a significant historical distance from them: they are old enough to reveal their historicity, yet recent enough to remain comprehensible.

To avoid formulaic explanations while retaining a familiar model, the present study has given a central place to metaphor and to the generalist periodical, and, more tentatively, to the idea of subject formation. These are not in themselves the mechanisms that account for the parallels: rather (if we must retain Hayles's image), they are tools with which we may construct the mechanisms. In attempting to write about literature and science, we must also draw upon 'a whole constellation of associated and unsettled material':[2] the present study has touched upon steam engines, empires, department stores, urban riots, dinner parties, telegraph wires, flatfish, lawn bowling, and a schizophrenic judge. Summarized thus, the material seems wilfully eclectic, but it becomes a constellation because it has been examined only in certain of its metaphorical aspects. The material was selected not capriciously, but on the basis of the metaphors which shaped the scientific theories.

If, in spite of the wealth of this material, I have not created the explanatory mechanisms envisaged by Hayles, it is because the metaphor of a mechanism is irreconcilable with the fragmentariness of the printed and archival material. We can glimpse fragments of the mechanism—an author reading science in one place, an expository metaphor emerging in their writing elsewhere—but never the full machine; an author who left a full archival record of his creative processes would be suspect on other grounds. It is better, perhaps, to refer to the *institutions* that account for the parallels. The primary institution in this study is the generalist journal; this institution encourages, I have argued, interpretative practices of anti-disciplinary reading. However, institutions may consist of

---

[2] Beer, 'Science and Literature', 797.

much less formal arrangements: groups of like-minded writers meeting in restaurants and in private homes on a regular basis, discussing ideas of the moment. The popular science writer has similar importance as an institution. If J. W. N. Sullivan has loomed disproportionately large in this study, it is because he is the most relevant and completely documented embodiment of the institution.[3] Other scientists, popularizers and polymaths may have had equally significant interactions with literary writers; if these are uncovered by future research, they may modify the personal significance of Sullivan, but not the significance of the institution he represents.

It is dangerously easy, of course, to assert that 'everyone' was talking about a science, and far more difficult to uncover eyewitness accounts of such conversations. I suggested in the introduction that generalist periodicals may be used to fill out the missing details of conversations, but, rich though they are, even the generalist periodical provides an incomplete approximation; moreover, as an approximation it is more relevant to some writers—notably Woolf and Eliot—than to others. One reason why James Joyce has been a marginal presence in this study is that he was isolated both from the literary communities of London and from their literary periodicals. Whatever advantages this brought to his writing, it places the present form of cultural history at a disadvantage. The generalist journal is also an imperfect tool insofar as very few long modernist works were serialized, and those that were tended to appear in the little magazines. The generalist journals printed minor verse, such as the poems by Shanks and Gibson, but they printed contributions from the major modernists only in their roles as essayists and reviewers, not as poets and novelists. If we wished to draw our texts exclusively from the generalist journals, using them as a corpus rather than as a flexible tool, we would have a strange and impoverished view of modernism in which Mrs Dalloway, for example, existed only as a distant rumour. If we use the generalist journals to establish the contours of the literary culture, and do not mistake the contour lines for fences, there is some loss of methodological elegance, but a far greater gain in literary material.

---

[3] Though J. G. Crowther is better documented, on account of his papers being deposited at Sussex University, he became prominent only in the 1930s, and was much less closely associated with literary writers.

What the parallels signify depends on our vantage point; lines which appear approximately parallel when viewed locally may exhibit a more complex relationship when seen in full, from a distance. What this study tells us in general terms about modernism, modernity, and science depends a great deal on how we understand modernism in the first place. Some of my working assumptions may appear to diverge from the dominant models: most notably, while most readers and critics have argued that modernism was an international movement, I have foregrounded the local and British aspect of its networks and publications. The divergence here is perhaps more apparent than real: after all, this study has examined theories which were mostly developed in continental Europe; if local networks have been emphasized, it is because even an international movement must manifest itself in local and material media. To speak of the international character of modernism without recognizing this is to come close to speaking of a *zeitgeist* that transmits its force instantaneously without regard to national or social boundaries.

A further reason for treating the internationalist model sceptically is that Britain experienced modernity much earlier than much of continental Europe, both in its technological aspects and its social and organizational ones.[4] Most critics of modernism have seen it as a response to the experience of modernity, though they have continued to debate what sort of response: celebratory or condemnatory; expressive, compensatory, or a dialectical combination of both.[5] These disagreements reflect the complexity of modernism, but that complexity is compounded by treating all its local manifestations as directly comparable. If we accept that Britain had begun to experience modernity in the first thirty years of the nineteenth century, then we must understand British modernism not only as a reaction to modernity, but also as a reaction to a reaction. The Victorian 'sages' had already responded prolifically to modernity— understood as 'mechanism'—as had, less directly, many Victorian poets: the British modernists responded to the perceived sentimentality and pomposity of the Victorian response.

Because of this complex background, British modernist writers were less inclined than their continental counterparts to define themselves in opposition to 'science'. That they have been presented

[4]   Sheppard, 'The Problematics of European Modernism', 7.

as a reactionary anti-science movement is due to a failure to respect the distinction between pure and applied science. The distinction was, as we have seen, strongly contested during this period, but it was if anything strengthened and clarified by the 1914–18 war. The presentation of modernism as an anti-scientific movement was exaggerated by the New Critics, and continues in works such as Calinescu's *Five Faces of Modernity*. I would suggest, very broadly, that the pure sciences provided a language—though by no means the only one—in which British modernist writers expressed their response to modernity. Because this 'language' consisted of scientific models and metaphors, it does not manifest itself primarily as a specifiable vocabulary, though certain key images recur in novels and poems, and more frequently in essays and reviews. Rather, it manifests itself as literary form.

The metaphors of literary form, I have suggested, have much in common with the metaphors of the self. We can approach the topic of modernity and subject formation by returning to Lakoff and Johnson, who argue that many of our activities are shaped around key metaphors, such as 'time is money': 'Much of cultural change arises from the introduction of new metaphorical concepts and the loss of old ones.'[6] If we develop Lakoff and Johnson's account of metaphor into an account of subject formation, it follows that cultural change affects not only the metaphors which structure our activities, but the metaphors in which we live. The metaphors of modern science may serve both to reflect modernity and to compensate for it, according to the situation of individual subjects. In *The Waves*, Bernard's and Louis's self-realization through telephone lines and rays of light combine both aspects. The modernist subject positions studied in the present work do not combine to form a single coherent or exhaustive model for the self: there are points of similarity between them, but there are also points of conflict. Framing all of them is the modernist subject's sense of the incompleteness due to intellectual specialization. Examining the metaphors internal to science, we see the modernist subject as a container filled with identical, fluid particles, in constant danger of entropic leakage; in this we may contrast it with earlier selves (and bodies) which were filled with four 'humours' or other contrasting basic elements. We see it as a receptive surface, almost without

[5] Jameson, *The Political Unconscious* (London: Methuen, 1981), 236.
[6] Lakoff and Johnson, *Metaphors We Live By*, 145.

depth, in danger of being overwhelmed by sensations, passive except in its ability to sort those sensations into patterns. In Chapters 5 and 6 it emerged as a porous or semi-translucent substance capable of extending beyond its position in space and time; it extends itself by means of radiation, fields of force, filaments, and rays of light; it is open to penetration by external forces. In Chapter 7, its flatness was again evident, and may be contrasted not only with the assertive muscular self proposed by Lodge and by Lewis, but also with the flatness seen in Chapter 3. While the flat surface of the consumerist self was susceptible to impressions, suggesting at least a residual quality of depth, the surfaces of 'non-Euclidean humanity' are absolute. The worst that could happen to the receptive surfaces of Chapter 3 was that they might be overwhelmed by sensations, but the traumatized non-Euclidean lives in fear of terrors and desires.

The metaphors of flatness are particularly interesting, both because the postmodern has often been characterized in such terms—or in the more nostalgic and negative terms of 'depthlessness'[7]—and because *The Waste Land* provides very clear evidence for the relation of flatness to traumatic memory. Though *The Waste Land* encourages us to identify the trauma as the 1914–18 war, I would argue that the quality of flatness is a response to the deeper trauma of modernity. Gaylord LeRoy and Ursula Beitz establish the socio-historical grounds for this argument. They locate the crisis in the last third of the nineteenth century, during the transition to imperialism, though the exact moment is less important than the character of the crisis:

in the epoch of monopoly, the decision-making process becomes invisible, the real decisions coming to be made more and more by those in command of the monopolies; ordinary people, even those in somewhat privileged positions, come to feel—and justifiably—that they lack the kind of leverage that the humanist tradition had always made one feel entitled to command.[8]

The humanist metaphor of 'leverage' implies the metaphor of depth: the humanist will, at the centre of the body and the centre of the self, is capable of shaping the world around it and controlling its own destiny; the body is one of its levers. Denied that control, the

---

[7] Jameson, *Postmodernism, or, the Cultural Logic of Late Capitalism* (London: Verso, 1991), 12.

[8] Gaylord LeRoy and Ursula Beitz, 'The Marxist Approach to Modernism', *Journal of Modern Literature*, 3 (1973), 1158–74 (p. 1159).

self comes to resemble T. E. Hulme's description of archaic Greek sculpture where 'the arms are bound close to the body'; for Hulme, such sculpture anticipates the anti-humanist tendency of modernist art.[9] Though Hulme (following Worringer) attributes this form of sculpture to 'space-shyness', we might reinterpret it as due to apathy in the face of powerlessness: there is little point in extending one's arms if they have no leverage. The 'lack of order and seeming arbitrariness'[10] which characterized the natural world for primitive man also characterize the social world of monopoly capitalism for modern man. If we place the metaphors of deep and flat selves at the centre of our account, then the other available metaphors for the self appear not as exchangeable equivalents, but as compensations. The possibility, for example, of reaching out with rays of light and invisible filaments into distant spacetime looks like a fantasy of control. The depths of spacetime compensate for the shallowness of the self. More directly, and less metaphorically, the power of selection that derives from consumer choice compensates for the lack of control over production and exchange.

The lack of depth which characterizes the individual subject also comes to characterize knowledge. We characterize arguments metaphorically as journeys: as Lakoff and Johnson show, we 'set out' to prove something, we stray from the 'path' of the argument.[11] The traditional journey metaphor implies that arguments have determinate beginnings and endings. The characteristically modern turn comes with the recognition that the journey takes place on a finite unbounded surface: it can move freely, but it is always in danger of returning tautologously to its starting point; it can never rise into an extra dimension above the linguistic surface.[12] It is tempting to present the history of the flatness metaphor purely as a history of ideas, because the philosophical consequences of the linguistic turn have been explored so thoroughly in post-structuralist writing. However, LeRoy and Beitz's outline of monopoly capitalism is compelling, and suggests that the idea of 'flat' knowledge arose because of the crisis in the humanist model of the self. In the humanist model of the self, language was, like the body, a technology through which the will expressed itself. Meaning existed in the depths of the self,

---

[9] Hulme, *Collected Writings*, 275.   [10] Ibid., 273.

[11] Lakoff and Johnson, *Metaphors We Live By*, 89–91.

[12] For a variant of this argument, explicitly invoking geometry, see Michael Roberts, *The Modern Mind* (London: Faber, 1937), 118–19.

prior to expression through language. After the crisis, language becomes a corporate entity over which the individual has no control. Saussure compares changes in a linguistic system to successive states of play on a chessboard, but recognizes that the analogy breaks down at one crucial point: 'If the game of chess were to be like the operations of language in every respect, we would have to imagine a player who was either unaware of what he was doing or unintelligent'; as Roy Harris puts it, language is 'impervious to interference although open to development'.[13] In granting explanatory priority to social history, I am aware, however, that we lack a history of cultural change in the terms described by Lakoff and Johnson: LeRoy and Beitz's metaphor of leverage (and implicitly, of depth) is only one of the possible descriptions of the impact of modernity.

---

[13] Saussure, *Course in General Linguistics*, 89; Harris, ibid., 74–5, n.2.

Select Bibliography

Bibliographical details for less frequently cited and less significant items may be found using the index and the footnotes.

ANDRADE, E. N. DA C. 'The Theory of Relativity', *New Statesman*, 14 (22 Nov. 1919), 215–16.

BEER, GILLIAN. *Darwin's Plots: Evolutionary Narrative in Darwin, George Eliot and Nineteenth-Century Fiction*. London: Routledge and Kegan Paul, 1983.

—— *Open Fields: Science in Cultural Encounter*. Oxford: Clarendon, 1996.

—— 'Science and Literature', in R. C. Olby, G. N. Cantor, J. R. R. Christie, and M. J. S. Hodge (eds.), *Companion to the History of Modern Science*. London: Routledge, 1990, 783–98.

—— *Virginia Woolf: The Common Ground*. Edinburgh: Edinburgh University Press, 1996.

BELGION, MONTGOMERY. [review of *The Universe around Us* by James Jeans], *The Criterion*, 9 (Apr. 1930), 529–33.

—— [review of *New Pathways in Science* by A. S. Eddington], *The Criterion*, 14 (July 1935), 707–14.

BELL, IAN F. A. *Critic as Scientist: The Modernist Poetics of Ezra Pound*. London: Methuen, 1981.

BENSON, A. C. (ed.). *Cambridge Essays on Education*. Cambridge: Cambridge University Press, 1917.

BENTLEY, J. M. [review of *The Grammar of Science* by K. Pearson], *Philosophical Review*, 6 (1897), 523.

BISHOP, EDWARD. 'Re:Covering Modernism—Format and Function in the Little Magazines', in Ian Willison, Warwick Gould, and Warren Chernaik (eds.), *Modernist Writers and the Marketplace*. Basingstoke: Macmillan, 1996, 287–319.

BODANIS, DAVID. *Web of Words: The Ideas Behind Politics*. Basingstoke: Macmillan, 1988.

BRADBURY, MALCOLM, AND JAMES MCFARLANE (eds.). *Modernism 1890–1930*. Harmondsworth: Penguin, 1990.

BRADSHAW, DAVID. 'The Best of Companions: J. W. N. Sullivan, Aldous Huxley, and the New Physics', *Review of English Studies*, 47 (1996), 188–206, 352–68.

BROAD, C. D. 'Euclid, Newton and Einstein', *Hibbert Journal*, 18 (Apr. 1920), 425–58.

CAILLARD, EMMA MARIE. 'The Human Telephonic Exchange', *Contemporary Review* 87 (Mar. 1905), 393–401.

CAMPBELL, NORMAN. 'The Common Sense of Relativity', *Philosophical Magazine*, 6th ser. 21 (Apr. 1911), 502–17.

CAREY, JOHN. *The Intellectuals and the Masses*. London: Faber, 1992.

CARR, H. WILDON. 'Einstein's Theory', *Times Educational Supplement* (22 Jan. 1920), 47.

—— 'The Principle of Relativity and its Importance For Philosophy', *Proceedings of the Aristotelian Society*, 14 (1913–14), 407–24.

CONRAD, JOSEPH. *The Collected Letters of Joseph Conrad*, ed. Frederick R. Karl and Laurence Davies, 5 vols. to date. Cambridge: Cambridge University Press, 1983–96.

—— *The Secret Agent* ed. Bruce Harkness and S. W. Reid. Cambridge: Cambridge University Press, 1990.

—— *Youth, Heart of Darkness, The End of the Tether*. London: Dent, 1946.

CROMMELIN, A. C. D. 'Einstein's Theory', *The Observer* (16 November 1919), 9.

CUNNINGHAM, E. 'Einstein's Relativity Theory of Gravitation', *Nature*, 104 (4 Dec. 1919), 354–6; ibid. (11 Dec. 1919), 374–6; ibid. (18 Dec. 1919), 394–5.

DAVIES, HUGH SYKES. [review of *The Mysterious Universe* by James Jeans], *The Criterion* 10/40 (Apr. 1931), 514–16.

DEERY, JUNE. 'Cultural Trespass? : Aldous Huxley's Forays into Modern Physics', *University of Dayton Review*, 21/3 (1992), 73–84.

DENTON, F. M. 'The Modern Theory of Relativity', *Times Educational Supplement* (4 Dec. 1919), 605–6.

DINGLE, HERBERT. *Relativity for All*. London: Methuen, 1922.

DIXON, E. T. [review of *The Grammar of Science* by K. Pearson], *Nature* (July 1892), 269.

EDDINGTON, A. S. 'The Domain of Physical Science', in J. Needham (ed.), *Science, Religion and Reality*. 1925; London: Sheldon Press, 3rd impr. 1926, 187–218.

—— 'Einstein on Time and Space', *The Quarterly Review*, no. 462 (Jan. 1920), 226–36.

—— 'Einstein's Theory of Gravitation', *Monthly Notices of the Royal Astronomical Society* (Feb. 1917), 377–82.

—— 'Einstein's Theory of Gravitation', *The Observatory* (Feb. 1917), 93–5.

—— 'Einstein's Theory of Space and Time', *The Contemporary Review*, 116 (Dec. 1919), 639–43.

—— 'Foreword', in A. Allen Brockington, *Mysticism and Poetry*. London: Chapman and Hall, 1934, pp. vii–ix.

EDDINGTON, A. S. 'Gravitation and the Principle of Relativity', *Nature* 101 (7 Mar. 1918) 15–7, and ibid. (14 Mar. 1918) 34–6 [a discourse first delivered at the Royal Institution, Friday 1 Feb. 1918].

—— *The Nature of the Physical World.* Cambridge: Cambridge University Press, 1928.

—— 'The Philosophical Aspect of the Theory of Relativity', *Mind*, 29 (Oct. 1920), 421–2 [a symposium with W. D. Ross, C. D. Broad, and F. A. Lindemann].

—— *Report on the Relativity Theory of Gravitation.* London: Physical Society of London, 1918.

—— *Space, Time and Gravitation.* Cambridge: Cambridge University Press, 1920.

ELIOT, T. S. 'Ben Jonson', *TLS* (13 Nov. 1919), 637–8.

—— *The Collected Poems and Plays of T. S. Eliot.* London: Faber, 1969.

—— 'Contemporanea', *The Egoist* 5/6 (Jun.–Jul. 1918), 84.

—— 'The Idea of a Literary Review', *The Criterion*, 4 (Jan. 1926), 1–6.

—— *The Letters of T. S. Eliot*, ed. Valerie Eliot, 1 vol. to date. London: Faber, 1988.

—— 'London Letter', *The Dial*, 70 (June 1921), 686–91.

—— 'Modern Tendencies in Poetry', *Shama'a*, 1/1 (April 1920), 9–18.

—— 'Religion and Science: A Phantom Dilemma', *The Listener*, 7 (23 Mar. 1932) 428–9.

—— *The Sacred Wood.* 1920; London: Methuen, 1928.

—— *Selected Prose*, ed. Frank Kermode. London: Faber, 1975.

EMPSON, WILLIAM. [review of *The Metaphysical Foundations of Modern Physical Science* by E. A. Burtt], *The Criterion*, 10/38 (Oct. 1930), 167–71.

FLAMMARION, CAMILLE. *Lumen* (1872), trans. A. A. M. and R. M. London: William Heinemann, 1897.

—— *Popular Astronomy: A General Description of the Heavens*, trans. J. Ellard Gore. London: Chatto and Windus, 1894.

FREUNDLICH, ERWIN. *The Foundations of Einstein's Theory of Gravitation*, trans. H. L. A. Brose. Cambridge: Cambridge University Press, 1920.

FRIEDMAN, ALAN J., AND CAROL C. DONLEY. *Einstein as Myth and Muse.* Cambridge: Cambridge University Press, 1985.

GIBSON, W. W. 'Chambers', *The Athenaeum*, no. 4654 (11 July 1919), 583.

—— 'Windows', *Fortnightly Review*, 113 (Apr. 1920), 570–1.

GRANT, MICHAEL (ed.). *T. S. Eliot: Critical Heritage.* London: Routledge and Kegan Paul, 1982.

HAYLES, N. KATHERINE (ed.). *Chaos and Order: Complex Dynamics in Literature and Science.* Chicago: University of Chicago Press, 1991.

—— *The Cosmic Web.* Ithaca: Cornell University Press, 1984.

HAYNES, ROSLYNN D. *From Faust to Strangelove.* Baltimore: Johns Hopkins University Press, 1994.

HEILBRON, J. L. 'Fin-de-Siècle Physics', in Carl Gustaf Bernhard, Elisabeth Crawford, and Per Sörbom (eds.). *Science, Technology and Society in the Time of Alfred Nobel* Nobel Symposium, 52. Oxford: Pergamon, 1982, 51–73.

HOLTON, GERALD. *Thematic Origins of Scientific Thought*. Cambridge, Mass.: Harvard University Press, 1973.

—— *The Advancement of Science, and its Burdens.* 1986; Cambridge, Mass.: Harvard University Press, 1998.

HULME, T. E. *Collected Writings*, ed. Karen Csengeri. Oxford: Clarendon, 1994.

HUXLEY, ALDOUS. *Antic Hay*. 1923; London: Flamingo, 1994.

—— *Crome Yellow*. 1921; London: Flamingo, 1994.

JEANS, JAMES. *The Mysterious Universe*. Cambridge: Cambridge University Press, 1930.

—— *The Universe Around Us*. 1929; Cambridge: Cambridge University Press, 2nd edn. 1930.

JOSEPH, H. W. B. [review of *The Analysis of Matter* by Bertrand Russell], *The Criterion* 6 (Dec. 1927), 548–54.

KERN, STEPHEN. *The Culture of Time and Space 1880–1918*. London: Weidenfeld and Nicolson, 1983.

KIEVE, JEFFREY. *The Electric Telegraph: A Social and Economic History*. Newton Abbott: David and Charles, 1973.

KILLEN, JUDITH. 'Virginia Woolf in the Light of Modern Physics' Ph. D. thesis. University of Louisville, Kentucky, 1984.

KUHN, THOMAS S. *The Structure of Scientific Revolutions*. 2nd edn. Chicago: University of Chicago Press, 1970.

LAKOFF, GEORGE, AND MARK JOHNSON. *Metaphors We Live By*. Chicago: University of Chicago Press, 1980.

LAWRENCE, D. H. *The First 'Women in Love'*, ed. John Worthen and Lindeth Vasey. Cambridge: Cambridge University Press, 1998.

—— *Letters of D. H. Lawrence*, ed. James T. Boulton et al., 7 vols. Cambridge: Cambridge University Press, 1979–93.

—— *The Rainbow* ed. Mark Kinkead-Weekes. Cambridge: Cambridge University Press, 1989.

—— *The Trespasser*, ed. Elizabeth Mansfield. Cambridge: Cambridge University Press, 1981.

—— *Women in Love*, ed. John Worthen, Lindeth Vasey, and David Farmer. Cambridge: Cambridge University Press, 1987.

LEANE, ELIZABETH. 'Contemporary Popular Physics: An Interchange between Literature and Science', D. Phil. thesis. Oxford, 1999.

LEWIS, [PERCY] WYNDHAM. *Time and Western Man*, ed. Paul Edwards. Santa Rosa: Black Sparrow, 1993.

LINDEMANN, F. A. 'Einstein's Theory: A Revolution in Thought', *Times Educational Supplement* (29 Jan. 1920), 59.

LODGE, OLIVER. 'Einstein's Real Achievement', *Fortnightly Review* 110 (Sept. 1921), 353–72.

—— *Ether and Reality*. London: Hodder and Stoughton, 1925.

—— 'The Ether Versus Relativity', *Fortnightly Review* 113 (Jan. 1920) 54–9.

—— 'The Geometrisation of Physics', *Nature*, 106 (17 Feb. 1921), 795–800.

—— *Letters from Sir Oliver Lodge*, ed. J. Arthur Hill. London: Cassell, 1932.

—— 'The New Theory of Gravity', *The Nineteenth Century*, 86 (Dec. 1919), 1189–201.

—— 'Popular Relativity and the Velocity of Light', *Nature*, 106 (4 November 1920), 325–6.

LOTKA, ALFRED J. 'A New Conception of the Universe: Einstein's Theory of Relativity, with illustrative examples', *Harper's Magazine* (Mar. 1920), 477–87.

MACH, ERNST. *The Analysis of Sensations*, trans. C. M. Williams, revised from the 5th German edn. by Sydney Waterlow. Chicago: Open Court, 1914.

MACMURRAY, JOHN. [review of *The Nature of the Physical World* by A. S. Eddington], *The Criterion* 8/33 (July 1929), 706–9.

MAETERLINCK, MAURICE. *The Life of Space*, trans. Bernard Miall. London: Allen and Unwin, 1928.

MARVIN, CAROLYN. *When Old Technologies Were New: Thinking About Electric Communication in the Late Nineteenth Century*. Oxford: Oxford University Press, 1988.

MAURON, CHARLES. 'On Reading Einstein' tr. T. S. Eliot, *The Criterion*, 10 (Oct. 1930), 23–31.

MIND. [review of *The Grammar of Science*, by K. Pearson], *Mind*, n.s. 1 (1892), 429–30. [Unsigned.]

MIVART, ST GEORGE. 'Denominational Science', *Fortnightly Review*, 64 (Sept. 1895), 423–38.

MONIST. [review of *The Grammar of Science*, by K. Pearson], *The Monist*, 2 (1891–2), 623–7 [unsigned].

MORLEY, FRANK. 'When and Where', *The Criterion*, 15 (Jan. 1936), 200–9.

MURRY, JOHN MIDDLETON. 'Literature and Science', *The Times* (26 May 1922), 16.

—— *The Things We Are*. London: Constable, 1922.

NEEDHAM, JOSEPH. 'Religion and the Scientific Mind', *The Criterion*, 10 (Jan. 1931), 233–63.

—— (ed.) *Science, Religion, and Reality*. 1925; London: Sheldon Press, 3rd impr. 1926.

NORDAU, MAX. *Degeneration* translated from the second edition of the German work. London: Heinemann, 'fourth edn.' 1895.

NORDMANN, CHARLES. *Einstein and the Universe*, trans. Joseph McCabe. London: T. Fisher Unwin, 1922.

PALL MALL GAZETTE. 'Science as Shorthand', *Pall Mall Gazette* (26 July 1911), 5.

PATER, WALTER. *Marius the Epicurean*, ed. Michael Levey. Harmondsworth: Penguin, 1985.

—— *The Renaissance*, ed. Donald L. Hill. Berkeley, Ca.: University of California Press, 1980.

PEARSON, KARL. *The Grammar of Science*. London: Walter Scott, 1892.

—— 'Politics and Science', *Fortnightly Review*, 62 (Sept. 1894), 334–51.

PEPPIS, PAUL. *Literature, Politics and the English Avant-Garde*. Cambridge: Cambridge University Press, 2000.

POINCARÉ, HENRI. *Science and Method*, trans. Francis Maitland. London: Thomas Nelson, n.d. (*c.* 1914).

RANDALL, A. E. 'Relativity', *The New Age*, 28 (21 Apr. 1921), 298–9; ibid. (28 Apr. 1921), 309–10.

READ, HERBERT. 'Readers and Writers', *The New Age*, 29 (18 Aug. 1921), 187–8.

—— 'Readers and Writers', *The New Age*, 30 (8 Dec. 1921), 67–8

—— [review of *Science and the Modern World* by A. N. Whitehead], *The Criterion*, 4 (Jun. 1926), 581–6.

RICHARDS, JOAN. *Mathematical Visions: The Pursuit of Geometry in Victorian England*. San Diego: Academic Press, 1988.

ROBERTS, MICHAEL. [review of *Philosophy and the Physicists* by L. S. Stebbing], *The Criterion* 17 (Apr. 1938), 542–5.

RORTY, RICHARD. 'Texts and Lumps', *New Literary History*, 17 (1985), 3–16.

ROUSSEAU, GEORGE S. 'Literature and Science: The State of the Field', *Isis*, 69 (1978), 582–91.

RUSSELL, BERTRAND. *The ABC of Atoms*. 1923; London: Kegan Paul, Trench, Trubner, third impression (revised), 1925.

—— *ABC of Relativity*. 1925; London: Routledge, 1993.

—— 'Einstein's Theory of Gravitation', *The Athenaeum* (14 Nov. 1919), 1189 [signed 'X'].

—— *The Problems of Philosophy*. 1912; Oxford: Oxford University Press, 1980.

—— 'Relativity, Scientific and Metaphysical', *Nation and Athenaeum*, 31 (16 Sept. 1922), 796–7.

—— 'The Relativity Theory of Gravitation', *The English Review*, 30 (Jan. 1920), 11–18.

SACKVILLE-WEST, VITA. 'Books in General', *The Listener*, 4 (19 Nov. 1930), 844.

SAINSBURY, GEOFFREY. 'Anthropomorphic Universe', *The Adelphi*, 1 (Jan. 1931), 338–41.

SATURDAY REVIEW. 'Einstein's Reaction on Philosophy', *Saturday Review* (22 Nov. 1919), 481–2 [unsigned].

SEDLAK, FRANCIS. 'Einstein's Theory or Pure Thought', *The New Age*, 29 (18 Aug. 1921), 188–90.

SEWARD, A. C. (ed.). *Science and the Nation*. Cambridge: Cambridge University Press, 1917.

SHANKS, EDWARD. 'Astronomy', *The New Statesman*, 14 (29 Nov. 1919), 248.

SHEPPARD, RICHARD. 'The Problematics of European Modernism,' *Theorizing Modernism: Essays in Critical Theory*, ed. Steve Giles. London: Routledge, 1993, 1–51.

SHINN, TERRY, AND RICHARD WHITLEY (eds.). *Expository Science: Forms and Functions of Popularisation*. Sociology of the Sciences, 9. Dordrecht: D. Reidel, 1985.

SILBERSTEIN, L. *The Theory of Relativity*. London: Macmillan, 1914.

SINGER, E. A. [review of *The Grammar of Science* by K. Pearson], *Philosophical Review*, 9 (1900), 448–50.

SLOSSON, EDWIN. *Easy Lessons in Einstein*. London: George Routledge and Sons, 1920.

SMITH, CROSBIE. *The Science of Energy*. London: Athlone, 1998.

SNOW, C. P. 'The Two Cultures', *New Statesman and Nation*, 52 (6 Oct. 1956), 413–14.

—— 'The Two Cultures and the Scientific Revolution', *Encounter*, 12/6 (June 1959), 17–24, and 13/1 (July 1959), 22–7.

SOLOMON, JOSEPH. 'The Philosophy of Bergson', *Fortnightly Review*, 96 (1911), 1014–31.

SQUIRE, J. C. (as 'Solomon Eagle'). 'Books in General', *The New Statesman*, 14 (22 Nov. 1919), 223.

SULLIVAN, J. W. N. *Aspects of Science*. London: Cobden-Sanderson, 1923.

—— 'A Crucial Phenomenon', *The Athenaeum* (9 May 1919), 303.

—— 'Dissolving Views', *The Athenaeum* (19 Dec. 1919), 1361–2.

—— 'The Entente Cordiale', *The Athenaeum* (9 Apr. 1920), 482.

—— 'The Equivalence Principle', *The Athenaeum* (6 June 1919), 433.

—— The Justification of the Scientific Method', *The Athenaeum* (2 May 1919), 274–5.

—— 'The Notion of Simultaneity', *The Athenaeum* (23 May 1919), 369.

—— 'On Learning Science', *The Athenaeum* (4 July 1919), 559.

—— 'On Relative Motion', *The Athenaeum* (16 May 1919), 337.

—— 'Scientific Education', *The Athenaeum* (12 Sept. 1919), 885–6.

—— 'The Union of Space and Time', *The Athenaeum* (30 May 1919), 402.

TANDY, GEOFFREY. [review of *The New Background of Physical Science* by James Jeans], *The Criterion*, 13/51 (Jan. 1934), 310–13.

TUNZELMAN, G. W. DE. 'Physical Relativity Hypotheses Old and New', *Science Progress* (January 1919), 475–82.

TURNER, FRANK. *Contesting Cultural Authority.* Cambridge: Cambridge University Press, 1993.

TURNER, MARTHA. *Mechanism and the Novel.* Cambridge: Cambridge University Press, 1993.

TYNDALL, JOHN. *Fragments of Science.* London: Longmans, Green, 5th edn., 1876.

WATERLOW, SYDNEY. 'The Philosophy of Henri Bergson', *Quarterly Review*, no. 430 (Jan. 1912), 152–76.

WELLS, H. G. *The Invisible Man*, ed. Macdonald Daly. 1897; London: Dent, 1995.

—— *The Time Machine.* 1895; London: Dent, 1993.

WESTERN, R. W. 'The Principle of Relativity', *New Age*, 25 (27 Nov. 1919), 54–6.

—— 'Relativity and Metaphysics', *New Age*, 25 (1 Jan. 1920) 137–8; ibid. (8 Jan. 1920), 154–5; ibid. (15 Jan. 1920), 171–2.

WHITEHEAD, A.N. 'A Revolution of Science', *The Nation* (London), 26 (15 Nov. 1919), 232–3.

—— *Science and the Modern World.* 1926; Cambridge: Cambridge University Press, 1927.

—— 'Space, Time and Relativity', *Proceedings of the Aristotelian Society*, 16 (1915–16), 104–29.

WHITLEY, RICHARD. 'Knowledge Producers and Knowledge Acquirers', in Shinn and Whitley (eds.), *Expository Science.* Dordrecht: D. Reidel, 1985, 3–28.

WHITWORTH, MICHAEL. 'The Clothbound Universe: Popular Physics Books, 1919–39', *Publishing History*, 40 (1996), 53–82.

—— 'Inspector Heat Inspected: *The Secret Agent* and the Meanings of Entropy', *Review of English Studies*, 49 (1998), 40–59.

—— 'Physics and the Literary Community'. D. Phil. thesis, University of Oxford, 1994.

—— '*Pièces d'identité*: T. S. Eliot, J. W. N. Sullivan and Poetic Impersonality', *English Literature in Transition* 39 (1996), 149–70.

—— '"Within the Ray of Light" and Without: The New Physics and Modernist Simultaneity', forthcoming in the *Proceedings* of the 1999 Leiden October Conference, ed. Valeria Tinkler-Villani.

WOOLF, VIRGINIA. *Collected Shorter Fiction*, ed. Susan Dick. London: Hogarth, revised edn., 1989.

—— *The Diary of Virginia Woolf*, ed. Anne Olivier Bell, 5 vols. London: Chatto and Windus, 1977–84.

—— *Essays of Virginia Woolf*, ed. Andrew McNeillie, 4 vols. to date. London: Hogarth, 1986 onwards.

—— *Jacob's Room*, ed. Sue Roe. London: Penguin, 1992.

—— *Mrs Dalloway*, ed. Stella McNichol. London: Penguin, 1992.

WOOLF, VIRGINIA. *Night and Day*, ed. Julia Briggs. London: Penguin, 1992.
—— *To the Lighthouse*, ed. Stella McNichol. London: Penguin, 1992.
—— *The Waves*, ed. Kate Flint. London: Penguin, 1992.
—— *The Years*. London: Penguin, 1968.

Index

Printed in the United Kingdom
by Lightning Source UK Ltd.
127334UK00001B/13/A

9 780198 186403